DOUBLEDAY
CELEBRATES
100 YEARS OF
EXCELLENCE

Also by Jonathan Kramer and Diane Dunaway Kramer

Why Men Don't Get Enough Sex and
   Women Don't Get Enough Love

DOUBLEDAY

New York   London   Toronto

Sydney   Auckland

Losing the Weight of the World

A Spiritual Diet to Nourish the Soul

Jonathan Kramer, Ph.D.
and Diane Dunaway Kramer

PUBLISHED BY DOUBLEDAY

A division of Bantam Doubleday Dell Publishing Group, Inc.
1540 Broadway, New York, New York 10036

DOUBLEDAY and the portrayal of an anchor with a dolphin are trademarks of
Doubleday, a division of Bantam Doubleday Dell Publishing Group, Inc.

Library of Congress Cataloging-in-Publication Data
Kramer, Jonathan.
    Losing the weight of the world: a spiritual diet to nourish the
soul / Jonathan Kramer and Diane Dunaway Kramer. — 1st ed.
        p.   cm.
    Includes bibliographical references.
    I. Spirituality.   I. Kramer, Diane Dunaway.   II. Title.
BL624.K72   1997
291.4—DC20   96-34324
                                                   CIP

_____

To the Spirit within us all—

May all beings be happy and whole, enlightened and enlivened by the spark of life.

The Spiritual Diet is a combination of the basic principles common to the world's major religions, and the knowledge and techniques of modern psychology. It's designed to help modern people with households and careers, by providing a menu of choices to lead a more spiritual and personally fulfilling life.

It's offered in the hope that it will help us to be strengthened and sustained by Spirit.

May we lose the weight of the world and realize that life is a feast to be enjoyed!

Acknowledgments

It's been said that gratitude takes three forms: a feeling in the heart, an expression in words, and a giving in return. Many people have helped and supported us along the way. With heartfelt words and this book as at least a small, partial offering in return, we'd like to thank:

Loretta Barrett, a great agent with a great heart; Rob Robertson, for his friendship, and unflagging support and editorial expertise; Lori Lipsky, for her clear instincts; Laurie Bernstein, for her invaluable interest and insight.

Our readers, for their giving of their time, effort, and encouragement, and for their many thoughtful and helpful suggestions: Erin Grady Alcaraz; Lee Faver, Ph.D.; Michelle Joseph; Marcia Jourdane; Stan Terman, M.D., Ph.D.; Jan Wahl.

The staff at Warner Springs Ranch, San Diego, for helping create a Garden of Eden in which to write and rest.

All those who play important parts in our lives, both those

who are and aren't mentioned by name—our families, friends, students, therapy clients—we thank and appreciate what we receive from you.

We would also like to offer a deep bow of love and appreciation to our invaluable teachers, stars shining in an endless, clear blue sky. We've never met in the flesh, but we've known and learned from you intellectually, emotionally, and spiritually: Siddhartha Gautama, Jesus Christ, Moses and the Prophets of the Old Testament, Jiddu Krishnamurti, Chogyam Trungpa, A. H. Almaas, Dalai Lama, Bhagwan Shree Rajneesh, Mother Theresa, Thich Nhat Hanh, Ram Dass, Ken Wilber, Shunryu Suzuki, and all our spiritual friends mentioned in our References and Recommended Reading section.

Contents

Chapter 2
The Breath of Life   25

Preoccupation and stress are main courses in modern life. But when we learn to pay attention, and focus our mind, we can calm down, and awaken to the ever present spiritual reality within and around us.

Chapter 3
Living Here and Now   52

We're preoccupied with the past and the future, but we only feel at home when we truly learn to *be* in the present. When we wake up in the present, we're on intimate terms with life and our spiritual nature.

Chapter 4
Soul Food   74

Excessive self-criticism and guilt create psychological wounds. We are healed and changed when we discover our basic goodness and are nourished by it.

Chapter 5
Singing the Body Electric   107

It's common to be out of touch with our senses. When we learn to inhabit our body, we deepen our intimacy with life, as we discover we're living in a spiritual temple, within a magical world.

Chapter 6
Endless Lust

Our personality is endlessly desiring and frustrated. We can find ful-fillment and satisfaction when we understand and meet our basic needs and gain a spiritual perspective.

Chapter 7
Jumping Monkeys

Our mind jumps from one thing to another, making us scattered, unable to concentrate, forgetful, and confused. We can have greater spiritual awareness when we learn to watch and understand our thinking process and use prayer, mantras, and holy thoughts.

Chapter 8
Inner Streams

Our emotions are complex. We often avoid and/or get stuck in them. When we learn to fully digest our emotions through under-standing, awareness, experiencing, and letting go, our spiritual feel-ings come forth.

Chapter 9
Why Am I Here?

Modern people race from one chore and responsibility to another. But we find peace of mind in the midst of this activity when we dis-cover our purpose in living and use it to guide our daily life.

Chapter 10
Too Much Me   228

We naturally strive to meet our needs and satisfy our wishes for a rich life. But individualism can be taken too far, making us unhappy by further separating us from our unity with all other living things. We can learn to spiritually enrich ourselves by growing beyond our individual self to interconnectedness with the One.

Chapter 11
Barefoot in the Spring   262

Our many burdens make millions live halfheartedly. We can enjoy a vibrant, juicy life and find spiritual nourishment when we lighten our load and live more fully.

Chapter 12
Luscious Living: A Daily Spiritual Diet   282

Daily pressures and habits make it hard to change, but by cooking up our own Spiritual Diet recipes, we can live an enriching life that integrates our personality and spirituality and helps us lose the weight of the world.

References and
Recommended Reading   309

Index   315

Losing the Weight of the World

Introduction: The Whole Truth

The most beautiful and profound emotion we
can experience is the sensation of the mystical.

ALBERT EINSTEIN

We're born with the need to create a personal identity
that separates us from our spirituality. As a result, we
share common psychological burdens that make us feel
we're carrying the weight of the world.

Spiritual Hunger

People are hungry for more spiritual, meaningful, and joyful lives. In the past twenty years, we've seen this to be true among friends and family, among those Jonathan sees in his psychology practice and among the students in Diane's university classes.

Children and Generation X-ers are fearful about the future. The baby-boom generation is moving from midlife to maturity, wondering what it all means. Seniors are sensing their mortality. The burdens of daily life with careers and chores, and the limitations of materialism, leave people of all ages yearning for a life that's uplifting and inspiring, with greater closeness to a "higher power," whether we call it *God, Jesus, Buddha, Allah, Yahweh, Brahman* or the *Great Mystery.*

But a nourishing and fulfilling spiritual life is difficult to experience because it's eclipsed by the everyday tornado of activities and thoughts, feelings and sensations, nearly all of which seem to focus primarily on our personal dreams and desires, and so little on *that which is beyond words.*

What we're suggesting is a "spiritual diet," not in the sense of depriving us, but conversely, a diet that feeds us a healthy blend of spiritual ideas and techniques that nurtures our psychological side and nourishes our soul.

We've both been on lifelong spiritual journeys. Jonathan grew up in a reform Jewish family that celebrated every December with a menorah and a Christmas tree. Diane's family was liberal Christian and celebrated the Jewish holidays with their closest friends and neighbors. As adults we've personally explored and extensively studied Eastern and Western philosophy, psychology, religion, prayer, and meditation. In the 1960s, Jonathan studied philosophy and religion for six years at New York University and the New School for Social

Research. He wrote his doctoral thesis in 1975, an Eastern religious view of Western psychotherapy, and has been using these ideas and techniques with people in therapy ever since. Diane has for many years used our ever-evolving Spiritual Diet philosophy with her students in her university classes and in her own writing.

In 1986, with our growing experience, we began compiling notes for a book that would help people from many spiritual backgrounds. We wanted to provide a "spiritual diet" that would help individuals lighten the load of the burdens we all carry, and thus *lose the weight of the world*.

As householders with careers, chores, and children, we've struggled to integrate the power of Spirit into our own busy, everyday lives. We've worked on the Spiritual Diet for many years, allowing it to evolve as we've grown through helping ourselves and others.

Students and therapy clients often confide their hopes, their dreams, their fears and concerns, and they often ask for guidance. While our advice is aimed at helping individuals resolve their specific personal problems, it's also aimed at encouraging and freeing them to move closer to their own spirituality.

For example, a student has a problem finishing an assignment. With discussion, it becomes clear that the underlying issue is actually grounded in excessive self-criticalness, low self-esteem, or other difficulties associated with her spirituality being buried beneath her particular "weight of the world."

Giving the student specific advice about the assignment will only help in a limited way, but addressing the underlying burdens of self-esteem and self-criticalness (for instance, by putting her in touch with her basic goodness, as discussed in Chapter 4) will help her with every other assignment in life, and increase her connection with her own goodness and joy.

And that's exactly what happens. Over and over, people in therapy, students in classes, and others who've used the Spiritual Diet's recipes for losing the weight of the world have found their burdens feeling lighter and their lives feeling happier, brighter, and more contented.

The Dalai Lama, Tibetan Buddhist world leader, as well as other world religious leaders, has suggested the need to find "a universal, secular spirituality." We hope the Spiritual Diet adds to this by embracing the major religious traditions, offering techniques and understandings that nurture both those with an existing set of beliefs and those who simply want greater spiritual consciousness within our everyday lives.

With the Spiritual Diet, you don't have to believe in any system in particular. It offers spiritual techniques that are compatible with most belief systems, and they can stand on their own. You don't have to believe, you just have to do it. It works if you work.

Lao-tzu, the unintentional founder of Taoism, wrote, "As rivers have their source in some far-off fountain, so the human Spirit has its source. To find this fountain of Spirit is to learn the secret of heaven and earth." This source is the focus of all spirituality, and all religions point to it, though in different words, forms, and images.

We've used the basic principles of the *Losing the Weight of the World* Spiritual Diet for many years, with people from many faiths (Christians, Jews, Buddhists, Hindus, Unitarians, and unaffiliated). We've mixed together those ingredients and directions that have helped people the most and seem best able to coexist with the pace of our modern Western lives at the cusp of a new millennium.

The Spiritual Diet is a blend of the essence of many religious teachings that nourishes the soul by putting people in touch with their spirituality.

By lightening the load of our personal problems, balancing our personality and Spirit, focusing our awareness, helping us discover our basic goodness, and

showing us how to live more fully and freely, the Spiritual Diet will help us lose the weight of the world.

Finding Our Way

Be a light unto yourself.
Be your own confidence.
Hold to the truth within,
  as to the only truth.

GAUTAMA BUDDHA

Losing the Weight of the World can be read straight through, teaching and encouraging you to practice the Basic Spiritual Diet (Chapters 2 and 3), then moving through the eight courses that follow (Chapters 4 to 11), and ending with ways to integrate your spiritual recipe(s) into your daily life (Chapter 12).

Or you can read Chapters 1 to 4 and follow the directions on page 68, "The Basic Spiritual Diet Recipe." You'll learn how to combine the Basic Spiritual Diet with one or more ingredients from the other eight chapters. In this way, you'll create personalized spiritual recipes you can "cook up," creating a Spiritual Diet that suits your own tastes.

Each of us must prepare what we need for our own psychological health and spiritual growth, so as you read, think about what will help and nourish you the most, identifying the Spiritual Diet recipes that appeal to you.

Readers are often pressed for time. If this is true for you, then just read the chapters and the "What Can I Do?" sections that seem most appropriate for you. If at some point you find yourself feeling stuck or setting the book aside, go to the assessment of burdens at the end of Chapter 3 and move on to what is currently your heaviest weight of the world. Of course, you can also focus on using a recipe you've already found that works for you.

Keep in mind that there are many important things in life that appear simple, yet require time, effort, patience, and perseverance to experience and embody. Old patterns have a life of their own and keep pulling us back to what's familiar. But we can keep growing if we just keep ourselves gently moving forward.

Reading this book may be like going to a salad bar or a smorgasbord. We get the freedom to pick and choose what we want until we fill up our plate. Then we can sit down and enjoy the feast of life set before us.

Chapter 1

Life Is a Feast

This is the day which the Lord hath made; we
will rejoice and be glad in it.

PSALM 118:24

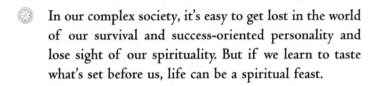 In our complex society, it's easy to get lost in the world
of our survival and success-oriented personality and
lose sight of our spirituality. But if we learn to taste
what's set before us, life can be a spiritual feast.

Coffee on the Run

In a flash, we awaken after a long night of darkness and dreams. Our personality coalesces and the one we think of as our *self* returns to waking consciousness. Modern people with jobs, families, and homes, we rise from our beds, planning and preparing for the day ahead. So many things to do. So much to handle.

Our feet touch the floor and we're off and running. We aren't relaxing in the Bahamas or living in a monastery or a nunnery. Regular life each day consists of work, chores, bills, family, friends, sleeping, then awakening to do it all over again.

We slide out of bed and go for our toothbrush, to the toilet and the shower. We put on our clothes and get ready for work. We eat our breakfast on the run. We get the kids ready for school. A whirlwind of activity envelops us.

The dog needs to go out, the phone rings, the coffeemaker springs to life. Suddenly, we're lost in a tornado of thoughts and deeds, conversations and responsibilities, feelings and desires. We need to bake cookies for the Brownies, fix the leaking tire, feed the cat, grocery-shop, worry about Mom's fall, get the kids to soccer, face the boss, and buy sympathy and birthday cards. Oh yeah, pick up a cake for the party, call the TV repairman, commute to work, and somehow pay those taxes and credit card bills. Ugh.

We often go through the day preoccupied, not fully in the present, trying to maximize the available time. It's a life of fast food and quick conversations.

Our attention is consumed by the next thing on our agenda and we're often trying to do two or three things at once. We're all so busy, even healing has become a rushed affair.

Mrs. Davis suffered an injury in a car accident and needed

surgery. When she went to see the surgeon under her new health care plan, he said to her, "We keep things moving pretty fast around here. The first day after surgery, you have to be up and walking around the room. The next day, we expect you to walk three laps around the fourth floor. Then you're sent home." The doctor looked at his watch and rose to leave. "Now, if there aren't any questions," he said, heading toward the door.

Mrs. Davis quickly called, "Just one, Doctor. Do I get to lie down during the operation?"

Time is at a premium with high expectations about what we're supposed to be accomplishing. Our responsibilities and concerns preoccupy us. We can't really relax in the present because our thoughts are traveling to the past, looking ahead to the future, or off in some imaginary time and place. We're busy handling and coping as best we can.

We're so busy and preoccupied that even fun activities can be difficult to enjoy because we're not totally "there" to enjoy them.

Sometimes we have the sense that we're rushing through life without really living it.

Yes, there is joy in what we do, but as we anticipate the day ahead, a heaviness descends upon us and we think to ourselves, "I wouldn't want to give up this life I'm living, but sometimes it's hard and it seems like something's missing."

It's as if our daily diet of fast living is like fast food. It lacks the essential vitamins and minerals to keep us healthy, contains a lot of fat that weighs us down, and the soda never quenches our deepest thirst.

Millions of us intuitively feel there's much more to life. We sense our spiritual connectedness and reach for it. We go to churches, synagogues, temples, meditation centers, museums, music, and Mother Nature seeking something greater.

We're hurried, harried, and hassled.
We want to be happier, less frustrated, less stressed.
We want to feel calm, cool, and contented.
We want to live meaningfully and with worthy goals.
We want a greater sense of love and peace.
We want great joy and spiritual awakening.

But we don't have these things, and millions feel something's wrong. Many spiritual leaders have diagnosed these problems as being widespread. Vietnamese Zen master Thich Nhat Hanh writes:

> There is a deep malaise in society. We can send e-mail and faxes anywhere in the world, we have pagers and cellular telephones, and yet in our families and neighborhoods we do not speak to each other. There is a kind of vacuum inside us, and we attempt to fill it by eating, reading, talking, smoking, drinking, watching TV, going to movies, and even overworking. We absorb so much violence and insecurity every day that we are like time bombs ready to explode. We need to find a cure for our illness.

Mother Theresa says, "There is hunger for ordinary bread, and there is hunger for love, for kindness, for thoughtfulness; and this is the great poverty that makes people suffer so much."

Marilyn Youngbird, North Dakota Native American, adds, "In the majority world, humanity isn't taught self-worth, self-acceptance, self-love—ingredients absolutely necessary to be mentally, physically and spiritually well. I feel these are reasons why we are experiencing a spiritual famine."

Millions of people are hungry for spiritual nourishment and so they feel they're carrying the weight of the world.

But what is there to do except just go on? This is real life. We're not giving it up, abandoning our possessions, bills, families, or jobs. Even if we downsize and simplify our life, we've still got a big load.

In the midst of having coffee on the run, we wonder if there's a way to find the spiritual nourishment that would help us solve some of our difficulties and feel stronger, healthier, and happier.

In fact, there are ways to lighten our load, but first we have to look at some of the weight we carry, the common psychological problems, what we call *burdens*. They are:

The burden of being preoccupied and out of touch with our spirituality

The burden of being unable to live in the moment

The burden of being out of touch with our basic goodness

The burden of not being able to fully experience and enjoy our body and physical sensations

The burden of being dissatisfied with what we already have

The burden of being unable to concentrate, of being forgetful or confused

The burden of not knowing the best way to deal with our emotions

The burden of not living with meaning

The burden of being disconnected from others and life

The burden of not living to the fullest

These burdens can cause a wide range of problems: stress, loneliness, meaninglessness, the sense that something's missing, that we're not "centered," boredom, disappointment, irritation with our life as it is, fear, guilt, confusion, lack of energy, and excessive self-criticism and/or criticism of others, to name some of the possibilities.

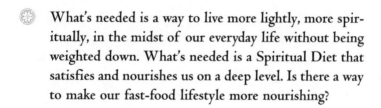

What's needed is a way to live more lightly, more spiritually, in the midst of our everyday life without being
weighted down. What's needed is a Spiritual Diet that
satisfies and nourishes us on a deep level. Is there a way
to make our fast-food lifestyle more nourishing?

Heavenly Spirit, Earthly Personality

If you want the truth, I'll tell you the truth:
Listen to the secret sound, the real sound, which
is inside you.

KABIR

We live two lives. One open, one in secret.

Our open life is the one we develop as we go along each day,
the one we know best. It's our world as a **personality,** a whirlwind of
activity we call our life.

Our personality is a combination of our personal identity, our temperament, our frame of reference, our
will, our defenses, our processing of experience, and
our sense of direction.

Our personal identity is what we think of as our self,* and
what we refer to when we use our name or say "I," "me," or "my-

---

* Our "self" is a complex system. For a theoretical overview of the ego or self
structure and its composition, development, and evolution, see, for example, Ken Wilber's
Transformations of Consciousness.

self." When we wonder "Who am I?" or are asked who we are, we often say "I'm a teacher" or "I'm a doctor," as if our career captures our essence, when in fact it's a part of our personal identity and a role we play in society and at work. Other roles we fill might include being a mother or father, son or daughter, mortgage holder, bill payer, errand runner, family chauffeur, first-aid consultant, and homework adviser. We think what we do is what we are.

In addition to our personal identity, our personality includes: the tendencies with which we're born (such as our temperament); how we organize our world (our frame of reference); our efforts to achieve our current goals (our will); the ways we protect our self from pain, discomfort, and threat (our defenses); how we feel and make sense of the world (our processing of experience); and how we go toward or away from what we like and dislike (our sense of direction in life).

Our personality organizes and interprets our experiences in terms of our self and is the center of most of our thoughts, desires, actions, and preoccupations. We express our will, giving life a sense of direction, by aiming to get our needs met—as, for example, we work to get a new car, promotion, or other goal. We're endlessly hungry for reassurance of our worth and security, and crave love, specialness, safety, and much more as we seek pleasure, avoid pain, and struggle to survive, succeed, and feel satisfied.

Our personality is an essential part of us as human beings and is invaluable in helping make us feel special and solid—qualities we must have to survive and succeed in our society.

But our personality also causes us to separate from the rest of humanity and the world as we identify with our body, our feelings, our thoughts and opinions, our accomplishments, our job, our family, our history, our nationality, our political beliefs, our religion, our likes and dislikes, our goals, and our possessions. **We come to believe that our personality is all we are.**

Our Secret Life

Our other life is a secret life. It's our inner light, the life of the *Spirit*, the source of our soul. Spirit is ever present, eternal, and shared with all living beings.

Spirit creates and animates all life. Whether we call the eternal spiritual energy *God, Jesus, Buddha, Allah, Krishna, the Divine, the Sacred, the Great Spirit, the Great Mystery, the Tao, Yahweh, I AM, Being, It, G-d, the Nameless, Big Mind, Brahman, the Creator, That-Which-Is-Beyond-Words, the Giver of Life, Good Spirit,* or *The Force,* we can find a healthier life and a lighter load by uncovering our secret life and discovering eternal spiritual awareness.

Spirituality is the mode of consciousness beyond thought and words, through which we're connected with the whole cosmos. We think of it as a "deeper" or "higher" order of intelligence, greater than even our combined selves. We feel it when we hold a baby in our arms or kiss someone we deeply love. We sense it when we sit quietly by a waterfall or hear Ave Maria, Kol Nidre, a heartfelt sermon, or a moving Zen poem.

Spinning through space, we walk the earth as spiritual creatures clothed in physical bodies, living complicated earthly human lives. We are the light of consciousness manifested in physical form, angel Spirit in animal bodies. We are biological, spiritual, and psychological at the same moment. Animal, Spirit, and householder personality in one. We are animated with the spark of life. We are the life force that exists everywhere in all living things, the Spirit that animates us in life and leaves our body in death.

When we feel our Spirit's life-giving power, our sense of self is enlarged. It connects us with the baby and our beloved, with the redwoods and the Rockies, with the people in the next pew and the

Eskimo in a frozen igloo, with the Bedouin in a desert oasis, and the sailor out at sea.

On a spiritual level, we are connected with all our ancestors and all our descendants, with the deer in the deep woods, with the eagle soaring in the cloudless sky, and with any creatures who might possibly be living on planets unknown to us earthlings circling unknown suns millions and billions of light-years away.

Spirituality is eternal, and the basic spiritual principles have been around for thousands of years. All are rooted in the deeply felt mystical experience of their founders, whether it's Jesus, Moses, Buddha, Muhammad, or Lao-tzu. It is the direct knowledge of what we call God.

But it's not just humanity's religious geniuses who can awaken to that which is beyond words and thought. All of us can experience the spiritual. Albert Einstein said:

> The most beautiful and profound emotion we can experience is the sensation of the mystical. It is the sower of all true science. He to whom this emotion is a stranger, who can no longer wonder and stand rapt in awe, is as good as dead. To know that what is impenetrable to us really exists, manifesting itself as the highest wisdom and the most radiant beauty, which our dull faculties can comprehend in their primitive forms—this knowledge, this feeling, is at the center of true religion.

The American teacher and author Ram Dass says:

> I believe there is a spiritual dimension to life. I believe who we are is not what we think we are and what is seeable. Who we are is more than the body and personality . . . Spirit resides in every human heart, and there is life, or awareness, or continuity of awareness, beyond death and before birth.

Spirituality is not simply a belief in God. It is an experience of the sacred in the midst of everyday life.

What is the relation between who we are and what we think we are? The Hindus describe the personality's relationship with spirituality using a metaphor of actors in a play. Each actor has a series of masks for his or her part. Some of the masks have smiling faces for when the character is happy. Other masks reflect other expressions such as fear, sadness, rage, curiosity, guilt.

The actors expertly exchange these masks of character and mood. They play out the role of each mask they put on. Indeed, the word "personality" comes from the Latin *persona,* which means "mask." Of course, during the play, there's always the true identity behind the mask which remains the same no matter what part is played.

The true identity behind the mask of personality is Spirit, the eternal Self, the inner Seer. It quietly watches the play, ever ready for the masks to be put away and the actors to return "home" by becoming aware of their spiritual Self.

Our masks are the personal identities we act out in the world—the expressions we show, the needs we feel, the roles we play. But unfortunately in life's drama, the curtain never falls and the play never ends until death. As a result, many of us continue acting out our roles until, eventually, we forget our true identity, and believe the masks and the roles and all they engender are who we really are. The more we're identified with the play and our roles, the more we're separated from our eternal Self.

Forgetting How to Fly

As infants, our spirituality is already present, ready to be nourished by the "feast" life sets before us. As Hindu's ancient Upanishads puts it, "The soul is born and unfolds in a body, with dreams and desires and the food of life."

A baby is the human embodiment of light. We see a divine spark in the infant's eyes and a purity in her actions. She coos with contentment, cries with hunger, and giggles with delight at a familiar smile. So natural. No pretense. Arms flail, feet kick. Totally enmeshed in each moment, each child is enlivened by sparks of light from the life force flowing infinitely throughout the universe. Just seeing the guileless innocence in her wide eyes lighted from within, we sense a sacredness about our shared human existence. We look into the baby's face and see the pure light, knowing we're seeing a miracle, a Spirit from heaven.

Yes, this baby, and all of us, are born with animal bodies that crave food and fluids, yet always within is the eternal light of consciousness, the Spirit that never dies. Yoga master Swami Satchidananda says, "Spirit is always light...You are that light, the spirit." And the Bible tells us, "God is light."

Originally, babies are lost in the immediacy of their senses, unable to distinguish between self and other, but, after a time, they begin to develop a sense of "self," a personal identity distinct from everything else, a personality that gradually feels ever more separate from its divine origin as it learns to handle the problems of living as an earthly human.

We are "skin-encapsulated egos," as Alan Watts put it, body-encased personal identities with an artificial sense of separation from Spirit.

As we travel through many stages of development, our sense of self evolves. Our built-in tendencies are shaped and molded by millions of bits of experience. Our personality asserts itself, even imposes itself, on our world. It makes choices to keep us safe and comfortable, and acts to avoid danger, unpleasantness, and pain. Babies quickly develop a separate self whose personality is busily making choices, desiring and rejecting, and vigorously solidifying. "I want,"

"I don't want," "More," and "Yech!" Already, the two-year-old yells "No!"

"No" to yucky creamed spinach. "No" to the doctor's cold stethoscope. "Yes" to ice cream and cookies. "Yes" to snuggles and tickles.

Desiring that which feels good and rejecting that which feels bad is the basis of our personality, as it learns to survive in a physical body, becoming separate from an outside world. The pioneering father of modern psychology, Sigmund Freud, wrote, "Originally the ego includes everything, later it detaches from itself the external world. The ego-feeling we are aware of now [as adults] is thus only a shrunken vestige of a far more extensive feeling—a feeling which embraced the universe and expressed an inseparable connection of the ego with the external world."

Within the first year of life, we develop a physical sense of self; between one and three, we grow an emotional self; between three and six, we gain a mental self—the first three major stages of self-development.

As we grow, our personality is reinforced and developed. As children and teenagers our spirituality is still an intuitive connection with the infinite. But as time goes by and we're taught to focus on our personality, we're increasingly separated from our inner self. We're told to get dressed, stop playing, stop imagining, and to get on with our homework.

Soon we can barely recall the magical moments of early childhood when our senses were still fully awakened, our house seemed like a mansion, and the blue sky was a million miles high. That first ripe strawberry was ambrosia to our child's taste buds, and a trip to the park seemed like an Alaskan adventure. In time, we lose the magic. Millions become at least mildly depressed over this loss of childhood wonder and feel some degree of aloneness.

In adolescence, many teens feel distressed over these and other changes (without really understanding what's changing). Some drop out and avoid developing an adult sense of self. Some don't "find" themselves until later in life, and some never do. Many temporarily hide in herds and fads, before moving into adulthood armed with a personality sufficiently strong to create a successful life in modern society. Yet often these same adults will continue to experience the loneliness of this sense of separation to one degree or another, without understanding the reason or its source.

As in Steven Spielberg's movie *Hook*, Peter Pan grows up to become an attorney and becomes so heavily weighted with responsibilities and worries that he loses touch with his happiness and forgets how to fly.

Those of us who manage the transition find that over time, as we strengthen our personality, we become preoccupied with our body, self-identity, thoughts, jobs, possessions, children, ambitions, and opinions, and become immersed in our technological culture. We come to believe that this is all of who we are. What we overlook or even forget is our spiritual nature.

It's interesting to note that in some, more "primitive" cultures, it's just the opposite—they stay more fully connected to Spirit and may have little connection with technology, careers, and possessions.

KARRANA'S CALL FOR HELP

In some cultures, Spirit is primary, and ambition and possessions are of little importance. People from such cultures who come to our world have great confusion over how we live so apart from our spiritual connection.

Friends of ours, Nora and Sam, tell a story about a Mexican woman, Karrana, who'd been displaced by local fighting near her mountainous village, a place so remote that no one who was trying to help her even knew what area she was from. Somehow, she had ended up on a fishing trawler that had brought her to the United States.

Karrana was trying to get back home when Nora and Sam met her and agreed to let her stay with them until a way back to her village could be found. Within a day of her arrival two facts about Karrana clearly stood out. One was that she was completely unfamiliar with modern indoor plumbing, electricity, or gadgetry. And the second was that Karrana had a tremendous sense of calmness, even in so foreign an atmosphere, a calm that seemed to arise from a deep spiritual connection with all living things. This calm connectedness was obvious as she lovingly examined the plants in their garden and spoke to their dog and cat as if they were her children. Karrana spoke of *Dios* (God) often, prayed every morning and night, and chanted prayers throughout the day.

Nora and Sam, who knew enough Spanish to communicate the basics, began to show Karrana how to use some modern devices, particularly the telephone, including how to dial 911 *(nuevo uno uno)* in case of a problem.

Karrana was attentive, listening to every word, nodding her head and intoning *"sí"* throughout the lesson. But while Karrana obviously had great experience with inner peace and spiritual calm, she'd had almost no experience with numbers.

Still, at last, she seemed to get the idea, and Nora felt comfortable leaving Karrana alone for an hour while she ran a few errands.

"Now," Nora said, wanting to review the emergency procedure one more time before leaving, "show me who you call in case of fire."

Karrana remained calm and serene, but ignoring the phone, she instead stretched her arms out to the sky, tilted back her head, and called loudly, *"¡Dios!"*

After staring at her long enough to realize Karrana wasn't making a joke, Nora shook her head. "No," she said. "Remember what I showed you. In our world we call *nuevo uno uno.*"

"*¿Nuevo uno uno?*" Karrana asked in her pleasant way.

"*Sí,*" Nora said, nodding.

A new comprehension crossed Karrana's face. "Yes, of course," she said with a small laugh at herself. "Now I understand."

"Okay," Nora said, "then who do we call in case of a fire?"

Karrana beamed confidently with her new knowledge. This time she stretched out her arms, tilted her head back, and called to the sky, "*Nuevo uno uno.*" Then turning to Nora, she said with a smile, "You call him a different name, yes?"

Karrana was accustomed to a way of life so connected to Spirit, she couldn't imagine relying on anything else. Yet most of us have become so accustomed to relying on all our technological aids and social organization, we have put our faith in them while the spiritual world that nurtures our soul slips out of sight.

It's not that we're doing anything wrong. We're simply striving to protect and promote our "self," and master our life within a modern culture. Unfortunately, the side effect is that of being cut off from our source of spiritual connection that nourishes our soul.

By being cut off from our spiritual connection, our life is spent preoccupied, worried, and asleep to the Spirit within.

By being preoccupied, worried, and asleep, we reduce our openness, our creativity, and our intimacy with life.

By not being open, creative, and intimate, we lose sensitivity and are out of touch with the present.

By not being present in the details of our life, by armoring and anesthetizing ourself, we lose our ability to notice the nuances of our senses.

By not appreciating the nuances of our senses, we can't fully drink in the richness and beauty that surround us.

By not being nourished by the richness and beauty that surround us, we forget how to love and be light enough to "fly."

In our culture, most of us are weighed down with burdens, as our human "doing" outweighs our human "being." Our load keeps us from the endless source of comfort and support that's ever present and ever ready to help us carry our burdens and lighten our load— our spirituality.

The Great Mystery

The one essential thing
is that we strive to have light in ourselves.

ALBERT SCHWEITZER

The Great Mystery we must solve is how to stay in touch with our spiritual essence while living in physical bodies with personalities that are endlessly preoccupied with getting the bills paid, eating well, raising our kids, and lowering our golf score.

Even spiritual professionals struggle to find the proper balance. Rabbi Cohen and Father Casey had been friends for many years. One evening the father and the rabbi were sharing coffee together after a fine dinner when Father Casey leaned across the table and said softly, "Tell me honestly, my good friend. Have you ever tasted bacon?"

The rabbi's face reddened. "Once many years ago, when I was

a teenager, I did have a piece," he admitted shyly. He paused, sipped his coffee, and eyed his friend. "And you tell me, Casey. Have you ever been with a woman?"

This time, the father's face reddened and he nodded sheepishly. "Once, many years before I was ordained."

Father Casey leaned closer and whispered, a bit sadly, "It's better than bacon, isn't it?"

> The challenge is to find a sense of balance between our physical, emotional, and mental personality that's ever striving to meet its needs and be satisfied, and the eternal Spirit that's our basic Being.

How do we reunite our basic Spirit with our body and personality? That's what the Spiritual Diet recipes are designed to offer.

The Psychospiritual Tug-of-War

At this point, your personality might have the following conversation with spirituality:

Personality: I'm busy trying to accomplish my goals and get the best life that I can for myself. What's spirituality and the Spiritual Diet going to do for me?

Spirit: Haven't you noticed that in the midst of trying to meet your goals, you're missing something?

Personality: I do feel there's something missing, but I don't want to give anything up.

Spirit: On the contrary, there's more available than you know. We can feast on all that surrounds us and find our whole life greatly enriched.

Personality: That's hard to understand when there are so many hassles, frustrations, and disappointments in life. What am I supposed to do?

Spirit: We need to awaken, to actually experience being, and live in ways that are life-affirming and bring us greater peace of mind.

Personality: I don't understand, but maybe I can't at this point. What can I do to cooperate?

Spirit: Have a cooperative and receptive attitude. When you're going through the Spiritual Diet, have an open mind and a warm heart, with good intentions and the willingness to make the effort to bring it to life in your own daily life.

Personality: Well, I can try. I'm ready to go on.

Spirit: That's all that's needed. Just keep aware, with sensitivity and care. In this way, you can experience greater intimacy and spirituality in your life as it actually is right here, right now.

Chapter 2

 ――――――――――――――――――――――――――――――

The Breath of Life

And the Lord God formed man[kind] of the
dust of the ground, and breathed into his
nostrils the breath of life; and man[kind]
became a living soul.

GENESIS 2:7

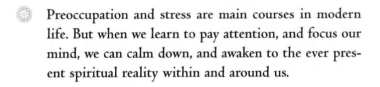 Preoccupation and stress are main courses in modern
life. But when we learn to pay attention, and focus our
mind, we can calm down, and awaken to the ever present spiritual reality within and around us.

A Jungle River

I'm so <u>busy running</u> and trying to do it all that at night it's hard to slow down. Even when I finally get the chance, I don't feel relaxed.

It's as if <u>something important is missing in my life</u>, but I'm not sure what it is or how to get it. It's like there's a hole or a missing piece to a puzzle.

Sometimes I feel <u>nervous</u> and I get light-headed and weak. I have aches and pains in my neck and back. My chest is tight and I could use a long massage. But who has the time or money?

I get so <u>preoccupied.</u> I wish I could concentrate better, but it seems like I've got so many things to think about that <u>it's hard to keep my mind on one thing.</u>

Life is like a river in the jungle. We're all in the river, even if we think we're on the banks watching it go by. In fact, all of us are being swept along in life's flow.

For most modern people, daily life is a hard swim against the current. When the river is tough and treacherous, and we're overly stressed with too much physical, mental, and emotional pressure, we go into "survival mode."

We constrict our chest and breathe shallowly, thus slowing the flow of oxygen and blood to our brain. The result can be light-headedness and concentration problems that make efficiency and effectiveness even more difficult.

Check yourself. Is your breathing constricted or relaxed? Do you have areas of tightness in your head, neck, shoulders, or back? Do you feel you could use a massage? Move your arms and shoulders, observe your natural breathing, and see for yourself. Chances are

your breathing is fairly shallow and you're just using the top portion of your lungs.

What we need is something to help us rise above life's stresses and navigate the river. Learning techniques that teach us to be aware of our spirituality is like building a raft on life's river. At first, it may be difficult. We may have only one small log (technique) to grab onto, to keep our self afloat. But, little by little, we add more logs (techniques, understandings, experience) until we can confidently crawl onto the raft. Then we can "go with the flow," riding reality safely and comfortably, wherever the river carries us. When we can successfully navigate life's twists and turns, the River of Life offers us spiritual nourishment.

But how do we construct a spiritual raft while we're stressed and preoccupied, being carried along by the rushing currents of real life? The first and most fundamental "log" of the raft is to *pay attention.*

A Raft on the River

Twenty-five hundred years ago, Siddhartha Gautama was the royal prince of a kingdom in what is now Nepal. At twenty-nine, he left home and throne to follow a spiritual path, and after many years of intense effort, he saw the light and became the Buddha (meaning "the Enlightened One").

One afternoon, as the Buddha sat under a tree at the edge of a clearing in the jungle, a woman went up to him, bowed with respect, and asked, "Sir, are you a god?"

"No," the Buddha answered simply.

"Are you an angel?"

"No."

"Then what are you?"

"I am awake."

The rest of us, like Siddhartha before his enlightenment, are only partially awake. Spiritual masters often say that the normal person with a job and household is sleepwalking through life. But we, too, can awaken.

Obviously, they're not talking about physical sleep. They mean that, like the Buddha, we can become conscious and awake spiritually. We're asleep in the sense that we're personality-dominated, with hundreds and thousands of preoccupations. The modern Zen Buddhist master Shunryu Suzuki wrote, "Most people have a double or triple notion in one activity. There is a saying, 'To catch two birds with one stone.' That is what people usually try to do. Because they want to catch too many birds they find it difficult to be concentrated on one activity, and they may end up not catching any birds at all!" Or as the Indian teacher Bhagwan Shree Rajneesh wrote, "You walk, you talk, you do a thousand and one things, but ... You don't live in awareness. When you listen to the awakened ones ... [and] they tell you, 'Wake up!' they mean: Be totally conscious so that nothing unconscious and dark remains in your being."

We can awaken and become conscious in the present. By learning to pay attention, we can more fully awaken to the Spirit within, fulfilling our potential as intelligent beings with a powerful consciousness.

The more we pay attention, the more logs we gather and the stronger our raft. The stronger our raft, the more awake we become. The more awake we become, the more effectively we can navigate the river.

Paying attention strengthens us spiritually, but it also strengthens us physically. It is well documented that the act of focusing the mind leads to the "relaxation response," described by Harvard physician Herbert Benson. Focusing our mind slows our heart and respiration, relaxes our muscles, and reduces stress-induced hormones and brain chemicals. The relaxation response helps 75 percent of insomniacs to sleep normally, 34 percent of pain sufferers to reduce their need for painkillers, and 35 percent of "infertile" women to become pregnant.

Yet at first, it seems impossible that paying attention could be important at all. Paying attention seems like a small, boring, inconsequential thing, but that's simply an error of our personal perception. Our personality is based on an unfocused, busy mind that misunderstands and underestimates the significance of focused attention. The silent Sufi sage Meher Baba wrote, "The ego takes all that is unimportant as important and all that is important as unimportant."

Paying attention is the first and most important technique of the Basic Spiritual Diet. By learning to be aware, we begin to know what's truly in and around us, so we can come to realize that a feast has been set before us.

Traditionally, focused awareness has been used (along with prayers) by the world's major religions to help spiritual seekers come closer to God. (Prayers and mantras will be discussed in Chapter 7.) The power of awareness—consciousness, attention, awakeness—has been known to the few, but lost to the many:

In the first century, Rabbi Jacob said:

Better a single moment of awakening in this world than eternity in the world to come . . .

Why?

A single moment of awakening in this world is eternity in the world to come.

The inner peace of the world to come is living in this world with full attention.

The two are one, flip sides of a coin forever tumbling and never caught.

An early father of the Christian Church, St. Simeon, in the fifth century, said, "By keeping your mind attentive . . . and repeating the Jesus prayer, this will teach you everything." In the eleventh century, Rabbi Bahya ibn Pakuda said, "Because the mind is unstable our sages have composed the Order of Prayers" to help maintain attention, and in the sixteenth century, Rabbi Judah Albotini, similarly concerned about inattention, recommended that "those who practice concentration . . . close their eyes." At that time, Jewish *Kavannah*, or concentration and meditation, became Kabbalah, a regulated set of prayers to create a sacred union through focused attention on God and his teachings.

The sixteenth-century Christian mystic St. Francis of Sales said, "If the heart wanders bring it back to the point quite gently," suggesting that even if one spent the whole hour of prayer repeatedly bringing one's attention back to the focus, "your hour would be very well employed."

In Islam, prayers are used five times daily to focus the mind. The seeker is told to "give full attention" to the prophet Muhammad's words *"La ilaha illa Allah"* (There is no god but God).

Gautama Buddha said:

Wakefulness is the way to live.
The fool sleeps
As if he were already dead,
But the master is awake
And he lives forever.
He watches.
He is clear.

How happy he is!
For he sees that wakefulness is life.

In prerevolutionary Russia, Russian monks and laypeople were instructed to "purify the intellect" by repeating "Lord Jesus have mercy on me" with each outgoing breath, thus directing attention to their personal savior, Jesus.

Zen teacher Joko Beck writes that paying attention changes us, for "when we become open awareness, our ability to do necessary thinking gets sharper, and our whole sensory input becomes brighter, clearer . . . and there's a richness which is just our natural state if we are not blocking our experience with our tense, worrying minds."

Awakened Attention

Many spiritual teachers tell us that attention is important. So what do they really mean by "attention"? In fact, we already know how to pay attention. We did it in school and we do it at work. The difficulty is that mostly we're lost in our thoughts, activities, and preoccupations, with several things going on at the same time (or in quick succession), and we simply drift in and out of attention.

In contrast to these usual limp moments of awareness, all of us have memories of times we've been keenly aware and alert, our attention riveted in the moment. Such "truly awake" moments may be stimulated by an emergency or by great joy.

For example, people surviving an accident often speak of how time seemed to slow down as they watched everything with intense attention. A young friend, Morgan, recently survived being hit by a truck. She said it all happened in slow motion—the truck seeming to come at her slowly at about five miles an hour, her body rising eight feet in the air as she watched the pavement drop away below her. Yet her sister Stephanie reported that the whole thing happened in an instant.

People experiencing great joy also awaken from their everyday dreaming. Sharon said that when she and Matt got married, it was as if everyone and everything were intensely happy along with her. She imagined the music was even coming through the flowers and everything was vibrantly alive.

These are examples of intense attention during special situations. At these moments we become acutely aware of the essence within us that's always paying attention.

The *one* who is watching during the accident is the inner observer who sees so clearly it can seem like life is in slow motion.

It is the same *one* who's aware during moments of joy. At such times, we often know in some vague sense that there's something inside us, something even deeper than the watcher. We can watch, but we can also watch our self watching. Spirit is this source of our awareness, that within us *which knows that it knows.* Often this recognition of our true identity is accompanied, at least for a while, by great clarity, euphoria, or well-being.

Such moments of emergency or joy are rare for most of us. But we don't need big emergencies or peak experiences to calm our personality, clarify our mind, and be more spiritually awake. With practice, it can happen at any moment, even in the midst of regular life.

Big Bangs, Little Bangs

We can slow down enough to pay attention right now as we're reading these words. We can notice the small things that are with us here and now: the colors in the room, a sound from outside, the feeling of our body resting in our chair. We can allow ourselves to be more fully where we are, more conscious of the details that surround us. We can notice the feeling in our hands and fingers as we touch the paper and hold this book. We can pay attention at any moment, even now.

We live with the illusion that what counts are the *big* things: the promotion and the raise, the Super Bowl, winning the lottery, a wedding, a new car or house. These experiences are exciting and can be of value in meeting personality's needs. But they quickly become fading memories, special desserts rather than our regular meal.

In personality's efforts to achieve life's climaxes, we fail to enjoy the foreplay. By craving the Big Bang, we lose all the little bangs of which life is made and we miss out on the good stuff along the way. As Robert Fulghum humorously illustrates:

"What I do" is literally "how I spend my time" ... I figure in my life so far I have spent 35,000 hours eating, 30,000 hours in traffic getting from one place to another, 2,508 hours brushing my teeth, 870,000 hours just coping with odds and ends, filling out forms, mending, repairing, paying bills, getting dressed and undressed, reading papers, attending committee meetings, being sick and all that kind of stuff. And 217,000 hours at work. There's not a whole lot left over when you get finished adding and subtracting. The good stuff has to be fitted in somewhere, or else the good stuff has to come at the very same time we do all the rest of the stuff.

The vast bulk of life is made of all the so-called small things that surround us all the time, but they contain the possibility of great satisfaction and enjoyment: walking down a street holding a loved one's hand; the smell of fresh bread; holding open a door for an elderly person; a bright white full moon against a dark blue sky; fresh shoots of green grass in the spring; the tinkling of a wind chime; the taste of a juicy orange.

Moments of intimacy are ever possible and ever present. If we fail to be aware of what is in and around us, we've missed life's greatest source of natural nourishment, and life's feast that surrounds us goes uneaten and undigested.

But as we learn to pay attention, we notice that we feel more alive. In time, we'll begin to find the observer who watches the flow of life, and if we keep paying attention, we will, in time, we become spiritually awakened and vibrantly alert as our mind focuses and attends to what's here and now.

Paying Attention
Through Breath Awareness

How do we pay attention when our life is so demanding, hectic, and preoccupying? How do we build a raft on the river when our attention must be shared by so many demands? And how do we pay attention when what life seems to offer is often not peaceful, pleasant, or beautiful?

It's easy to say "Pay attention!" But how do we really do it?

We've seen that all religions emphasize paying attention. It's also true that every religion teaches us that the source of spiritual experience lies within:

Christianity: The kingdom of heaven is within you.

Judaism: The path to God is within your heart.

Buddhism: Look within, thou art the Buddha.

Hinduism: God lies hidden within the hearts of all.

Siddha Yoga: God dwells within you as yourself.

Shinto: God is found in man[kind]'s own heart.

Islam: He who knows himself knows his Lord.

Confucianism: What the underdeveloped man [or woman] seeks is outside; the advanced man [or woman] seeks within.

What is within is found through paying attention. The traditional way to pay attention is to focus within, using one or another technique. One of the most frequently used techniques is our breath.

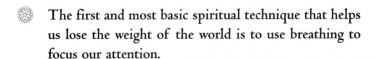 **The first and most basic spiritual technique that helps us lose the weight of the world is to use breathing to focus our attention.**

We can breathe consciously as our breath goes in, and breathe consciously as our breath goes out. Paying attention to our breath keeps us afloat on the river, in the rapids or in the calm spots.

Conscious breathing is a basic technique that's been used for thousands of years in many spiritual traditions to help focus and strengthen our ability to pay attention. Our breathing is simple, natural, and available to each of us every moment we're alive. The more we use our breath to focus ourselves, the more readily we can. Yet it is also natural to resist the idea that breath awareness is of such great use. After all, breathing is so commonplace—too boring and ordinary, too invisible to really be important. Everyone breathes. Adults don't think about it at all, unless they have asthma or otherwise have trouble breathing. And children play with it by holding their breath as long as they can. But this is more than a game. We typically don't see its essential unity with life until we're kept from it or see someone else who's not breathing. Such life-and-death illustrations are not easily forgotten.

A SPECIAL BREATH

I (Diane) was a horse-crazy nine-year-old whose mother always told people my first word was actually a neigh. But whatever the truth (which I suspect that wasn't), it's safe to say that getting a horse for my ninth birthday had been the answer to a long-recited prayer. From that moment on, my entire life revolved around the care, feeding, and adoring of Naco Sue, a chestnut mare, who had the gentlest brown eyes I'd ever seen. Every day we'd greet each other in traditional horse language, her blowing gently into my nose, and I blowing gently into hers. Then one day when I learned that my adored darling was going to have a baby, I felt I'd come as close to heaven as I possibly could.

Anyone who has seen a baby horse knows how they can steal your heart: the oversize brown eyes, the legs at once graceful and impossible, the wispy fuzz that passes for a mane and tail, and the tiny velvet nostrils lined in baby pink.

Each day my father (who was just as horse-crazy, but with far more dignity) and I crossed another square off the calendar as we waited for the eleven-month gestation. June the third stood out, starred in red, with "SUE DUE" written in. Sue Due, Sue Due. As I repeated it to myself, the rhyme played in my head like a mantra with a crescendoing beat, as the due date actually came and then marched on for seven more agonizing days until time had slowed to a moment-by-moment "Is she in labor yet?" vigil.

The night before the event that none of us ever forgot, my father and I "slept" in the barn, locked in what is best described as a staring contest, we in our cots in the barn aisle, the mare hanging her head over her stall door, the only action the mare's stomach occasionally rolling, like a great washing machine on delicate cycle. And with every turn, her stomach seemed to sink lower, and often she uttered something between a sigh and a groan.

It was ten at night before Sue's sighs had unmistakably become groans. Then beginning to circle, she at last lowered herself into the two-foot-thick depth of pine chips.

Horse labor is designed to be a sprint, not a marathon. It should be a quick, even violent, set of contractions that collapses the mare from her rib cage to her flanks and should produce a foal in twenty minutes or so.

When ninety minutes of these powerful contractions had come and gone, I realized what my father must have known for some time: that we were in terrible trouble.

My fourth-grade teacher had suggested I record the event for class by taking notes. I still have them in their childish scrawl, their stark simplicity conveying the growing desperation of events.

1:30 A.M.—Call Dr. Davidson. He is out on another emergency.

2:15 A.M.—Mare is kicking at her own stomach.

3:45 A.M.—Call Dr. Logan. He's on his way back to office but is still 2 hours away.

4:00 A.M.—Sue's sweat is running down her face and dripping in her eyes.

4:15 A.M.—She has stopped letting us get near her.

It is one of the most vivid of all my memories. Sue, no doubt desperate with pain, came to her feet and pulled the halter rope from my father's hand and staggered out the door to the center of her corral. She suddenly threw herself down on her bulging side with such force that it shook the ground even as she bellowed a heart-rending groan. Then, if that wasn't horrifying enough, she pulled herself to her shaking legs and again threw herself down on the opposite side with the same gut-crunching force that seemed destined to kill both mare and foal with the sheer intensity of impact.

I begged my father to make her stop. But she wouldn't let anyone get near her now as pain whipped her into a foaming frenzy.

I'd stopped taking notes, paralyzed by what I would only years later recognize as the overwhelming helplessness we all feel when facing the death of someone we love and being powerless to intervene.

At last then, Sue dragged herself to her feet, and with her whole body contorted, staggered back to her stall, before throwing herself down again. But this time the force produced a golf-bag-sized projectile that burst from her and landed where the two cinder-block walls of her stall met in a sharp corner.

The projectile was hardly distinguishable as a foal and was clearly dead, its limp body within what looked like a wet waxed-paper bag, eyes closed, ears plastered back to its thin head, its body so collapsed and apparently emaciated that its skin was molded to each rib like a wet T-shirt.

The sickening horror, disappointment, and rage hardly had a moment to sink into my abdomen before a new emergency added to it all. Sue, perhaps unaware she'd had a foal, or perhaps in too much pain to care, rolled onto her back and began suddenly writhing and thrashing. One of her hind steel-shod hooves kicked high in the air, smashing my father in the shoulder and knocking him down. Then her whole body rolled toward the dead foal, her hooves lashing out.

My father, with the speed and strength born of fear, regained his feet, and, apparently unaware the foal was beyond help, was trying to restrain the mare's hind legs. Grabbing her hind fetlocks (ankles), he braced himself, holding her on her back and away from the foal. Through gritted teeth he said, "Drag the baby outside so it has a chance."

I realized then he must not be sure it was dead, at least not as dead as it would be if one of Sue's bone-shattering hooves reached it.

The foal weighed more than I did, a fact pointed out to me later. But somehow, as I grabbed its front legs, dragging it from harm's way out the stall door and into the dawn light flooding the corral, it never seemed heavy. I was only staring at the eyes, the lips—for any movement or sign of life—until, at a safe distance, I stopped, falling to my knees and taking the baby's limp head in my hands.

I remember thinking of all the pictures in those books my father had on horse birthing and the passages he'd read me. But now it all seemed like so much vapor. And then I must have realized the obvious. The baby wasn't breathing. It lacked the incredibly simple, yet absolutely necessary breath that kick-starts the life within all of us. It was cut off from its mother's life-giving oxygen and yet hadn't created the link that would connect it to the earth and all of life.

I don't know to this day why it occurred to me—perhaps from having seen lifesaving techniques around swimming pools—but without a further thought, I wiped the mucus from its nose and mouth and, cupping my palms around its muzzle, placed my lips on its nostrils and blew in a long exhale.

In the instant of a light switching on, the tiny nostrils jerked beneath my cupped hands. The huge lash-trimmed brown eyes opened into mine with a startled look and the sound of gulping air. Its chest inflated and it no longer looked emaciated. With its lungs expanded, it was clearly a real live fat and healthy baby horse, and looked me square in the eye with that curious newborn light of infinity, it nickered a soft gurgling baby noise that resonated from my head to my joyous toes.

The divine power of the breath of life was here in living form. Nothing could ever illustrate it more clearly to my young mind. It became a lifelong reminder that our breaths are our moment-by-moment connection with the earth and all of life within and around us.

Suddenly, my father was there, his cheek badly scratched and blood flowing from his ear, where Sue had grazed him with her hoof. (Sue recovered fully from the whole ordeal.) He must have been watching because as he looked down at me he said, "That was a real special breath you gave that baby."

And so, while the foal was christened a fancy registered name, he was always to be known simply as "Special," and for all of us a reminder of the thin line between life and death.

Breath, a gift of life in a burst of air. We can pass it along and share it, but it circulates among us—a gift from God.

Holy Spirit, Holy Breath

The word "spirit" comes from the Latin *spirare*, meaning "to breathe." Many ancient traditions reveal the connection:

In Judaism, *ruah*, "the breath," means the spirit of God that infuses creation. Job says in the Old Testament, "The spirit of God hath made me, and the breath of the Almighty hath given me life."

In Christianity, the Holy Spirit is the breath of life, for, as it says in the New Testament, "God that made the world . . . giveth to all life and breath."

In Hinduism, "Brahman," a word that comes from *br*, "to breathe," and *brih*, "to be great," refers to the ultimate reality beyond name and form.

In Chinese Taoism, *ch'i* literally means "breath," and is used to refer to our vital spiritual life energy, the Tao, the rhythm of life.

Over and over in religious traditions breath is considered to be a primary path to strengthen our spiritual nature.

As we're born, the Great Spirit blows the breath of life into us, and it is with us from our first moment to our last. Like many of the most valuable parts of life, it's invisible, yet in plain sight. It's an ever-present diamond lying beside the road which we miss because it's taken for granted, a "No big deal," a "So what?"

We're wrong.

Breathing can be important for both personality and Spirit.

Breathing can be, and often is, used simply as a valuable self-help technique to make us feel calmer and better, and meet our personality's goals of relieving bodily aches and pains and helping us to reduce stress and cope more effectively with our daily life.

But breathing as a self-help technique is only a start. Attentive breathing carries us beyond personality's goals to Spirit.

By bringing our consciousness to the present and adding the light of awareness, breathing helps spirituality emerge from the eclipse of personality and into our awareness.

Spirit is like the sun. Personality is like the moon. Mostly, we spend our life in the darkness of a partial or even total eclipse, as personality blocks out Spirit's light.

Our aim is for personality to learn to step aside and let Spirit shine more fully.

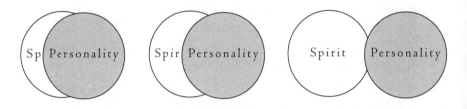

A. H. Almaas writes, "Liberation is really nothing but the personality becoming free in the moment; the personality loosens its grip, lets itself just relax. When your personality hangs loose you become like a child and you enter paradise."

Breathing Magic

Breathing is completely ordinary, yet it can bring us into contact with the vivid and brilliant reality in which we constantly live.

It may only happen for a fleeting moment at first. But as we consciously breathe and pay attention in the midst of our life, we realize that we exist *right now*. We realize that underneath our personality our basic spiritual nature is complete in itself. We feel alive, whole, good, and eternal.

The more powerfully we feel this and the more moments of awakeness we string together, the greater our spiritual awareness.

✳ Like a genie in a bottle waiting to be called forth, breathing with attention is the source of tremendous spiritual wealth and renewal. Breathing is the foundation for the Spiritual Diet and the first step in losing the weight of the world.

At any moment, we can take a full, slow Spiritual Diet breath, relaxing our stomach muscles and allowing our abdomen to gently rise and fall. We use the breath to calm down and focus our awareness as we go on breathing normally. **Do it for a moment right now:**

Sitting here, holding this book, my breath goes in, my breath goes out.

Simply aware, feeling the air as it enters and leaves my nose or mouth. For a moment, there's nowhere to go, nothing to do. I can relax and take it easy.

As I read these words, air enters my body and leaves my body.

Slowly, paying attention. In, out. My abdomen gently rises and falls, the lower part of my lungs filling and emptying. Aware, the breath enters; aware, the breath leaves as I'm reading these words.

As I continue to breathe consciously, I slow down. If I can allow myself to follow another breath in and out, and another, I settle down and relax even more and can be more fully attentive wherever I am, whatever I'm doing.

We can do this anytime. We can breathe and focus our awareness, tasting life's sweetness. Relaxed, yet alert. Taking a conscious breath in, nothing mysterious needs to happen. Taking a relaxed breath out, no fireworks need to go off. We turn inward and focus our attention for a passing moment. Just breathing here and now. We let our self feel more comfortable where we are.

We focus and attend to what's in and around us as our breath reminds us to be attentive.

Our personality may want to control the breathing and set itself up as the judge and the judged: How am I doing? Am I relaxing enough? Am I breathing right? Am I following my breath carefully enough? Am I able to be attentive enough long enough? Personality wants to get high with challenges and intensity, quickly pursuing its immediate goals and striving for success.

We can let go of these worries and just enjoy a relaxing moment as we pay attention, using our breath to calm down and go beyond personality to find the spiritual, the watcher, within. As our ability to maintain this attentive state grows, we can awaken to the real world here and now, to the spiritual essence that is behind the watcher and between the thoughts.

What Can I Do?
The "Breath of Life" Recipe

Learning to be conscious by breathing with attention is the first course of the Basic Spiritual Diet. Our challenge is to be attentive within our modern personality and life—while answering the phone, putting on our socks, sitting in a laundry, typing on our computer, commuting to and from work, or walking down the street. The following suggestions can help.

    1. Whenever you can, take a full, slow, "beginning" breath in and out, your stomach and abdomen gently expanding and contracting, initiating the awareness process. Then resume normal breathing, aiming to stay attentive, taking another full conscious breath.

    This is just the beginning. As we go on, we'll see how to combine conscious awareness with the other courses on the Spiritual Diet, to cook up spiritual recipes that suit your specific needs and tastes.

    Do it every day, even if only once a day. Maybe you can aim at ten or more full, slow, conscious, "beginning" breaths a day. Wherever you are, whenever you can, sitting in your car or office, your kitchen or the train, focus your breath and become more aware. No tension or concern is needed, just an awareness of your natural breath going in and out of your body. Feel your lungs filling and emptying, your abdomen rising and falling, as the breath enters and leaves your nose or mouth. By simply paying attention to our breath, we increase our ability to generally be more fully attentive. Be awake and aware! Ninety percent of meditating is just showing up.

You might note if your breaths are long or short, deep or shallow, light or heavy, constricted or relaxed, silent or soundful, conscious or unconscious. Awareness, rather than any effort to alter the breath, is the point.

By integrating beginning breaths into our day, our personality will grow more comfortable with spiritual awareness. We can take one breath at a time, or we can take many.

Use reminders or routines to help develop a habit of using breath to increase awareness. Put up signs or reminder notes at home and work. Breathing in, breathing out. Put a little *B* in your appointment book each day. Take beginning-breath breaks—if only for one breath or one minute. Use drive time each day or while washing the dishes each night to be the time and place for breathing to increase awareness.

Think of yourself as taking a few minutes vacation each day to breathe in the sky. Author Diane Ackerman writes:

> Look at your feet. You are standing in the sky. When we think of the sky, we tend to look up, but the sky actually begins at the earth. We walk through it, yell into it, rake leaves, wash the dog, and drive cars in it. We breathe it deep within us. With every breath, we inhale millions of molecules of sky, heat them briefly, and then exhale them back into the world. At this moment, you are breathing some of the same molecules once breathed by Leonardo da Vinci, William Shakespeare . . . Air works the bellows of our lungs, and it powers our cells. We say "light as air" . . .

Whenever possible, try to create conditions that foster awareness. The more time we're paying attention, the more our spirituality can emerge, and any time we spend being awake and aware is valuable. But don't set yourself up for failure. It's preferable to ask less and accomplish our aim, rather than to ask too much, feel frustrated, and give up. In the beginning of any endeavor it's extremely important to encourage and engineer success. So have achievable expectations and keep at it for the long haul. As the ancient Chinese *I Ching* repeatedly says, "It furthers one to persevere."

2. Breathing instructions for simple, structured mindfulness meditation. If you can find the self-discipline and the time, in addition to beginning breaths here and there, it's very valuable to set aside five, ten, or twenty minutes once or twice a day for more intense spiritual awareness.

It's helpful if we *have a quiet, peaceful place in which we can sit comfortably* on a chair or a cushion, where we're least likely to be interrupted.

If we *have something natural nearby,* such as a window with light, sky, or tree, or somehow make our space attractive and inviting, as with a vase of flowers, that can help us settle down and feel at home.

We should *wear comfortable clothing* that won't cut off our blood circulation.

We *keep our back erect but relaxed,* leaning neither left nor right, tipping neither forward nor back. Straight but not rigid.

We *rest our hands in our lap, palms up, one hand cradling the other.*

Ears in line with shoulders, mouth slightly open, breathing in and out through our nose (or mouth, if we find that works better).

Eyes half-open and unfocused, gazing at the floor a few feet in front of us or at a blank wall or nature, without looking at anything in particular, allowing our eyes to relax.

Allow our chest, lungs, stomach, and abdomen to relax. Notice now, as we breathe fully, that our entire body expands, our shoulders and back become straighter, our head lifts higher. It can be so relaxing to feel our body fill and empty of air, our abdomen expanding and contracting, lightening our whole being.

Aim at breathing targets. Breathing in through our nose or mouth, pay attention to the place in our nostrils or mouth where we actually feel the air. Now exhale and notice the spot in our nose, mouth, or lips where we actually sense the air leaving our body. Those are our *breathing targets,* and focusing on them helps us pay attention.

Counting our breaths can help us maintain awareness: Breathing in, one, breathing out, one. Breathing in, two, breathing out, two . . . Or: Breathing in, one, breathing out, two, breathing in, three, breathing out, four . . . Count up to 10 and then go back to 1 again. Breath counting is an excellent way to grab hold of our attention when the waves in the River of Life are strong and feel like they're sweeping us away. Counting breaths helps us build a raft on which we ride the waves.

Increase your lung capacity. At least once a day, take two out breaths in a row, exhaling more air than normal. This simple exercise strengthens your abdominal muscles and increases your lung capacity.

Let thoughts come and let thoughts go. We don't worry or berate our self when attention inevitably wanders away. If we are worried or self-critical, then we can be aware of that. Just come back to the breath over and over again when our attention is distracted. This will happen repeatedly and is to be expected. Simply, gently, come back to breathing awareness over and over, breathing in, one, breathing out, two. Breathing in, three, breathing out, four . . .

This is basic meditation posture. As busy people with jobs and households, we may not have an ideal situation in which to rest quietly. But whether it's a corner in our bedroom or a chair in our study, we can always breathe with attention, attuning to the fact that we're already, always breathing and conscious.

BREATHING IN, BREATHING OUT

In time our mind will become quieter, our body will begin to relax, and we'll start to feel more at home in the world, and we increase our level of conscious alertness. As Almaas writes:

> Watchfulness is a way to develop awakening. When you are awake you are watchful without being watchful. When you're a light bulb, you don't need to look. So awakening is called the perfection of non-watching. You watch and you watch and you watch until you become the watchfulness. Then you don't put any effort into watching, you're just awake. You don't have to look in order to see, just by being there you see. Then you don't watch anymore. But first you need to watch for a long time. You have to develop watching until you become the watching.

There's a progression that comes with experience. In the beginning, we're like a half-awake archer. We're not yet fully conscious, and we can barely see the target of mindfulness and attention. We draw back the bow and aim. But like the sleepy archer, we can barely keep the target in our sights. Our attention drifts away and we even forget all about the target for a while. It's the same as we watch our breath and pay attention.

We accept that we won't be able to fully keep our eye on the breathing target until practice gives us focused consciousness, and we can more strongly and more often maintain our focus. In the meantime, we simply aim and return again and again to our aiming. We drift off and we return to our aim, we drift off and we return to our aim.

We lighten our load by having a lighter attitude. Don't try to control and dominate the breath. We don't want to be harsh and demanding with our self if we want to lose the weight of the world. We should aim at breath awareness and come back to it whenever we can. The effort we make is more valuable than the results. Wherever we are, we need to find self-acceptance, imperfect as we may be. Breathing helps us learn this.

Pema Chodron, Buddhist nun, writes:

I'd like to encourage us all to lighten up, to practice with a lot of gentleness . . . Sitting here being gentle with ourselves, we're rediscovering something. It's like a mother reuniting with her child; having been lost to each other for a long, long time, they reunite . . . Let the whole thing be soft. Breathing out, the instruction is to touch your breath as it goes, going out into big space and dissolving into space . . . You're simply relaxed outward with your breath . . . Loosen up, lighten up . . . Just let it be.

BORED WITH BREATHING

Many busy modern minds find breathing with attention difficult and boring. Feeling a lack of stimulation and challenge, we fight the slowing down and we avoid resting. By grasping this simple act of breathing, we can see our resistance and grow beyond it.

There's an old story about a Zen student who complained to the Zen master about being bored with breathing. After listening patiently, the master suddenly grabbed the student and plunged his head in a nearby trough of water, holding him under as the student struggled to come to the surface. When the master pulled the student's head from the water, he asked, "Did you find your breath boring just now?"

If we're bored, just breathe and feel bored for the moment.

Feeling bored can't hurt us, so don't fight it or run from it. Breathing in, "bored," breathing out, "bored." It will come and go.

⚜ **Don't battle with your self. Personality enjoys setting up goals, competitions, and struggles. It likes intensity, challenge, and mastery. But spirituality is a state of acceptance and awareness of what is.**

ALL IN GOOD TIME

Gradually, over time, it becomes easier, and we learn to find our attentive mind more quickly and easily. Even in the midst of a busy or chaotic day, we can focus on breathing with attention. In time, and with effort and experience, we'll find peace of mind and spiritual awareness.

Listen to the words of an accomplished master who was deeply intimate with life, the world teacher of choiceless awareness, Jiddu Krishnamurti:

> The blade of grass was astonishingly green; that one blade of grass contained the whole spectrum of color; it was intense, dazzling and such a small thing, so easy to destroy. Those trees were all of life; the lines of those sweeping hills and the solitary trees were the expression of all time and space ... It was incredible to see, feel all this by just looking out of the window. One's eyes were cleansed.
>
> Meditation is this attention in which there is an awareness without choice of the movement of all things, the cawing of the crows, the electric saw ripping through the wood, the trembling of leaves, the noisy stream, a boy calling ... And in this attention, time as yesterday pursuing in the space of tomorrow

and the twisting and turning of consciousness has become quiet and still.

We should not try to be Krishnamurti or anyone other than our self, for each of us must live within our own life and our own experiencing. But each of us can be more awake and aware and on more intimate terms with our life by using our breathing to pay attention.

If we think of awareness as light, at first we see that we are only able to focus a narrow beam of awareness at our breath and we're easily drawn away. But as we keep shining the light, our ability to pay attention strengthens, as our comfort and ability grow. Soon, our awareness no longer encompasses just our breath. It broadens and strengthens, growing beyond our self to encompass all that is within and around us. We see beyond our preoccupations and thoughts to the truth of our connection, and we see, smell, and taste the feast of life.

As we go on, we'll see how to apply our awareness to other aspects of life. Now we'll go on to the second course of the Basic Spiritual Diet and discover something essential—we're always home.

Chapter 3

Living Here and Now

And God said unto Moses,
I AM THAT I AM.

EXODUS 3:14

We must exist right here, right now. This is the
key point.

SHUNRYU SUZUKI

We're preoccupied with the past and the future, but we
only feel at home when we truly learn to *be* in the

present. When we wake up in the present, we're on intimate terms with life and our spiritual nature.

No One's Home

I have a <u>hard time staying with the present.</u> I spend a lot of time <u>off in my imagination,</u> thinking about who knows what. Sometimes it seems like I'm on another planet. Maybe that's why I have this sense of being <u>incomplete and never at peace.</u>

I'm always <u>thinking about the past</u> and I can't seem to let things go. I still dwell on the fact that my husband flirted with my sister at my birthday party, and that was over five years ago.

So much of the time I'm thinking about what's going to happen in the future and <u>I worry and rehearse and plan</u> for whatever lies ahead. All day today, I've been thinking so much about a presentation I have to make next week that I couldn't concentrate on what was happening today.

Mind chatter. We remember vacations and plan parties, think about things we have to do, worry about our concerns, and generally feel preoccupied as we travel to other places and imagined events.

"Amanda's party is going to be great fun next Saturday. The girls will be so cute all dressed up. Maybe we should have a chocolate cake. Oh, chocolate cake. That reminds me of her milk allergy. I'd better make an appointment with her doctor. But that doctor's bill will be expensive and we're still paying on the last vacation to Colorado. That was a kick riding in the mountains last summer . . ." And so it goes.

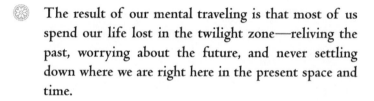 **The result of our mental traveling is that most of us spend our life lost in the twilight zone—reliving the past, worrying about the future, and never settling down where we are right here in the present space and time.**

When we don't live in the present, we're never in the only place that is solid and real. Instead, we're lost in our mind and emotions, inattentive, preoccupied, and separated from our spirituality. We become absorbed by our thoughts, our problems, and our worries to the point that they no longer seem external to us. We feel as if we *are* our thoughts and worries, and that they are our *real* self. We lose sight of our deeper identity and of spiritually true reality in the here and now.

Not being present in the here and now means that even when the present is pleasurable, the habit of not being in the moment keeps us from living deeply and fully. This means we can't enjoy the feast that's right here all the time. And when we're lost in thought or worry and never truly here, we have a deep sense of dissatisfaction. We feel that something's missing. It isn't until we're able to focus on this feeling and truly ask the question "What's missing?" that we realize *we're* what's missing; what's missing is *us.* Our body may be here, but our true presence is not.

Even if we're on a ski trip or relaxing with friends, we may have trouble really enjoying it, because we're preoccupied with other things. We're not here.

We may be aware of the problem, but we aren't certain how to change. We often tell ourselves we have to achieve our goals before being fully here and now. We all have many goals. Maybe we need a better job, more money, and a new car, or maybe we're just trying to make it to the weekend. Or maybe we'll have time when the baby starts school. We've got our eye on some point off on the horizon.

And we think—when we get there, *then* we'll be able to settle down and live in the present.

An anonymous writer describes the danger in this future, goal-oriented focus:

> *First I was dying to finish*
> *high school and start*
> *college.*
> *And then I was dying to*
> *finish college and start*
> *working.*
> *And then I was dying to*
> *marry and have*
> *children.*
> *And then I was dying for my*
> *children to grow old*
> *enough for school so I*
> *could return to work.*
> *And then I was dying to*
> *retire.*
> *And now I'm dying . . .*
> *And I suddenly realize I*
> *forgot to live.*

Personality is caught in time and space, traveling from one place to another yet never really arriving. This creates a background tension that interferes with our peace of mind. Our personal striving has taken control. We reject reality, the here and now of this moment. Life isn't acceptable as it is. Yet, as André Gide wrote, "It is now, and in this world, that we must live." If we are to find true peace and a way to lose the weight of the world, it is by finding ourselves in the present and learning to live in the midst of it all.

No Time Like the Present

Eternity's true name is Today.

PHILO

There are two types of time: clock time and eternal time.

Clock time is what our watch tells us. It's the way we keep track in the world of personality. As busy job- and householders we're traveling from the past to the future. We're striving, becoming, moving with the hands of clock time.

Eternal time is the endless present of spirituality.

Eternal time is the here and now. In the midst of life's ever-changing impermanence, it is always this tiny moment now and now and now.

When we allow ourselves to be here and now and now and now, we're opening to the eternal Spirit living within us. That's why Jewish Hasidism equates *shekinah* ("God's presence") with *yesh* ("that which is"), and why Christian mystics speak of prayer as "the practice of the presence of God."

Focusing on clock time, and not being truly present in the here and now, is another way our personality eclipses our spirituality and makes us feel we're carrying a burden that's weighing us down on the River of Life.

An old Native American tale illustrates our dilemma: Long ago, the People had no light. It was hard for them to be dark and cold, so the Mink took pity on them and, journeying to the other side of the world, he saw the Sun, and decided to take it and put it in the sky for all to share. Now there was light and warmth and the People were happy. Mink was praised and became so prideful that he decided to steal something else for them.

When the Europeans later arrived, the Mink heard that they had Time and decided to steal it for the People. He sneaked into their house and found that time was kept in a box on a shelf, made strange noises, and had two arrows that moved in circles. Mink stole the powerful Time, but quickly found that he had to endlessly watch the hands move in circles, and keep winding it, and he no longer had time to do the things he used to do, like fish and sing songs. Now he had to get up at a certain time and go to bed at a certain time. He had to go to work when the box of Time told him to go and to return home when the box of Time told him to go there. Mink had stolen Time and now it owned him and the People.

An Australian Aboriginal expresses how strange we seem from a primal person's perspective, when he makes this observation about westerners' lives and sense of time: "Mutants [white people] . . . have something in their lives called frosting. It seems to represent that they spend almost all the seconds of their existence in doing superficial, artificial, temporary, pleasant tasting, nice appearing projects and spend very few actual seconds of their lives developing their eternal beingness."

Computers, faxes, and highways take us through life at an ever-increasing speed, zooming away from here and now to get to a hopefully better there and then.

Our life is endlessly moving away from where we are, pulling us away from here and now. We may even become so lost that we doubt our very existence and seek some form of proof that we exist.

Sum, Ergo Sum

The French mathematician and philosopher René Descartes tried to find certainty about life and about his existence, and came up with *Cogito, ergo sum* (I think, therefore I am).

Unfortunately, great harm has come from Descartes's, and Western culture's, overemphasis on thinking and the artificial divisions of mind from body, and each of us from the rest of life.

In reality, if we tune into it, the most basic fact of life is not that we think, it's that we *exist*. We're always here, even when we're driving seventy miles an hour, talking on a phone, or waiting for a fax. We always have the basic being with which we were born and which survives our physical body when we die. Maybe that's why we've called ourselves "human **be**ings."

A more accurate formulation for the basis of human knowledge than Descartes's would therefore be *Sum, ergo sum:* I am, therefore I am, or even more simply, I am that I am.

I AM THAT I AM

Underneath our personality's daily preoccupations and divisions is Being. In the West's holiest book, the Bible, God tells Moses who He, God, is when Moses wants to know how to explain by what authority He comes to lead His people. God says: "I AM THAT I AM: and He said, Thus shalt thou say unto the children of Israel, I AM hath sent me unto you."

The Great Spirit asks and answers:

Who am I? I am that I am.

Who am I? I Am. I exist. Simple existence itself.

Who am I? The eternal life force. The ever-present Great Spirit.

Who am I? I am consciousness and presence.

Who am I? I'm here, I'm aware I'm here. Resting within, conscious and present.

Who am I? That which is beyond thoughts and words.

The Kingdom of God is within us in the form of presence, our basic Being, the moment-to-moment experience of resting with awareness in whatever presently exists.

Asked by his disciples, "When will the new world arrive?" Jesus said, "What you are waiting for has already come, but you don't recognize it." Millions of people accept Jesus as their personal savior and interpret this as referring to the person of Jesus. Others believe that conscious Being, the sacred Spirit in Jesus—and in each of us—is always, already here and now, ever ready for us to realize that we already have what we're looking for. We just don't recognize it because we're unable to settle down in the present with whatever actually exists.

In Hinduism, the ultimate reality is Brahman, the presence of Pure Being, Pure Consciousness, and Pure Bliss. To realize our ultimate nature, the Hindu saint Ramana Maharshi said, "Your duty is TO BE and not to be this or that. I AM THAT I AM sums up the whole truth."

As we breathe to awaken our consciousness, we gain a log for our raft to ride the waves of life. Now we add a second log—presence. We can breathe with awareness and relax in the present where we are right now.

BE QUIET AND STILL

Imagine all your personal needs have already been met. You've won the lottery, your loved ones love you and you love them. You've got some meaningful things you want to do and you can afford to do them. You have the possessions you desire. Your health is great, your mind is sharp, you've already achieved what you wanted.

The pressure is finally off. You can financially, emotionally, and mentally afford to slow down and relax. Think of it! You have it all! Take a restful breath in and a calm breath out. For a few moments, imagine not having to pursue anything. Nowhere to go, nothing to do.

Take a deep, relaxed, contented breath in and let a full, restful, satisfied breath out. Feel a sense of completion. Let a smile come to your face and enjoy the relief. For a few moments, allow yourself to imagine what it would be like for your personality to feel this fully.

When we fully experience this, we awake in the present. Our personality can rest because, at least for this breath and this moment, we don't have anything for it to do. And as our personality steps aside, Spirit can come forth.

Content and Complete

🌀 **To lose the weight of the world, we need to spend less time in the past and the future and a bigger portion in the present—aware of where we are, what we're doing, and how we're feeling.**

In the present, we can open to a deeper sense of contentment and completion that we cannot experience when we're lost in the past and the future. Clock time changes to eternal time when we're content and complete.

Presence is the key to awareness of Spirit, the light within us, that which animates us and never dies. The more fully present we're able to be, the more feelings of contentment and completion grow.

Who am I? I am content and complete. As A. H. Almaas, a contemporary master of Being and spirituality, puts it, "Presence is completeness. When you finally understand what presence is, when you are completely present, you are complete. There is the valuing of presence; there is the perception of completeness. When you're complete, you're content with being present. There's no need for anything else."

DO IT NOW

Resting here and now, I can feel that everything is fine as it is for the moment. I can let life be what it is, with nothing else needed. I'm finally good enough and so is life itself, for everything is exactly the way it's supposed to be.

For a moment, I feel what it's like to be content and complete. I lean back and am relieved, as I exhale and sigh. Finally, home sweet home. A looseness and re-laxation crosses my face, maybe bringing tiny tears or small sparkly smiles.

It's possible to be present at any moment, though naturally some moments are more inviting than others. Riding a horse in the deep woods or lying on a Maui beach welcomes us to being present and we may, momentarily, feel that we don't need anything else. But life is complex and many parts are hard or even painful, making it difficult to live in the present. We don't want it to be the way it is. The dentist's chair and the nurse's needle make us want to run and hide. Loved ones inevitably die or go away. We have problems in our relationships, job and money frustrations make us preoccupied, and we want the present to be different than it is.

Our personality picks and chooses, accepts and rejects. We crave what feels good and reject what we dislike. Spirituality, however, is an inner resting and an attentiveness in the moment to what is, whatever it is—even if we're ill or have problems.

But we don't feel content or complete. Our brows are furrowed with intense intent, our eyes looking at the next hill to climb. Our personality judges and strives, and we run from our pains and our problems into remembering the past and planning for the future, and we don't rest where we are. But Spirit can only come to us and through us when we rest here and now and realize our inherent spiritual worth as a being. Almaas writes:

> What's important? You're important. You don't need to do anything important to be important. You don't need to achieve enlightenment or accomplish any noble action to give importance to your life. You're very special, always ... You are important because of your nature ... You are important because without your actual presence, there is no significance in life, no value in life. When you are conscious of your existence the experience is unmitigated pleasure. This pleasure is there regardless of what you're doing—scrubbing floors, going to the bathroom, creating something wonderful. Every moment is precious, and lived to the fullest. You are not the feelings or the thoughts or the content of your awareness. None of these are who you are. You are the fullness of your Being, the substance of your presence.

This does not mean we give up meaningful goals and meeting our basic needs. In fact, learning to be aware and present is, at least in the early stages, a goal. We continue with our life and our work, but now we are present with the ups and downs. We are still ourselves, a precious being: as Almaas puts it, "the *you* that is really *you* regardless of what *you* do, your preciousness as a being" (emphasis added).

> ⊛ Our "preciousness as a being" can be felt at any and every moment if we rest here and now.

When we rest here and now, we realize what Rabbi Abraham Heschel meant when he said, "Just to *be* is a blessing. Just to live is holy." Rabbi Moshe understood this, for after his death, Rabbi Mendel asked one of Moshe's disciples, "What was most important to your teacher?" And the disciple answered, "Whatever he happened to be doing at the moment."

THE PRESENT'S TINY POINT

Spirituality is always in the present and we must be present to be fully in touch with spirituality.

Imagine awareness as the host of your house and presence as your guest. Presence is constantly knocking on the door, but awareness isn't home. It's in the past, the future, or some imagined place and time. The guest (presence) continues knocking, but it is only when we're awake and at home that we hear. We can open the door to the tiny point of the now. We can see what is here all the time, ever changing, impermanent, yet eternal. We can realize Spirit in our own life in this very moment, and feel content and complete.

When we let ourselves be in the present, it's not that we stop thinking about the past or planning for the future. Instead, we're able to rest ever more fully in the midst of it all.

RESTING IN
THE MIDST OF IT ALL

The awareness that you are here, right now, is
the ultimate fact.

SHUNRYU SUZUKI

I'm sitting in my office and memos are flying, faxes are coming and going, and my coffee cup has just been knocked over. My mind is on the last phone call, a new client wanting help, but also on having to shop for food on the way home tonight, a business meeting this afternoon, whether I can leave the office in time to catch the train, and now the phone light is blinking with a caller on hold while I'm trying to mop up the spill.

Breathing with awareness, I can be present here and now. Now I can rest, content and complete, at peace deep inside. For the moment, there's nowhere to go, and nothing to do. Just this, here, just this, now.

Responsibilities, stresses, annoyances, frustrations, and demands pull me in ten directions. It's a jungle out there, and so it's a jungle in here. Yet if I breathe and allow myself to settle into the moment, I can be here with greater calm. I can feel clearly that *the me that's me regardless of where I be* operates through it all. I am aware in the present in this place. I don't have to just do something, it's enough that I can do it while reading these words, breathing here, breathing now.

Sinking into my chair, aware, awake, alert, attentive to what's in and around me. Cars go by, a blue jay calls outside, the wind blows through the trees.

The result will be an improved experience on a practical, personality level and greater power on a spiritual level. As soon as I return to the task at hand, I can prioritize and be as efficient as I want or need to be, taking the next call, able to brush off extraneous thoughts and mop up the coffee with an inner shrug and a chuckle. We can find some breathing room in the middle of the muddle. Spills happen. Life goes on. When we allow our self to be aware of our present being, we gradually discover a vivid, magical quality to life that lightens our load.

What Can I Do?
The "Living Here and Now" Recipe

In the last chapter we discussed the importance of breath awareness as a way of focusing and paying attention—the first course of the Basic Spiritual Diet.

Now we see that breathing serves a second, equally important aim—to help us to be present. Using breathing as a focus, we can bring our attention here and now, contented and complete. This is the second course, and the "second" breath, of the Basic Spiritual Diet.

1. Breathe and be at home in the universe. Even if we can only do it for a moment or two, wherever we are, we can bring our attention to the present. We can take a "beginning" breath to focus our attention (awareness, consciousness . . .) and a "second" breath to be here and now (present), resting with contentment and completeness.

We can simply be here with what we're doing when we're doing it. Quiet down. Look around. Notice the details in the room. Hear a sound, see a color, feel your presence. Nearby is a lamp we picked out years ago; since we see it all the time, we've forgotten how beautiful it is, but now we can notice its lines, textures, and colors.

When we pay attention here and now, we can see the small jewels that lie within and around us—the outline of a winter tree against a blue-black, moonlit sky; the vase of yellow flowers on a secretary's desk; the feel of our clothes on our body; the succulent sweetness of a rich, ripe strawberry in the midst of a hurried lunch; a warm hug from an old friend. Anywhere we are, it's possible to feel at home, content and complete.

2. Return to the present again and again, if only for a breath or two each time. In spite of preoccupations and thoughts, we can repeatedly sink into the moment, wherever we happen to be. It's possible to set aside time to do this on a daily basis, but whether or not we have the discipline for structured presence, we can let our self return to the moment again and again throughout life.

3. Unite Spirit and personality. We can be spiritually resting in the midst of our personal striving. In the middle of doing whatever we're doing, we can be present. In other words, we can Be while meditating, but we can also Be while making a sales presentation or answering a phone.

Try it now: Take some full, slow breaths to focus your consciousness in the present. Breathing in and out, awake here and now. What do you notice? Perhaps you hear your child's voice, so familiar and dear. How does it sound? How does it make you feel? Notice the light slanting through the window, its golden glow illuminating the carpet. Breathe and be in the midst of becoming, resting where you are, noticing what's in and around you, losing the speed and numbness that's kept you from fully living in the middle of your life. Off in the distance a crow is cawing; out the window a tree branch is waving in the wind. For the moment, breathing, being, and becoming, feeling a sense of contentment and completeness.

4. Chores, routines, and problems can be reminders to be in the moment. Doing the dishes, brushing our teeth, listening to the phone ring, and even worrying about the future can awaken us to where we are at the moment. Anything can be used as a reminder to take a "beginning" and a "second" breath, and be aware in the present.

5. Look for small opportunities to be present. When we look, we discover small spaces in life when we can actually Be here and now: a thirty-second elevator ride, a two-minute walk out to the car, a coffee break, waiting for a friend at a restaurant, driving home at the end of the day, sitting on the toilet, commercials that can be muted on the TV—all opportunities to be present in the midst of doing something else.

6. Pay attention even when you're not being present. Paying attention to *what is* is simple, natural, and ever available. At the same time, it's difficult because it slows personality's momentum, changing our sense of self (our dearest possession). Especially in the West, Being seems almost unnatural. Being at rest is not something we're used to doing.

Personality: It's boring to just be here now.

Spirit: Breathe consciously in the present, content and complete. Awaken and rest, here and now, letting our preciousness as a Being come to the surface of awareness.

Personality: I don't want to slow down and just Be. What am I getting out of this? It's uncomfortable. I'm used to going and doing and solving and accomplishing, and "just Being" somehow seems like a waste of time and energy.

Spirit: When we see that the burdens we're carrying are a result of our lack of presence, we see the value of being present to lose the weight of the world. Until then, all we're aware of is our going and doing and running away from here and now. We can allow ourselves to return to the present with awareness again and again.

> It is only when attentive in the present that we can taste life's juiciness and discover the natural nourishment that life offers.

Many feel better when they're present. "I no longer go into a room of strangers and feel foolish or defensive or shy the way I used to," said Ann, a spiritual dieter we'd worked with for several months. "I used to worry about others' opinions a great deal. Now I know myself in a deeper way and value myself more. I used to have to talk all the time because I didn't feel comfortable with gaps in conversation. Now I can *Be* where I am, even with others, and I listen much better to what others say and mean. I can relax more fully where I am, as I am."

We can lose the weight that comes with being out of touch with the present. We can drop the heaviness of being weighted down by the past and future, and allow the present to support us and nourish our soul. Over and over, we can come home into the welcoming present. Home sweet home, here and now.

The Basic
Spiritual Diet Recipe

The Basic Spiritual Diet consists of taking two deep, slow relaxing breaths to get going. A "beginning" breath in and out to be aware, and a "second" breath in and out to be present. Then, returning to normal breathing, aim to continue being aware and present.

In the beginning, you may only be able to pay attention and be present for a fleeting moment, but as you gain experience, your ability to maintain attention in the present will grow stronger. In this way, the beginning and second breaths of the Basic Spiritual Diet will nurture your spiritual essence—to be awake in the ever-changing here and now—and bring forth basic goodness, love, compassion, and intimacy with life as a sacred experience.

The two Basic Spiritual Diet staples of awareness and presence can be used alone or in combination with any of the many ingredients offered in the following chapters to create Spiritual Diet recipes that suit your taste. To summarize the Basic Spiritual Diet:

1st step: Take a full, slow, beginning breath, aware of your breath going in and out, your stomach and abdomen expanding and contracting.

2nd step: Take a full, slow, second breath in and out, resting here and now. Then continue breathing normally, maintaining awareness in the present.
You can also add a third step to lighten a specific burden or to grow in one or another area.

3rd step: Add your own Spiritual Diet ingredient(s) with the third breath in and out, to create your own recipe(s).

If you were caught in a pattern of excessive sadness and wanted to counterbalance your sadness with better feeling, then with the third in-breath you could say to yourself "happy" (while reminding yourself of a real reason for being happy); on the out-breath you might say to yourself "ahhhhh," with a sense of satisfaction. Or if you wanted to feel more spiritual love and support, try saying to yourself on the in-breath "God" and on the out-breath "loves me."

The possibilities are endless. Each of the following eight chapters offers ingredients and recipes (prayer, love, happiness, compassion, basic goodness, wholeness) which will be explained and which you'll learn to use. Pick whatever appeals to you and will best help you lose the weight of the world.

Don't limit yourself to three breaths. You can use your spiritual recipe for three breaths, three minutes, or three hours. We recommend that you make a commitment to yourself to use your Spiritual Diet Recipe at least once every day—more if you can. Some people use their current recipe at least five times each day; others aim for twenty-five. It's up to you and your degree of eagerness to unburden yourself and nourish your soul.

It's helpful to use the three steps and three breaths as outlined above. But *with experience, you may simplify the whole process to one breath that you use each day,* as your awareness, presence, and prayer (or other ingredient) blend together.

You don't have to use the same recipe every day, any more than you cook up the same food every day. However, as each of us has favorite meals that we frequently prepare and eat, so, too, can we create our own Spiritual Diet Cookbook of our favorite spiritual recipes. So as you read, identify the ingredients that will help lighten your burdens, write the recipes you want to use, then use them.

The Spiritual Diet aims to give you a spiritual experience, not just a belief in Spirit. It provides you with the conditions (awareness and presence) that help you settle down and open your personal self to spiritual Being. Of course, no book, person, or program can do the work for another; each of us must feed ourselves. But the Spiritual Diet offers the nurturance and sustenance to experience psychological and spiritual health and wholeness.

You can (1) approach what follows in a casual manner by simply reading straight through from beginning to end, experiencing, absorbing, and identifying the most helpful recipes to lighten your heaviest burdens as you go. As you read, ask yourself, "Is this a weight I'm carrying right now?" If it is, make note (keep your own Spiritual Cookbook) and use the techniques that appeal to you from the recipes at the end of the chapters.

Or (2), you can assess your heaviest burdens at the moment and read just those chapters that relate to your most pressing needs (though we urge all our readers to read at least Chapters 1 through 4).

Identify Your Burdens

If you read *Losing the Weight of the World* from the beginning, you'll probably be able to identify the burdens that weigh you down. Whether they're physical, mental, moral, emotional, social, or any other kind, when we're burdened, we're constricted and held back. When we understand what our burdens are, we are already one step closer to losing some of the weight we've been carrying.

Let's review the burdens covered in the Spiritual Diet and assess our self and our life. Think about yourself. Ask yourself to what extent the following applies to you. Focus especially on the heaviest burden you're carrying right now:

Do I feel that I'm busy running and it's hard to slow down? Does it feel as if something important is missing in life? Do I feel stressed or nervous, and have a hard time relaxing? Do I get preoccupied or have a hard time keeping focused? Is my mind inattentive and unfocused? If so, see Chapter 2, "The Breath of Life."

Do I have a hard time staying in the present, mostly lost in the past, the future, and imaginings? Do I feel incomplete and never really at peace within myself? Do I worry and rehearse and plan for the future? Do I spend a lot of time reliving and recalling past memories? Do I have a hard time letting annoyances go? If so, see Chapter 3, "Living Here and Now."

Am I demanding and self-critical? Do I feel that whatever I do I should do still more? Do I carry around bad feelings, like guilt, shame, or embarrassment? Am I out of touch with my basic goodness? Do I wish I had more self-confidence and self-esteem? Do I doubt myself? If so, see Chapter 4, "Soul Food."

Am I suffering from being out of touch with my body? Do I have less pleasure sexually than I would like? Am I preoccupied and not really noticing what's around me? Do I wish that I had more touching and tenderness? Does my body feel like it's just another responsibility that takes time? Am I only barely aware of my sense of taste, touch, sight, sound, and smell? If this is true for you, see Chapter 5, "Singing the Body Electric."

Do I never seem to have enough, forever craving something new, bigger, or better? Do I have the sense that I haven't yet made it? Do I want still more even though I might not have the money to meet my real needs? Do I feel frustrated and that my needs aren't being met the way they should? If so, see Chapter 6, "Endless Lust."

Do my thoughts jump from one thing to another? Do I wish I could concentrate better? Do I feel preoccupied and have trouble remembering what I'm supposed to be doing? If I try to quiet down, does my mind jump all over the place? Do I feel ungrounded and lost in thought? If this is true for you, see Chapter 7, "Jumping Monkeys."

Do I sometimes have trouble getting out of bed in the morning? Are anger and irritability a problem for me? Do I dwell on things too long? Do I feel jittery and worried and I'm not sure why? Do I have trouble feeling good and wish there was a way to feel happier? If so, see Chapter 8, "Inner Streams."

Does it seem like I'm lost in what I'm doing and just getting through the day? Do I sometimes wonder why I'm doing what I'm doing? Do things seem routine and boring? Do I feel a lack of meaning or purpose in life and wonder what it's all for? If so, see Chapter 9, "Why Am I Here?"

Does it seem like it's everyone for themselves? Do I sometimes feel lonely or isolated even when I'm with other people? Do I feel separated from others? Do I feel preoccupied with myself and my world? If so, see Chapter 10, "Too Much Me."

Use the Spiritual Diet material to further your own psycho-spiritual evolution. How you use it all depends on you.

Do I feel that I am living half-heartedly, holding back, never living fully? Do I wish I felt freer and more alive? Do I want to carry a lighter load? Do I want to have more fun? If so, see Chapter 11, "Barefoot in the Spring."

Do I feel caught in the momentum of my old patterns and have a hard time changing to something new? Do I know how to keep myself on a healthier, happier spiritual path each day? If so, see Chapter 12, "Luscious Living: A Daily Spiritual Diet."

The Spiritual Diet is nourishment for your soul. By reading and practicing what follows, you'll be personally healthier and spiritually stronger

Chapter 4

 ────────────────────────────

Soul Food

Every human being has a basic nature of
goodness, which is undiluted and unconfused.

CHOGYAM TRUNGPA

Excessive self-criticism and guilt create psychological
wounds. We are healed and changed when we discover
our basic goodness and are nourished by it.

Hungry Souls

No matter how much success I have or how much I earn, <u>I still don't feel like it's enough. I know I'm too demanding and self-critical,</u> but I don't know what to do about it. My therapist says that's why I'm so picky with my family and employees—I'm just doing to them what I do to myself.

<u>I wish I had more confidence and self-esteem.</u> There's really no reason for it, but I have this <u>doubting about myself.</u> I act like I'm sure of myself, but that's just hiding how I really feel.

I know no one tells the whole truth all the time, but <u>I still feel bad when I purposely leave things out or tell white lies.</u> I don't know why such small things should bother me so much.

So far, we've talked about the Basic Spiritual Diet: Wherever we are, whenever we can, take a full, slow, beginning breath to be aware and a full, slow breath to be present. We then continue breathing normally, maintaining awareness in the moment, to the extent possible.

Now we add the dimension of basic goodness.

What is basic goodness?

Basic goodness is food for our soul. Like a healthy and delicious entrée, it nourishes, empowers, and enlivens our life. The word "goodness" itself comes from the Old English for "God."

Some of us feel goodness intimately within us; others have lost touch completely. But whether we feel it or not, basic goodness arises out of our essential spiritual nature. Our sense of spirituality emerges when we are conscious (Chapter 2), ever present (Chapter 3), and good.

As it says in Genesis, "And God looked at everything He had made, and behold, it was very good." And as the biblical Psalm says,

"The Lord is good," and "The earth is full of the goodness of the Lord." All of us have an ever-present basic goodness that arises out of Spirit's inherent goodness within each of us.

Spirit's basic goodness can be covered over and hidden from view, but it can't be destroyed. We begin to feel it once we begin using breathing to pay attention and be present, or when we simply begin to recall our own good feelings.

You can do it right now. Even if you can only do it for a moment, *take a slow, full breath in and out, bringing your attention to the present. Then recall any life-affirming things you've done in the past few days. Perhaps you did a favor for someone, encouraged a child, or talked with a troubled friend. Perhaps you reached out to someone with an open hand and a friendly smile. Maybe it was simply that you picked up a friend in need of a ride or got an item at the grocery you knew a neighbor wanted. It needn't have been a major event. Good acts, large or small, come from the same source within us, the wellspring of basic goodness.*

Caring and a desire to help also come from basic goodness. Compassion is evoked when we experience and relate to others' pain, whether it's people we know or those we read about. Our caring about another's plight brings us closer to those who suffer, and we share some measure of their pain. Like our good acts, our compassion is also a manifestation of our basic goodness.

Caring and compassion are more comfortably evoked when we think of our love for a special grandmother or grandfather, a good parent, a helpful aunt or uncle, our own or another's child, or a loyal, loving pet. When we think of these relationships, we feel warmth, softness, openness, and caring flowing through us.

Thinking of all these feelings of caring, compassion, and the desire to help, we glimpse the basic goodness that lives within us.

Of course, not all of us feel this warmth in our heart. Many of us have uncomfortable feelings arise when we breathe and bring our attention to the present, or we just can't seem to find or experience our sense of kindness, compassion, or love. Or perhaps we can't breathe and be present because every time we attune to the present, what arises are our feelings of "badness," of guilt, or shame, or anger, or some other form of negativity that blocks our sense of basic goodness. Our soul is undernourished and hungry.

Sometimes we're lost in the storms of our personal life (guilt and self-criticism), but spiritual consciousness is always shining above the clouds, ever present, whether we're aware of it or not.

No matter how out of touch we may be, no matter how undeveloped or unrecognized our basic goodness, it always exists within each of us, ever ready to be uncovered and developed into a source of sustenance for our soul. What we must learn is a way to get beyond the bad feelings that we experience when we're present so we can find and experience the goodness within.

In the Beginning

Although the details and the metaphors differ, in nearly all major religions, human life comes from Spirit.

We can think of Spirit as an ocean of consciousness, all-good and all-knowing, vast and eternal. We can imagine this vast ocean at some point differentiating itself into waves, rising and cresting at the surface.

We can think of our self as one of these waves, a specific soul emerging from the vast ocean of Spirit, and ultimately manifesting in our incarnation in human form. Out of that grows our personality and our individual human life.

Throughout life, spiritual consciousness is always part of us, our secret sound, our true identity, here with every breath we take. While we're always part of it, we're not always aware of ourselves as manifesting spiritual consciousness.

> **Spiritual consciousness is knowingness, and it is everywhere about us, within us, and beyond us. Consciousness is the source of our awareness, that within each of us that *knows*, and that knows that it knows.**

As all of creation is spiritually good, we, too, are born basically good. But once born, we now have our body and life to support within a physical and social world that presents us with endlessly complex problems to solve. This creates a "fall from grace," as we develop a personality where both our awareness and our goodness are filtered through our personal perspective and needs.

The personality is essential to keep our body alive, and to groom, nourish, and protect us, to successfully function in society and to meet our many needs. Personality is what makes us feel separate from the ocean. It governs our endless choices based on our likes and dislikes, and on our drive to survive and succeed on our own in the world.

For example, as infants we begin by knowing and experiencing as "good" those things that feel good: warm milk sliding easily into our tummies, soft, clean diapers, a smiling face with gentle hands rocking and holding us. We're aware of all that feels good and helps us grow and survive. If it *feels* good, it *is* good. Our infant sense of a personal "good" is largely based on simple physical needs.

As our personality develops, we begin to learn that not everything that feels good actually *is* good. We also begin to learn that there exists a "greater" or a "higher" good, which may not personally feel as good, but nevertheless is good. This higher good is embraced by all religions and is largely based on our spirituality.

It may be fun to throw our food, to eat dessert first, to take another's toys or hit a playmate who displeases us. But parents, teachers, and others who've already learned these lessons teach us that our personal good may not be appropriate behavior by the standards of the higher good. And we begin to judge our behavior and learn self-discipline even in the face of temptation.

We become aware of what's good, but is it to be our personal good (what feels good to our body and personality) or the higher good (guiding our actions by our social and spiritual conscience)? Constantly deciding between the two creates within us an ongoing struggle. We all face this inner tug-of-war, but children feel it most powerfully as they first try to cope with the dilemma of being "naughty or nice." Our daughter Amanda was no exception.

NAUGHTY OR NICE

When Mandy was four years old, our family attended an annual Christmas party held by some dear friends, Chuck and Kate. This party had developed its own traditions over the years, among them Jonathan playing Santa Claus and Chuck playing Chuckles the Elf.

Every year, sometime after dinner, both men would disappear and dress up in their elaborate costumes, transforming themselves into their holiday roles. Then, with the sound of sleigh bells and a lot of clanging and thumping, they appear, speaking in new voices as they cavort and hand out presents as everyone has a turn on Santa's lap.

Four-year-old Amanda, for whom Santa Claus was an unquestioned reality, was eager as ever for Santa's yearly visit. But that year, as our daughter looked into Santa's face, we knew the fantasy had come to an end. Amanda's eyes locked with her father's, and recognition followed by shock crossed her little face. With an almost miraculous poise for her age, Mandy didn't say a word. After momentarily closing her eyes and burying her face in Santa's shoulder, she continued the ruse, had her photo taken, accepted her gift, and jumped off Santa's lap to allow the next child a turn.

We had a parent huddle at the first opportunity, both of us keenly aware of Amanda's recognition, and decided to ask her if there was anything she wanted to discuss. Amanda, however, didn't want to talk about it at all.

Instead, assuming her most polite four-year-old self, she simply joined the other children, making no comment as they showed off their toys and relived Santa's visit.

During the following days, we both gently hinted at the topic and were surprised that Amanda still seemed unready to discuss it. Far from seeming upset or disillusioned, she seemed fine and even more well behaved than usual, cleaning up her room on her own and coming to ask permission to eat candy that her friends had given her.

Concluding that either we'd been mistaken about the recognition or Mandy simply didn't want to give up the fantasy of Santa Claus being real, we decided not to bring it up until she was ready, and we dropped the subject.

It wasn't until a year later that we understood the truth. A few hours before the annual Christmas party, we were talking about how great the previous year had gone when five-year-old Amanda said firmly, "I don't think it's been so great. It's been really hard."

"Hard? Why do you say that?" Diane asked.

Looking shy and as if she wasn't sure it was okay to say what she'd kept inside, Mandy said, "You know, because of you, Dad, and . . . the secret," she confided hesitantly. "But I've been good, haven't I? I clean my room and I help, right?"

"Of course you've been good. But what about Dad? And what secret?"

Amanda twisted with the discomfort of suddenly being the focus of our combined attention.

"I know about him," Mandy went on, pointing a finger at her

father. "I found out at the party last year. I wanted to tell, but I knew it was a secret."

"What secret?" Diane asked.

"Well, you know about the song?"

"What song?"

"You know," she said, looking at us now as if we were both slightly imbecilic. "The song, You'd better not shout, you'd better not cry 'cause Santa will know if you're naughty or nice. You know that song. Well, before I thought Santa wouldn't know everything. But when I saw that Santa is really my dad. Wow!" Her eyes grew huge. "I knew right then I had to be *really* nice!"

Poor Amanda. Imagine the pressure of thinking your father was the real Santa and that he was right in your own house where he'd know every instance of your good or bad acts, and that he'd keep a list and check it twice, just to find out if you were naughty or nice.

A serious sit-down discussion immediately followed, with the truth being told that the original Santa, St. Nicholas, lived in the fourth century ("a long, long time ago"). And while he's no longer alive, the loving Spirit that gives and cares lives on in us all. And we remind each other to give and care by dressing up in costumes and living it out with trees, lights, cards, and presents every year.

By keeping the secret so as not to reveal her father's special identity, Amanda had demonstrated a basic consideration and self-control older than her years. But she'd also shown another common element of human nature.

The idea of being naughty or nice is taught very young and very simply. If you're nice by the standards set for you, you'll be rewarded; if naughty, you're in trouble. But at some point we begin asking ourselves who's determining what's naughty and what's nice. Who's really watching? And how likely are they to punish us?

This learning is crucial to our relationship not only to the world but, more important, to ourselves and our spirituality. As we get older and become more sophisticated, we learn that "naughty" behavior is often tolerated, or even rewarded as we see that some people who break the rules get richer and more successful as a result.

Indeed, by emphasizing individual, material, and social success, society often ignores or penalizes those who are good, brave, truthful, compassionate, caring, and honest and who pursue a spiritual path. "Good guys finish last" is a common, and often true, saying, if outer, material success is the measure. And since many of us are far removed from our spiritual nature, this common axiom for success may be the only one we have.

This means that opening to our Spirit's basic goodness is an ongoing process made more complicated by our society's emphasis on individualism and material success.

A Deficit of Decency

A famous interviewer couldn't give up her profession even after death. So upon entering heaven, she asked for an interview with the Virgin Mary. The meeting was arranged, and once the Virgin Mary entered and was seated, the interviewer began.

"Please, Virgin Mary, the mothers of the world want to know: How does it feel to be the mother of someone millions of people consider the son of God?"

"Well, frankly," the Virgin replied, "we'd hoped he'd be a doctor."

Being a doctor can certainly be, and is for many, a sacred calling, but the joke points to Western society's emphasis on practical, social success, which may actually go against our greater good. In so doing, a *deficit of decency* is created in which the motto is "Whatever it

takes to get ahead," along with an aggressively self-centered inter-
pretation of "God helps those who help themselves."

Whatever the reasons, most people commit at least minor
moral violations like white lies or "borrowing" things that aren't exactly theirs. And, as a result, while most of us want to follow a
higher good, sometimes the temptation to compromise our values
and go against our moral code becomes overwhelming in the face of
the powerful drive to survive and succeed.

Then, when we violate our principles, we feel bad—guilty,
ashamed, embarrassed, unworthy.

As a result, when we begin to seek greater spiritual awareness
and focus on being conscious and present, we are more aware of who
we are, including our self-criticism and guilt. We see that our personal deeds are out of alignment with our inner sense of goodness,
and our spiritual light is covered over by the darkness of our morally
deviant deeds.

One of Diane's writing students, Sara, recently called for a
consultation regarding a persistent case of writer's block. Sara had
already published a very successful science-fiction novel, but in spite
of her publisher's constant encouragement, she couldn't seem to
work on the next book. "I sit down but nothing comes into my head.
I feel really scared and I can't relax. It's as if I'm afraid to write this
book," she said, going on to describe her sense of despair.

After exploring the situation, it became clear that much of the
source of her discomfort was the feeling that she didn't deserve to
be successful or to feel good about what she'd accomplished. Once
she seriously considered this, she realized the source. Sara was
trapped in a job in which she was working part-time in the evenings,
telemarketing a pyramid scheme to seniors. She hated all the manip-
ulation: "We don't exactly lie to these people," Sara said, "but we
know how to use their fears of poverty and illness, and how to appeal to their greed to get rich quick."

Once she started talking about it, she realized just how unhappy she was. "I can't just quit my job. It's perfect hours for taking classes and writing, and it brings in regular money to pay the bills. But the whole thing is making me feel like I don't deserve anything good when I spend so much time doing things that are hurting these people."

It was clear that her sense of guilt was keeping Sara from feeling good about herself and was undermining her writing career.

Diane taught Sara the Basic Spiritual Diet, and when Sara began taking beginning and second breaths to be aware in the moment, she found feelings of unworthiness, guilt, and shame that kept her from resting comfortably in the present. Many people feel the same. We take a deep, relaxed breath and try to be fully awake, here and now, but we don't feel comfortable inside our own skin. Our sense of self feels tarnished. Some of us know the origin of our guilty and negative feelings. For others, the causes are unclear and we feel lost in the midst of bad feeling.

We're running from our self and don't want to see our self fully, because we're uncomfortable with what we see. We're hiding from our self, and our feeling of being tarnished blocks our spiritual awareness. We might feel down and depressed, or tense and busy, or we might be bingeing on food, shopping, or alcohol.

Whatever their source, bad feelings, like shame, guilt, and embarrassment, block our being fully in the present because they bring up these unpleasant feelings that make us uncomfortable, and we emotionally withdraw to where we can't feel them. For some, the negative feelings are warranted by negative things we've done or are doing. If I feel that I'm not okay, then how can I be awake and relaxed in the present?

On the other hand, many of us who are not violating our basic goodness feel guilty anyway. For such people, our shame and guilt may be undeserved, but exist nonetheless. Excessive self-criticism, unrealistically high expectations, and unwarranted shame and guilt make many people feel terrible, even though they basically act in keeping with their values and honor their moral codes.

⊛ **Not appreciating our expressions of basic goodness is like eating a good meal but failing to extract the nutrients.**

Violating our principles obviously creates a barrier that keeps us from aligning with Spirit, but an equally destructive block is *not* appreciating what we're doing right and being unnecessarily self-critical and not appreciating our expressions of basic goodness. This pattern of negativity unnecessarily deprives us of good feeling.

Excessive Self-Criticism

"I'm not good enough." Have you heard, thought, and felt this before? Virtually all of us have. Why?

While we are born with basic goodness, as we grow into children, teens, and adults, our value is increasingly measured against what we or others accomplish, what grades we get in school, how we look, our success in sports and other activities, how much we're fulfilling our potential, our likability and charm, and our general level of success in the social, job, and material world.

We're evaluated and learn to evaluate ourselves and others based on achievements and expectations. We're often taught to emphasize what's "wrong" rather than what's "right," so we find ourselves focusing most on our lacks and limitations, our errors and inadequacies, our shame and guilt, our faults and flaws. A common source of self-criticism was brought home to us one day by our son Nicholas.

THE RED −3

Nick, our oldest child, was always a happy, energetic kid who'd usually come running or skipping out of school. But one fall day, when
Nick was six years old, I (Jonathan) was parked outside at the curb
when I saw Nick walking slowly toward me. His curly head hung
low, his mouth turned down, a bunch of papers in his hand. Nick
seemed to drag himself along the sidewalk. He slowly pulled open
the car door and slumped into the seat.

"Hi, Nick. How are you doing?" I asked.

No response.

"What's goin' on? Did something bad happen today?"

Nick slowly nodded yes before turning his face away. But of
course I'm a psychologist—I couldn't control myself.

"Oh come on, Nick. Tell your old dad what's wrong," I prod-
ded.

"I'm bad," Nick said at last.

"Bad? Why do you say that?"

Nick handed over a crumpled paper.

Smoothing it out revealed rows of math problems. A big, red
"−3" dominated the top.

"Look," Nick said, tears running down his cheeks, his lips
quivering in an attempt at self-control. He pointed at the glaring red
mark. "Look, Dad, I got a bad grade."

After considering for a long moment, I said, "That minus
three doesn't mean you're bad or that you got a bad grade, Nick. It
means you missed just three problems on this whole paper. Your
teacher wants you to learn from your mistakes. But that's not all that
counts. How many did you get right?"

Nick had no idea. So I started counting up the correct ones
that weren't marked, pointing at each one as I went. By the tenth correct one, Nick had joined in the counting, and by the time we'd got-

ten to twenty-seven, Nick's tearstained cheeks were showing signs of happiness. I had him write a big black +27 next to the red −3.

"There. Twenty-seven right." Nick absorbed the truth for a moment before his usual bright smile reinstated itself on his little-boy face. The subject was changed and the day went on.

Nick was able to find a good lesson in the red −3. But most of us never learn this lesson. Most of us grow up with a barrage of criticism at home or school, be it direct or implied. Since we learn and adapt to what's familiar, our own inner voice criticizes us automatically, and we apply this criticalness to ourselves and the world. Frequently, we develop a radar system that takes for granted the things we do right, while it scans for what's missing or wrong in ourselves and in life. We come to feel that we (and maybe also our life, as well as others) are "bad"—inadequate, incompetent, incomplete, shameful, unworthy, or unlovable.

Of course, high expectations and learning from our mistakes are extremely valuable. They help us grow and improve.

But at the same time, excessive self-criticism and ever-rising expectations wound us, as we inwardly wonder, "Why am I not smarter, better looking, more successful, sexier in bed, earning more, thinner, more fun, less tired, saving more money, a better parent, more efficient, better at math, doing more exercise, and able to resist chocolate?"

And Western culture magnifies and reinforces these self-criticisms through magazines, TV, ads, etc. Of course, our expectations can bring out the best in us, and we do learn from our guilt and shame to correct our behavior. But *excessively* high expectations and *harsh* self-criticism are so common that nearly all modern westerners feel some degree of inadequacy and wounded self-esteem. The resulting anxiety and depression are among the most frequent reasons why people go to psychologists and other therapists.

Excessive self-criticism, deserved and undeserved guilt, separate us from our spirituality and weigh us down with a sense of "badness" that interferes with our good feelings. This leads to experiencing meaninglessness, depression, anxiety, phoniness, and feeling undeserving of whatever success we may achieve. It interferes with our being able to enjoy our self, or experience wonder, awe, and closeness with others.

Hiding our failings or inadequacies adds to the masks we wear. Embarrassment, frustration, and defensiveness all contribute to a hardening of personality and the creation of a thick layer covering our spiritual awareness.

Basically Bad

Many people feel bad. Guilt comes from those acts done or not done. Shame is created by what I am or am not. Embarrassment comes from feeling foolish. All of these wound our personality. Bad feelings make us unable to settle down and feel comfortable with our self. Our consciousness is scattered, our breath is constricted, and our light is clouded over.

Perhaps we felt deprived of love, attention, safety, or intimacy. Maybe we were emotionally, mentally, physically, or sexually abused. Maybe we were excessively self-centered or self-indulgent and have acted thoughtlessly. Maybe we've done things we know are wrong. Or perhaps we're just very self-critical and demanding.

Whatever the reasons, many of us feel inadequate and incompetent and have become depressed or dysfunctional. Feeling bad casts a darkness over one's whole life. Relationship problems, wrong decisions, and bad habits often follow like gray on a cloudy day.

Our inner problems may make being in touch with basic goodness harder, but each of us must also contend with the realities of a modern world, making it doubly difficult.

Living in the Real World
with Basic Goodness

We may want to nurture our goodness, but in the real world it's difficult to always make the choice of the higher good. We live with a constant adult version of the "naughty or nice" dilemma with which we saw Mandy struggle, after she found herself in the same house with Santa Claus.

Maybe we're doing what we shouldn't or not doing what we should. And, of course, we alone know the "whole truth" about our self. Maybe we feel guilty about something we have or haven't done, or ashamed about something we are or are not. And we don't know what to do about the real-world pressures.

When Richard began to use the Basic Spiritual Diet (breathing for attention and presence) along with awareness of his basic goodness, he realized more fully that he was habitually put in the position of supporting and agreeing with his dishonest boss's attitudes and actions when, in truth, he didn't agree with them at all. This made Richard feel terrible, and as he became more conscious of his circumstances, his job became more difficult, and he had trouble falling asleep at night.

Richard wanted to disagree with his boss, but several people in his family depended on his earnings, and he feared taking the risk. Often our life has been constructed without our spirituality in mind. And when we begin to be more fully present and awake, we may feel more frustrated with our current situation.

As Richard became more aware of his situation, he realized that there were several possibilities. He could (1) tell his boss he objected to his business practices and risk losing his job; (2) find a middle path where he might say nothing to his boss and try to somehow sidestep the problem; (3) try to change his position or role within the company or get a different supervisor; or (4) look for another job or start a business of his own.

The path of greatest truth has the greatest spiritual strength. But sometimes, putting truth back into our life is difficult when it hasn't been there in a long time.

Maybe we need to make big changes in our self or our circumstances that will take a lot of time and effort. Or maybe we need more self-discipline to modify our life. Or maybe we need to be more confident to take a risk. Or maybe we need better skills, so we'll successfully make the changes. Perhaps we need patience and perseverance.

Being aware in the present, Richard began to keep his eyes open for opportunities to make things better. This is often all that many of us feel comfortable doing, as we wait for a time when we can change our situation to be more in keeping with our basic goodness.

Richard felt that for the time being, he had to keep his job and continue backing up his boss. But in keeping with being present and aware, he refused to lie to himself and decided to (1) be present as he supported his boss's lies, consciously aware of what he was choosing to do; (2) accept the guilt he felt, realizing that it was separating him from his basic goodness; and (3) acknowledge that for the sake of his family, he was sacrificing himself and a part of his relationship with his spirituality.

Over time, by knowing and fully acknowledging what we're doing, we at least limit the damage that lying does to our self, we maintain consciousness, and, at the same time, we work to change our life situation so that, as soon as possible, we can escape the harmful situation.

🌸   **If you're guilty, you need to straighten up. If you're excessively self-critical, you need to lighten up.**

So we deal with our sense of guilt and wrongdoing by being conscious and doing our best to live out our basic goodness. Wrongdoing calls for a course correction in our behavior. And we can also deal with our excessive self-criticism and undeserved guilt by having compassion for our self.

Guilt can be softened by understanding the complexity of our situation, admitting past wrongdoings to our self, being aware of present violations of basic goodness, making amends for misdeeds whenever possible, and making strong and sincere efforts to do the right thing in the future. Then we're aligning ourself with Spirit to the extent possible at the moment.

It's important to deal with our negative feelings, for our personality hardens like a shell surrounding us and shuts us in, blocking our spiritual presence and awareness. Like a hungry soul, we are cut off from spiritual sustenance.

The more often and the more seriously we have (or believe we have) gone against our basic goodness, the thicker our shell. Fortunately, there's a good answer—soul food.

Good Spirit

As we said earlier, the great ocean of original Spirit of which we are made is inherently good and is the source of our basic goodness. Expressions of goodness include positive, life-affirming thoughts, feelings, and acts, all of which feed and nourish us when we do what's right and digest the results. That's our soul food.

The prophet Muhammad said, "What actions are most excellent? To gladden the heart of a human being, to feed the hungry, to help the afflicted, to lighten the sorrow of the sorrowful, and to remove the wrongs of the injured."

Jesus said, "Blessed are the pure of heart." A picture in a church shows Jesus with his heart surrounded by a halo of fire, his face the essence of serenity and beauty, a visual image of spiritual love and goodness.

St. Augustine believed that all of God's creation is good.

Judaism speaks of the importance of *yetzer ha tov,* good intentions needed to counteract evil. God bestows loving kindness on humanity.

The Buddha taught, "Speak or act with a pure mind, and happiness will follow you as your shadow, unshakable." And,

> *To refrain from evil,*
> *To achieve the good,*
> *To purify one's own mind,*
> *This is the teaching of All Awakened Ones.*

The Dalai Lama says, "My true religion is kindness . . . All religions and teachings teach us to be a good human being, to be a warmhearted person, to be honest and compassionate . . . The most important thing is to have a good heart."

A Persian proverb says, "We come into the world crying while all around us are smiling. May we so live that we go out of this world smiling while all around us are crying."

Bishop Gregory of Nyssa said in the fourth century, "Blessed are the clean of heart, for they shall see God."

The Polynesian Maori writer Cleve Barlow writes, *"Aroha* in a person is an all-encompassing quality of goodness, expressed by love for people, land, birds and animals, fish and all living things. A person who has *aroha* for another expresses genuine concern towards them and acts with their welfare in mind, no matter what their state of health or wealth. It is the act of love that adds quality and meaning to life."

All of these are expressions of spiritual goodness from different cultures and times. An eternal expression of basic goodness that appears in all the major religions is the Golden Rule. For millennia, the Golden Rule has been a way for us to heal bad feelings and to judge, measure, and control our behavior.

Golden Rules

As a bee goes to make honey, so too should we
produce the spiritual sweetness of good works.

ABBOT JOHN THE DWARF

The Golden Rule—Do unto others as you would have others do unto you—can be found in some form in nearly every religion.

American Indian Shawnee: Do no wrong nor hate your neighbor, for it is not he that you wrong; you wrong yourself.

Buddhism: Hurt not others with that which pains yourself.

Christianity: All things ye would that men should do unto you, even so do ye also unto them.

Confucianism: What you do not want done to yourself, do not do unto others.

Hinduism: Do naught to others which, if done to thee, would cause thee pain; this is the sum of duty.

Islam: No one is a true believer unless he desireth for his brother that which he desireth for himself.

Judaism: What thou thyself hatest, do to no man [or woman].

Zoroastrianism: That nature is good when it shall not do unto another whatever is not good for its own self.

The Ten Commandments, in one form or another, are also a universal manifestation of spiritual goodness that serve as a life-affirming guide to daily behavior. Worship one God (spiritual oneness), don't worship idols (the many and the material), have one day each week devoted to rest and holiness, don't dishonor God, honor your father and mother, don't murder, don't commit adultery, don't steal, don't lie, don't lust after your neighbor's house or wife (or husband) or anything else that doesn't belong to you. Each of these instructions aligns our personality's behavior with Spirit.

The Buddha's Eightfold Path to find freedom from unhappiness is also a manifestation of spiritual goodness, teaching us to practice correct action, speech, livelihood, mindfulness, concentration, effort, view, and thought.

Though morality is taught in our families and culture, basic goodness is inherent and runs deep in our spiritual nature. Even zoologists studying higher primates find that basic rights, justice, and fairness are common. Chimpanzees kiss to make up after a fight, they stroke and embrace each other to offer consolation, and they show sympathy and empathy for each other.

The Golden Rule fosters survival of community, the species, life, and growth, and is a way for all of us to assess and guide our actions.

Basic Goodness Account

A man's [and woman's] true wealth is the good
he [and she] does in this world.

MUHAMMAD

We can think of ourselves as each having a personal *Basic Goodness Account.* We make deposits into our account by acting in keeping with

Spirit and with society's highest values, and by being aware of our basically good acts.

When we follow the Golden Rule, Ten Commandments, Eightfold Path, or our own moral code, we add to our Basic Goodness Account. Our good acts and efforts enrich us personally and spiritually.

> When personality does good deeds and has good intentions, it aligns itself with Spirit. We gain more respect in our own eyes. We feel that we're a "better person" than we were before, and we grow more comfortable and fond of our self. Then when we're consciously being aware in the present, we can more easily feel our basic goodness.

When we violate the Golden Rule, the Commandments, the Eightfold Path, or society's codes of good behavior, we withdraw good feeling from our account. Guilt, shame, and self-disparagement debit our account of good feeling and we lose respect in our own eyes. But, while misbehavior debits our account, we can always seek our own forgiveness, God's (Jesus', Buddha's, the Great Spirit's . . .) forgiveness, or the forgiveness of anyone to whom we owe an apology.

We can acknowledge our wrongdoing and make efforts to correct the wrong, doing our best to make amends where and when we can, and not repeating the misdeed.

We'll never be perfect (from personality's perspective), but as we grow spiritually and morally, we find that recognizing and behaving in keeping with basic goodness is much more automatic. We find that basic goodness arises naturally from spending more time being awake and aware in the present.

Jesus said, "Love your enemies and pray for those who persecute you so that you may be children of your Father in heaven, for

He makes His sun rise on the evil and on the good, and sends rain on the righteous and the unrighteous." Jesus' showering of love on whoever is present is an expression of advanced spirituality that is beyond our personality's comprehension.

Buddha said, "Like a mother who protects her child, her only child, with her own life, one should cultivate a heart of unlimited love and compassion towards all living beings."

It is to the experienced student that Rajneesh is speaking when he says, *"First you be, and once you are then it is not a mission. Once you are blissful, then you don't go out of your way to help others—your very being is a help wherever you are; you don't make it a profession. The way you are, wherever you are, you help."*

This is part of what, in the East, is called the Royal Path, the inner wisdom of those who've evolved and matured as human beings. To walk the Royal Path is for personality to be merged with Spirit, so basic goodness is a natural outgrowth of normal living.

When we've grown enough to see that we are the world, and that others are also part of our larger Self as conscious humankind, then we act out of universal spiritual goodness rather than personal self-interest.

There are many specific ways to be in touch with and to express our basic goodness, all of which provide us with natural nourishment and add to our Basic Goodness Account. We can use the Basic Goodness Menu to see the good things we do each day, week, or month, feeding our self spiritual and psychological nourishment.

Read through the list below and see if you can add items of your own. Think about the small and big ways our efforts, intentions, and actions express basic goodness.

And keep in mind that since our old patterns have a life of their own, we may have to make great effort in the beginning of any change. Once a new pattern is established, we can let ourselves go with the spiritual flow. When we become a spontaneous expression of basic goodness, we're enriched and nourished.

The Spiritual Diet's basic goodness recommendation:

1. Each day, choose items from the Basic Goodness Menu to nourish your soul.
2. Aim your energies at more fully aligning your daily life with basic goodness.
3. Appreciate the good that you do, extracting the nutrients from your good intentions and efforts.

Basic Goodness Menu

Caring about others: tucking in our child with a kiss good night, sincerely asking how another feels and listening to his or her answer, being supportive of a friend with a family problem, being moved to sadness by another's plight, circulating a birthday card for a coworker, taking a pet out for a walk...

Helping others: calling a sick friend, running an errand for a family member, starting a neighbor's dead battery, volunteering or making charitable contributions...

Spiritual involvement: going to church, temple, synagogue, nature, or reading spiritual material, being attentive, praying, just being...

Moral actions: following the Golden Rule, the Ten Commandments, Eightfold Path, and other forms of ethical behavior (truth telling, not killing, not stealing)...

Being conscientious: trying to be conscientious and doing a good job at work and home, caring about our natural world (growing a garden, not polluting, cleaning up after ourselves, recycling), being a good parent/child/partner/friend, trying to understand the other's point of view . . .

Having good intentions: having the intent of doing the right thing, wanting to be helpful, aiming to be considerate, trying to be compassionate and forgiving, trying to understand the other's needs and points of view . . .

Consideration of others: letting a pedestrian or car go ahead, letting someone have his or her way, cleaning up after ourselves, thinking of another's point of view . . .

Forgiveness and compassion: letting things go that bothered, hurt, or annoyed us, being understanding of the other's side, empathizing with others . . .

Good manners: acknowledging others, using a genuine "Hello," "How are you?," "Thank you," "Please," handshake, pat on the back, a friendly hug . . .

Basic being: realizing our value and worth by virtue of simply being, feeling our warm heart of loving kindness, appreciating our underlying spiritual preciousness.

All of these are ways to nourish our soul and our personality, while aligning personality with spirituality's basic goodness. Each day we can look for opportunities to live out our basic goodness and learn to appreciate our actions and our effort, nurturing and nourishing both our personality and our soul and helping us lose the weight of the world.

Experiencing Basic Goodness

The point to be grasped is this, that HEART
means the very Core of one's being, the Center,
without which there is nothing whatever. The
Heart is the undifferentiated Light of pure
Consciousness.

RAMANA MAHARSHI

Awareness is the light of human consciousness, and presence is our
home. Goodness comes from our heart, the core of our being, the
light of our life, the warmth in our home. With attention and presence we calm ourselves, and connect with our spiritual side, our eternal Self, ever ready to greet us as our personality *rests, content and complete in the moment, if only for a moment.*

*We can allow our self to slow down while we're reading these words. Breath-
ing and being aware in the moment. Following a breath in and out, and then another and another until our thoughts begin to slow down.*

*For a moment, we're in the moment. Aware of where we are, the colors and
shapes, the sounds, the sense of having a physical body, the feelings within our body.
We're aware and we're present and we're present and we're present. Like the clear
tones of a bell awakening us in the moment. Bong! Bong! Bong!*

*For a moment, we can feel our self in the midst of the world. We can focus
attention on goodness by recalling some good things we may have done. Perhaps we'll
recall a time when we were a child and we loved something or someone very much—
maybe a dog or cat or a best friend or a close family member. We can all recall times
we've felt and acted compassionately and find a softness within, a sense of caring
and compassion for people or pets or places we love and loved.*

*We can feel warmth and goodness inside, making our personality feel good.
Think of instances of goodness and be present with these feelings.*

*Once we're aware of this sense of goodness, we can go more deeply and look
within to where the goodness comes from, to the impulse that made us care, nurture,*

and be compassionate. We can focus on the natural urge to help, love, provide, or protect. As we relax even more, we can take a full, slow, conscious breath and be where
we are. Nowhere to go and nothing to do right now.

Breathing, being, and caring. Following a conscious breath in through our
heart and a restful breath out through our heart.

In through our heart, out through our heart.

In, out . . .

There may be a warmth, an opening, a softening of our chest. Maybe tears
come to our eyes as our vulnerability exposes deeper, more hidden feelings. Maybe
sad feelings of family, friends, or pets we've loved and who are long gone come to the
surface. That's natural and cleansing. Let the wave of sadness and loss come and go,
flowing through us now, sadness and love. In through our heart, out through our
heart . . .

We can allow our self to relax where we are for a moment. Our breathing
targets (where the air enters and leaves our nose and mouth) help us aim our awareness and presence—breathing in, being here, breathing out, resting now, our abdomen
rising and falling. Breathing in, recalling a recent kindness, breathing out, feeling basic goodness. Imagine goodness inside, bright yellow, glowing, golden, filling us with
warmth. We can feel the glowing within our own chest and it feels so good, even if
only for a moment. Perhaps a smile comes to our face as we appreciate the living,
loving, and basically good consciousness that's always within us. Breathing atten-
tively and relaxing, feeling the good feeling. In through the heart, out through the
heart.

Awareness gradually expands beyond our personal self to include the spiritual source of basic goodness, as the personal and spiritual flow together like streams
into the sea.

When we take a full, relaxed breath, and rest where we are with a good heart,
we can smile with deep love. We can feel the fresh cleanness as we step from our
shower. We can enjoy a spring breeze on our skin and the fresh air in our lungs.

Our experience of goodness connects our personal, separate self with Spirit
and is a manifestation of Spirit. And, as we sense basic goodness and feel our caring, we realize it's not just our self that is important. As we feel goodness, we connect with others, sensing our self in them. We can open to the larger consciousness

of which we're all a part. We are the world. Each of us is woven into the fabric of life.

We see that when we experience and act in keeping with our basic goodness, we are an expression of God. Spiritual goodness lives itself out through our good acts, kind thoughts, and compassionate feelings, and makes the world a better and more loving place. Rabbi Aryeh Kaplan writes:

> We see that the commandments are a special means that God gave us to experience the Divine . . . Imagine that you are in love. You are constantly trying to do things to please your beloved and draw closer to him or her . . . The same is true of God's commandments. These are not acts that one does on one's own to express one's love for God, but acts that God has asked us to do as an expression of this love. If one keeps God in mind when observing a commandment, the experience can be one of overwhelming love for and closeness to the Divine.

Spirit manifests in the world through us. Each of us can be a clear and loving expression of our basically good spiritual nature. To the extent that we act out of goodness, the world is that much of a better and more loving place.

We eat and are eaten. We consume life and are consumed by it. We are part of the food chain, as our bodies ultimately return to the natural world from which we came—food for worms and birds, flowers and fruit, molecules floating in the air. The Upanishads says, "I am the food of life and I am he who eats the food of life."

The two staples of the Basic Spiritual Diet are awareness and presence. Feeling and acting on our basic goodness is one possible course of the Spiritual Diet. We can cook up a recipe that includes being awake, present, and good.

What Can I Do?
The "Soul Food" Recipe

1. Focus on feeling your basic goodness while consciously breathing and being present.

The Basic Spiritual Diet recommends taking daily breaths (full and slow, in and out with awareness, here and now). Then recognize and foster basic goodness.

An example of a Spiritual Diet Recipe would be a beginning and a second breath to be aware and present, and a third breath to be aware of our basic goodness. Perhaps we could say to our self with our third breath, "Fine as I am," while being aware of a recent good act. Or if we're struggling to align our daily life with our basic goodness, we could say to our self, "God (Jesus, Great Spirit . . .), help me" or "God, give me strength to change." We can repeat our recipe each day and especially whenever we feel our soul in need of nourishment.

We can make it our daily aim to be awake, present, and good as much as possible. The more fully we aim in this life-affirming direction, the more easily living a good life becomes. When we're aware of our basic goodness and are doing what we can to live it out, we can view our self positively and this helps us be present and comfortable with our self.

It's helpful to think of this as a *circle of goodness:* When we do good, we feel good, and then we can more fully rest where we are and how we are. Then we're more fully in the present and more aware. And as we're more present, we're more aware of our goodness, and then we more easily act in keeping with our natural goodness, and that makes us feel good—and so on as the circle of goodness keeps turning:

2. Eating good food nourishes our body, and a daily diet of basic goodness nourishes our soul. Look for opportunities to fill up with basic goodness, acting on the thought, feeling, or impulse to understand, care, and help. We can consciously breathe in and out *through our heart*, feeling our caring and acting on the inner impulse to love and help each day. And then we need to appreciate our good acts.

When someone needs something you can give, give what you can. Buy an extra can of food when you go shopping, and when you've filled a grocery bag, donate it to a homeless shelter. Look for small opportunities to care, help, and do some good. Appreciate what you're doing and recognize the spiritual source behind it all.

3. Everyday life can help us. Keep the Basic Goodness Menu on pages 97–98 in mind. **Keep alert for opportunities to make the world a bit better each day.**

Feel the glowing warmth in your heart, breathing in with awareness, breathing out with rest and relaxation. We will create a welcoming home sweet home of caring and compassion, for our self and others.

4. Regardless of our religion, or even if we don't follow an organized religion, we can all **welcome Jesus' teachings of love and the Dalai Lama's teachings of kindness** into our life and heart.

Love, kindness, charity, and compassion can be an important part of our daily Spiritual Diet philosophy of life.

5. Focus on healing and nourishing our self. Many people's personalities are heavily weighted with emotional wounds, and it's difficult to feel good and express our goodness when we're preoccupied with unhappiness, worries, or pain. (See Chapter 8 for ways to properly process unpleasant and uncomfortable emotions.) To heal ourselves we can *nourish our personality and soul with a Good Feeling File.*

Create a file in which you put anything that heals your wounds, makes you feel good about yourself, and shows evidence of your acting in keeping with basic goodness. A note of thanks from Grandma goes in the file, along with a certificate of appreciation. Any awards or good evaluations. And write down any nice comments made to you about yourself (with name and date). You can also put in pictures and names of people you care about. If you want, you can keep a log of your efforts to express goodness.

The Good Feeling File is nourishment for both personality and soul. It mends our emotional bruises, changes our perspective and behavior, and aligns our personal and spiritual life. We should develop a habit of adding good things to our file.

6. Find and develop a loving inner mother, father, grandmother, or grandfather. Many people are deeply wounded at some time during childhood, and throughout life have a sense of basic badness and a hard time finding their basic goodness. We can help and heal our self by finding and developing a loving inner mother, father, grandmother, or grandfather—a healthy, supportive, and caring part of our self that is centered in spiritual basic goodness. Whatever form it takes, we can find this older, calmer, wiser, and safer part of life and carry it in our own mind and heart.

7. We can care about our self, understanding and appreciating all we've been through. We can have compassion for our self and our suffering, and find forgiveness, allowing our self to more fully relax with who and what we are. We can soften excessive self-criticism and avoid excessively focusing on the three wrong answers and find the twenty-seven correct answers in our life. We can contribute to our Basic Goodness Account. Then we can feel a deep love for our self, for the pain and struggles we've endured. We can understand and find forgiveness, enabling us to let go and move on. And when we learn to have caring and compassion for our self, we can move beyond the hurt, guilt, or shame.

Our warm heart of love can create self-forgiveness and patience, and warm us with its glow, helping us to have more respect for our self. We can look our self in the eye and be on intimate terms with our self and our world, healing us and lightening our burden.

Learn to give yourself love, understanding, friendship, forgiveness, and compassion, diminishing your dependence on others for love and acceptance. Instead of the usual search for love and acceptance from the world outside, when we live out our basic goodness and appreciate it, we find that we contain an unlimited supply of inner intimacy, friendliness, and warmth.

8. Some people have serious problems that this book will not solve. These people should **seek life-affirming, professional help** to change their ingrained personality patterns.

9. We must live and act responsibly, with self-control and self-discipline, in keeping with both spiritual values and the highest values of society. But we don't need to beat our self up for wrongdoing. We can find forgiveness and follow Jesus' instruction to "go forth and sin no more."

10. Keep growing forward. Spiritual growth is not a matter of memorization or accumulation. In fact, we grow spiritually by a process of subtraction as we lose the weight of the world; less personal struggle and pain, more Spirit, presence, and peace.

What matters is awareness and presence, which deepen with time and experience. Our aim and intent are powerful psychological forces which we can use throughout life. When we aim and intend to breathe consciously in the present, in and out of our heart center, we grow in attention, presence, and kindness. In time—be it days, weeks, months, or years—the power and influence of the Spiritual Diet's heartfelt course of basic goodness will have its life-affirming effect.

Basic goodness brings about the possibility of being on intimate, caring terms with our self and the world around us. When we walk a path in accordance with our heart, honor our values, and are present and attentive where we are, we begin to appreciate the incredible gift we've been given by simply being alive.

Chapter 5

Singing
the Body Electric

Caress the divine details.

VLADIMIR NABOKOV

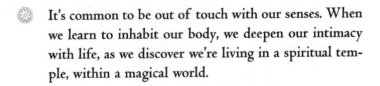

It's common to be out of touch with our senses. When we learn to inhabit our body, we deepen our intimacy with life, as we discover we're living in a spiritual temple, within a magical world.

Out of Touch

I can be so preoccupied that I hardly notice what's around me. It seems I eat without tasting or even smelling. Then suddenly I'm through my whole lunch and I hardly remember what I had.

I don't really enjoy sex as much as I wish I could. Sometimes it's because I'm thinking about something else or sometimes it's as if I'm numb or at least not very sensitive, so that touching doesn't feel as exciting as I wish it did.

A lot of the time my body is just another responsibility I have to handle. Bathe it, feed it, clothe it, beautify it, exercise it, medicate it, satisfy it, and hope it doesn't hurt or get sick.

A woman brought home two monkeys and wanted to keep them in her bedroom. Her husband objected, saying, "What about the smell?" His wife answered, "Don't worry about the smell. I got used to it. They'll get used to it, too."

We may be eternal Spirit, but we find ourselves in human bodies that are hairy, smelly, sweaty, and in need of showers. The Pulitzer Prize–winning author Ernest Becker vulgarly captured our complex situation when he wrote, "Man is a god who shits."

We are beauty and the beast. Each of us contains a beauty, the gentle soul of our spiritual nature, and a beast, the animal body in which we're housed that craves food, fluids, sleep, sex, and much more.

As a result, we humans have always had a love-hate relationship with our body. On the one hand, we glorify our physical form in paintings and sculpture, idolize beautiful men and women (automatically attributing success, niceness, and brightness to them), and devote enormous time, energy, and money to our physical appearance (clothing, makeup, cologne, hair care). And of course, we take great pleasure from our body (food and drink, music and dance, affection and sex).

On the other hand, our body's "animal" functions are embarrassing and usually kept private. They are also the origin of most curses and ways we express anger and aggression (full of crap, pissed off), not to mention the butt of endless jokes. So, while we enjoy our body, we're also often shy or even disgusted by it at the same time.

From early human history, people have viewed the body as vulgar and the Spirit as sacred. As early as the sixth century B.C., various religious groups began to reject their physical bodies as inhibitors of Spirit. "Purification" (by pain, deprivation, even fire) was used to detach from or be rid of the body so the soul could be released. Methods such as fasting, celibacy, and self-mutilation were used as ways of punishing and diminishing the power of the body and its seductive, animal pleasures.

Most of us are not so radical in our fear and rejection of the body, but, in more subtle ways, we all learn to control our physical behavior and suppress our senses.

The French obstetrician Frederick Leboyer wrote that as infants we're awash in sensation:

> What makes being born so frightful is the intensity, the boundless scope and variety of experience, its suffocating richness.
>
> People say—and believe—that a newborn baby feels nothing. He feels *every*thing.
>
> Everything—utterly, without choice or filter or discrimination.
>
> Birth is a tidal wave of sensation, surpassing anything we can imagine. A sensory experience so vast we can barely conceive it.

When we are babies, the senses are undivided, mixed together in a sea of nipple/mouth/eyes/skin/milk. Only later do we learn to separate out sight from smell, touch from taste, and sound from all the rest, and begin to experience them as more commonplace.

As children, we're still very sensorially focused. But soon, little by little, we're desensitized as we're taught to limit our senses. For example, it's common for parents to say things like, "Stop crying. That isn't so bad." So we learn to tune out the pain and control our reactions. And, "Clean your plate. You're not leaving this table until you've finished." So we learn to ignore our natural sense of taste (which tells us it tastes bad) and our stomach (which is saying it's already full). And, "Don't tell me you're tired. You're fine and you're going to school." So we learn to ignore physical fatigue in order to do what we're expected to do. And, "Stop staring out the window and finish your homework." So we learn to ignore what's around (and within) us in order to stay mentally focused on what we have to do.

This doesn't change as we get older. Indeed, while we may pay tremendous attention to our physical appearance, we only minimally sense our physical sensations. As writer/actor Robert Benchley joked, "As for me, except for an occasional heart attack, I feel as young as I ever did."

And the heavier our burden of responsibilities, the more this is true. Yes, we're concerned about how we feel, but only insofar as it helps us continue to get our job done. We may complain of aches and pains, but only because we can't ignore them and are annoyed when they're interrupting us. This is particularly true for parents of young children who must go on whether they are tired, sick, hungry, or whatever else. The more we have to do, the more we learn to ignore our body so we can continue on.

This is also true sexually. This "out of touch" mind-set contributes to inhibited sexual desire, frigidity, impotence, premature ejaculation, and more. Of course, self-control is essential and valuable, but there's a cost along with the benefits. Our socialization helps us learn self-control in order to produce law-abiding and productive citizens, but it also teaches us to ignore our physical sensations. Alan Watts described the results when he wrote that "awareness of our own existence is so superficial and so narrow that nothing seems to us more boring than simple being. If I ask you what you did, saw, heard, smelled, touched, and tasted yesterday, I am likely to get nothing more than the thin, sketchy outline of the few things that you noticed, and of those only what you thought worth remembering."

As our personality is caught up in the struggle to survive and succeed, our bodily needs often begin to seem like time-consuming chores, while our physical sensations become background noise.

We're too busy getting to work to notice our hands on the steering wheel. We're too preoccupied listening to our own thoughts to really hear the bird's song. We're too lost in conversation and newspaper to truly savor our food. And smells are mentally identified rather than sensorially experienced, as when we say, "Oh, that's a rose" or "That's a gardenia," naming it rather than fully enjoying its sweet perfume.

It's as if our thoughts and activities are jamming our system of senses. Mental static blocks out our senses and much of the rest of reality.

How sad, because we're losing the opportunity to live in a spiritual temple that can help lighten our worldly load.

While our body may be a hassle, it's also the primary way we have to fully experience life.

Coming to Our Senses

If we do come back into our body, we experience a vibrancy in the sheer act of living, and we feel more alive and fulfilled. We can discover the basic goodness of living in physical form with the simple reality of our senses.

> More fully inhabiting our body brings the real goodness of simple experiences, enabling us to relax and feel at home in the midst of our daily life.

The poet T. S. Eliot wrote that we must use what God has given us to serve God, that we are

> *joined spirit and body,*
> *And therefore must serve as spirit and body.*
> *Visible and invisible, two worlds meet in Man;*
> *Visible and invisible must meet in His Temple;*
> *You must not deny the body.*

Being conscious and awake brightens the light of awareness. Being present helps us relax, content and complete. Basic goodness adds the warmth of a good heart.

> Awareness of basic sensations helps us inhabit our sacred body and feel more at home inside our life.

As Chogyam Trungpa writes, "Discovering real goodness comes from appreciating very simple experiences. We are not talking about how good it feels to make a million dollars or finally graduate from college or buy a new house, but we are speaking here of the basic goodness of being alive."

We're alive in the flesh. The spiritual energy within us is manifested in a human body, and if we listen to that body, we can discover that a feast has been set before us.

Our waking consciousness has a natural inclination to be attuned to our senses. Using breathing to be aware in the present helps us consciously experience our physical sensations in the here and now. Then we and our sensations are one and the same; we are not a person with eyes who's seeing, but instead we become the act of seeing. We *are* the seeing. Chinese Zen master Garma C. C. Chang writes:

> When one discovers this self-awareness, he finds his whole being changed. While engaging in any activity, he talks and walks, but he feels that his talking and walking is not the same as before—he now walks with an opened mind. He actually knows that *it is he* who is doing the walking; the director—himself—is sitting right in the center of his mind, controlling all his actions with spontaneity. He walks in bright awareness and with illumined spirit . . . He then senses that ordinary people, blind to their innate, bright awareness, tread the streets like walking corpses!

Millions of us are spiritually comatose and fail to inhabit our body and our life. One of the few who awakened and walked with "bright awareness" was Krishnamurti, who described an experience of seeing with "illumined spirit":

> The earth was the color of the sky; the hills, the green ripening rice fields, the trees and the dry, sandy river-bed were the color of the sky; every rock on the hills, the big boulders, were the clouds and they were the rocks. Heaven was the earth and the earth heaven; the setting sun had transformed everything.
> The sky was blazing fire, bursting in every streak of cloud,

in every stone, in every blade of grass, in every grain of sand. The sky was ablaze with green, purple, violet, indigo, with the fury of flame.

The hills became transparent, every rock and boulder was without weight, floating in color and the distant hills were blue, the blue of all the seas and the sky of every clime. And the road that crossed the valley was purple and white, so alive that it was one of the rays that raced across the sky. You were of that light.

We can share our experiences by offering a delicious, ripe strawberry to a friend or sitting with a loved one watching a glowing sunset over the tree-covered hills. But each of us experiences our own sensations within our own body that intimately connects us with the world outside. When we're open to our awareness, without boundary, the strawberry, the setting sun, the mountain, our friends and loved ones are all interrelated with us. Our intimacy extends to the world and we love what is. Then we see that we are God's eyes and ears, a physical manifestation of Spirit.

God's Eyes and Ears

Christian mystic Meister Eckhart wrote, "The eye by which I see God is the same as the eye by which God sees me. My eye and God's eye are one and the same—one seeing, one knowing, one loving."

When we breathe to be aware in the present, we begin to more fully experience our self both as a spiritual being with the light of consciousness and as a physical personality with elaborate needs and desires.

Walt Whitman wrote, "If anything is sacred the human body is sacred." The body is our soul's housing, the result of billions of years of biochemical evolution. It's a physical mechanism of unimaginable complexity, unbelievable adaptability, and, when used properly, tremendous magic.

We reside within a temple, but we experience this fact only when we inhabit our body.

A beginning understanding would say that our body contains Spirit, but a more sophisticated understanding would go further, realizing the oneness of our senses with Spirit.

The Gospel of St. Paul asks, "Do you know that you are God's temple and God's spirit makes it home in you? . . . the temple of God is sacred and that is what you are."

The German poet Friedrich Novalis wrote, "We touch Heaven as we lay our hand on a human body."

Kahlil Gibran wrote, "Your body is the harp of your soul." The music of our basic nature comes forth when we play in the physical temple.

> **Mature souls, those who have highly developed conscious awareness in the present, realize that our Spirit is housed within the physical body with its needs and desires, pleasures and pains, and five senses. But the eternal light that shines within is not dependent on the physical for its existence. Spirit exists within and beyond the physical plane.**

By attending to our body, we gain access to Spirit as it manifests in our physical being. Our body can be a door into the dining room to enjoy a "meal" of conscious intimacy with our self.

As we return again and again to awareness of our bodily needs and desires, pleasures and pains, and the five senses, we can pay attention to what is. The body walks with awareness. The body sits with awareness. The body sees, smells, and hears with awareness. The body eats with awareness. The body breathes with awareness.

The body rests with awareness. The awareness animates us as it's channeled through our body and our bodily senses.

The spiritual presence is lived through the body itself. When we live more richly within our senses and learn to "caress the divine details," we can appreciate all that our body can experience in daily life, and realize that a feast has been set before us.

What Can I Do?
The "Magic Temple" Recipe

Fully digest our bodily senses. At any moment of life, we can live within our senses. We can do it even now. To reconnect with our body and our senses, we begin with the Basic Spiritual Diet before adding the recipe for awareness of sensations.

We take full, slow, conscious breaths in and out to be aware. Then we take second breaths in and out, to be here and now, focusing our attention in the flow of sensation in the ever-changing present.

Adding these nutrients to our system gets the basic spiritual "digestion" process going. It gives us the power of awareness and presence, producing the clarity and energy needed to focus more effectively on any burden—in this case on being in touch with the magic temple of our body, aware and present with our senses.

The "digestion" process of sensations begins with the Basic Spiritual Diet's beginning and second breaths for (1) awareness and (2) presence, continuing our normal breathing with awareness and presence. Then focus on

whatever sensations exist as they exist, (3) experiencing the sights, sounds, smells, tastes, and touches that come our way.

Try these three steps now. Breathe with awareness and presence until you're aware in the ever-changing moment, then focus on your bodily sensations:

A conscious breath in, feeling our arms, a breath out, feeling our arms.
A breath in, smelling the air, here and now, a breath out, feeling the air leave.
A conscious breath in, seeing a beautiful blue, a breath out, seeing a warm brown.
A breath in, hearing a plane, a breath out, hearing our breath right now.
A breath in, sensing our tongue, a breath out, tasting our saliva.
A breath in, inhabiting our body, a breath out, resting inside our clothes.

Air passing in and out of our nose and mouth, we can be aware and present, clothed or naked.

Once we've immersed our self in our senses, then the next steps in the digestion process of sensation are to (4) let go of the experience and (5) open to awareness and presence of whatever comes next, in an ongoing cycle.

Breathing in and out, aware and present with the colors before me—blues and browns, turquoise and maroon. A cat meows and the colors are less apparent as awareness and presence shift to the kitty running through the room. Letting go and opening to whatever comes next, be they sights, sounds, smells, touches, or tastes.

SIGHT— Incredible richness surrounds us if we have eyes to see. Wherever we are, we can take a moment or a minute (or five, ten, twenty) each day to attune to sight, noticing the colors, the shapes and shades, the shadows, designs, and movement that come with the gift of sight. Just look at colors, for example. Or just look at green—infinite intensities and textures in leaves and cars and clothes of every imaginable green. **Life is in living color! Look around!**

Try closing your eyes for a moment or a minute, and when you open them, pay attention to the incredible visible universe right around you. The color of this book, the quality of light falling on this page, the hue of your skin and clothing—the sights surrounding us are a feast for the eyes. We can enjoy and appreciate our eyes.

Now we let this fill us, surround us, pass through us, and we let it go, before opening to awareness and presence of whatever comes next.

Look into your eyes in a mirror each day. There's an ancient saying that "the eyes are the windows to the soul," and we can connect with our own soul by looking in our eyes each day (maybe appreciating a recent instance of how our basic goodness manifested itself), if only for a moment in passing. We can see who we are and how we're doing, as we slow down for a moment and really see ourselves.

Maybe we can slow down enough to see our true identity while we're brushing our teeth in the morning or when we're putting on makeup or brushing our hair or washing our hands before eating. We can take a full, relaxing breath and see ourselves.

SOUNDS— Now take a moment and shift to the sounds that are present. Breathe full and slow, in and out with awareness here and now. We can relax for a moment and a breath, and listen.

Close your eyes for a moment and be like an unobstructed, open microphone, hearing whatever sounds exist right now. Now let go and hear whatever comes next (the same or different sounds). It's quite simple, really. There are sounds in the foreground—a loud talker, a radio, a car honking. And there are background sounds—

the hum of the computer, cars whooshing by, ice cubes in a glass, a far-off jet, the wind through the trees. If we pay attention to our ears and our hearing, we can discover the world of sound.

Helen Keller, blind, deaf, and mute, wrote, "I am just as deaf as I am blind . . . Deafness is a much worse misfortune. For it means the loss of the most vital stimulus—the sound of the voice that brings language, sets thoughts astir and keeps us in the intellectual company of man . . . I have found deafness to be a much greater handicap than blindness."

Those of us who are not deaf and take our hearing for granted can appreciate the great gift of sound we've been given and heighten our sense of hearing with attention and presence. We can feast on sound.

SMELLS— Smells surround us throughout life and we can attune to them. Full and slow, consciously breathing in and out, here and now—the aroma of fresh coffee, tea, or chocolate in the morning; the smell of perfume or cologne that people wear at work; the fragrance of the flowers in the backyard; the smell of dinner cooking. We can pay attention to our sense of smell each day.

Without smell, our food is lifeless and bland. That's part of the reason why we so often lose our appetite when our nose is stuffed. We can appreciate our nose by noticing what we smell, letting go and opening to awareness of the smells that come next.

TOUCH— One afternoon, an old woman came to the Buddha and asked him how to meditate. He instructed her to remain aware of each movement of her hands and arms as she drew water from the well each day.

There are endless opportunities every day we're alive in the flesh to be awake and aware of how we touch the world and how the world touches us. We no longer go to the well for water, but when we go to the refrigerator for a snack or the sink for a drink, we can feel our mouth and teeth, as we bite an apple or drink a glass of milk.

Full and slow, consciously breathing in and out, here and now. When we wash our hands at the sink or do the dishes, we can feel our hands and arms, the sensation of the warm water on our skin. We take a conscious, present breath as we touch the world and the world touches us.

We can tune into our sense of touch at any moment. Right now we can feel our body resting in our chair, within our clothes, touching the pages of this book. Our arm brushes our leg and we feel our aliveness in the flesh more fully.

Rabbi Zalman Schachter-Shalomi teaches us to "feel the earth beneath you; feel the chair; feel how gravity upholds you. Gravity is the way earth loves you and attracts us. We should allow ourselves to be supported by that."

What a nice way to relax on the earth. The earth supports our body, holding us on the surface, keeping us in touch with the ground, constantly helping us to be grounded. Feel our feet resting on the ground, our buttocks and our back held in contact with our chair.

We can consciously touch the keys to our house or car as we leave for the day or arrive home at night. We can touch our pen or pencil or computer keys at work with awareness. Feel the thrill of touch. Don't unconsciously kiss your loved ones good-bye for the day or hello in the evening. Slow down for the few seconds that it takes, and actually feel your lips against the skin of your loved one's cheek. Then let that sensation go, and open to the next way life touches you. Even if we're only briefly conscious of touch, that moment of consciousness will nourish our spiritual nature and bring a greater degree of true intimacy to our life.

TASTE—So often we eat our food and drink our coffee/water/tea/soda/juice without sensing what's entering our body.

Slow down for at least a minute during each meal and attend to your taste sensations. Full and slow, in and out, aware here and now. The wetness of your drink, the flavor of your breakfast cereal. Hear the crunch of your carrot or potato chip at lunch; feel the smoothness of the peanut butter and the nutty flavor on your tongue. Salt and sour, sweet and bitter, connect us with what we eat and drink. Our senses act as a bridge binding us with the outside world as we incorporate it into our body.

The tastes lingering in our mouth, perhaps a hint of coffee or tea or a recent snack or toothpaste, can remind us to appreciate how much we enjoy our sense of taste. Letting the taste go, we open to whatever comes next. We can appreciate our mouth and tongue.

Experiencing "What Is" With Awareness

Whether we're an absolute beginner or an accomplished master, our awareness can repeatedly return to the moment we're living here and now. Breath is a special helper because its presence pulls us inside our body. Every moment of life we're breathing, and we can feel it in our mouth, nose, lungs, chest, stomach, abdomen, and back. If we sense it deeply enough, we can feel the oxygen from our breath reach our brain, fingers, and toes through our blood system. We can feel our aliveness in our bodily sensations at any and every moment, and our breath can remind us hundreds and thousands of times to awaken in the moment, living in our body.

If being out of touch with your senses is a particular burden for you, then your Spiritual Diet should focus on learning to consciously relax within your body each day:

Awakening each morning, we can feel our body breathing in and out.

Brushing our teeth, we can taste the paste and feel our teeth.

Eating our breakfast, we can breathe and be aware in the present and enjoy the relief and satisfaction of being able to end our morning hunger and add nutritious fuel to our system for the day ahead.

Driving to work, we can breathe and relax in the midst of our commute, hearing the cars whoosh by, seeing the blue sky and the white clouds.

At the office we can keep our ears and eyes awake, hearing the sounds and seeing the sights.

Inevitably our attention drifts away. Over and over again throughout our whole life, our attention is pulled to this thought or that worry, to a problem needing a solution or a plan to be put into action. Nevertheless, we can remind ourselves to keep our attention focused, to return to our immediate experience. We can rest for another moment, awake to a smell or sight or sound, aware of a touch or a taste.

Each moment of attunement is of great value, lightening the weight of burden that comes from being separate from Spirit's physical "home base." By being aware of our senses, we open to our spirituality and realize the inherent goodness of nature and of life itself. When we're awake, we're plugged into the life energy running through us.

Our vital energy is called *ch'i* by the Chinese Taoists, a word meaning "breath." Our breath fans the flames of life that vitalize and energize us. Our body is kept alive through breath, and our senses are how we merge with the world, the bridges of our interconnection. We see the world. We touch the world. We taste the world. We smell the world. We hear the world. Our senses are how we get information about the world and enjoy what's been created on the physical plane. If we merge with our senses, we realize *we are the world.*

Over time we can develop our awareness to the point that we stay aware and present more and more of the time. Gradually we can become very comfortable with all our senses, and as we learn to relax deeply into wherever we are, we become a reflection of all our senses. We are like a mirror that reflects what's seen, or a microphone that picks up the sounds.

Seeing Sound, Feeling Taste

Synesthesia is the mixing together of our senses, which happens when the barriers between our senses begin to fade. When that happens, we see and smell and taste the lasagna all at once, while the sound of chewing and the touch of the noodles in our mouth melt into one another in a delicious blending of sensation.

In the Bible, when the Ten Commandments were given to the Hebrews, "All the people *saw* the sounds," illustrating a merging and opening to boundariless sensations.

We can be open to sense combinations. We don't just *see* our plate of fruit or *hear* the sound of our spoon against the dish or *taste* a strawberry. In fact, they are intertwined in a stream of senses, which we have known ever since we were born. The senses blend together like currents into a river of sight/smell/sound/touch/taste. And we can be attuned to the combinations as they occur.

Let things in the physical world jolt us into a gentle awareness: the ring of a phone, the yellow of a scarf, the taste of coffee or juice, the whiff of a perfume, the feel of another's skin as we shake hands.

As we sit before our dinner, we can begin by breathing consciously in the present, feeling our lungs fill with air, feeling the air touch our mouth, lips, and nose, the smells all around us, the colors of our food, the bubbling of the soda. We're aware of what passes by. And within us arises a sense of appreciation that we have enough to eat. Right here and now, we breathe and rest as we see what's on our plate, content and complete for the moment. Right now, slowing down enough to notice the green of our lettuce, the tan of our bread. We notice the room we're in and are aware of the light where we're sitting. The sounds come in through our ears and we know what's being said around us. The aromas from our food drift into our nostrils.

We notice that as we chew and the food and fluids are ingested, the tastes subside. Swallowing, we feel the food moving inside us to nourish us and to remove our thirst and hunger. We intuit that we are a process, a movement or flow, craving fuel for energy, seeking and finding, digesting and satisfying, relaxing and relieving.

These sensations allow us to be connected to our life processes.

The Pain in Our Neck

Of course, not all sensations are pleasant and enjoyable. We all experience physical discomfort. The dentist's drill, the doctor's needle, the arthritic ache, the soreness of a nose that's been suffering with a cold or flu, the backache, neckache, or headache. Though we have many modern drugs to help us cope, we can never fully escape these pains even though our personality and body strive to eliminate them.

So we're all regularly confronted by the challenge of how to be aware and present with unpleasant or painful situations. We can take good care of our self to be as healthy as possible through exercise and good nutrition, but there's no escape from experiencing some level of discomfort.

We can't totally escape illness and pain. But we can learn to live with them. We can stop fighting the discomfort and allow it to travel its course while being aware of what is. This awareness allows us to dislike and reject the pain and discomfort. "I hate having a cold. I don't want to see my red, sore nose, or have to keep on blowing it. I don't want to be sick." This is a natural response. There's nothing that says we have to like all we get. That's just one of our personality's fantasies and wishes. Our body and personality have an automatic, deeply ingrained attraction to pleasure and reaction against pain. Our physical survival is rooted in pain avoidance. So it's natural to try to avoid pain and death and to seek that which makes us comfortable and promotes our life. But we all know we can't totally ignore pain. Rather, we have to learn to deal with it, and by doing that we lighten the burden of pain. The essential element is being awake in the moment. Breathe with awareness here and now even when we're angry that we have another headache, backache, or flu. Know it, see it, let it go. Know it, see it, let it go.

When we become one with the pain, we've removed one level of difficulty—our fighting against the pain—and can allow the uncomfortable process to run its course as we breathe and rest in spite of the problem. We can let our personality rest with a comforting "This, too, shall pass."

This doesn't mean we don't do whatever we need to do to end our pain and stop our suffering. But once we've done what can be done, it's healthier to just know that it exists and as much as possible relax, be aware, and let go.

Research reported in the *Journal of Personality and Social Psychology* (vol. 64, no. 2) shows that when we stifle or distract our awareness of physical pain, we prolong our discomfort. Those who suppress their pain actually become more highly sensitized to discomfort and overreact to all sensation, their radar scanning for unpleasantness. We find our attention actually drawn back to the pain we fear and avoid. On the other hand, those who accurately monitor their feelings of pain have the best chance of effectively coping with the unpleasantness, and recover most rapidly. So, even with discomfort and pain, awareness is the best policy.

If discomfort is a heavy weight, we may need to purposely balance our life with more comfortable feelings. We can *counterbalance the overweighted with the overlooked,* noticing enjoyable, pleasant, and comfortable sights, sounds, smells, tastes, and touches, as well as the unpleasant and the painful.

Losing the Physical Weight of the World

For most people, the taste, smell, sight, sound, and touch of food is a primary source of daily physical enjoyment (not to mention the many other needs our food meets). When we attune more fully to our senses, and we're enjoying our food, we're more likely to eat more slowly, get full more quickly, and thus lose physical weight. When we get physical satisfaction through sources other than eating, food can become a smaller focus, also enabling weight loss. A feast has been set before us in the form of life itself, if only we can learn how to enjoy it.

As we eat with awareness, we not only are nourishing our physical body, we're also nourishing our Spirit.

It takes about twenty minutes for our stomach to tell our brain that it's had enough, so taking time to eat, slowing down and enjoying each bite along the way, means we'll eat less, a natural form of dieting.

Be aware of the foods that are good for you and how they feel inside you.

Be aware of the life-diminishing foods and how they feel inside you.

Once aware, notice yourself feeling more comfortable. As you breathe and open to your senses, notice yourself relaxing more deeply. As you open your senses more fully, notice that greens seem greener, the peach seems juicier, and the sun seems brighter.

Once you actually experience how your food affects your body, you notice more clearly what's good and bad for you. And then you're more likely to avoid what's bad and seek what's good. Personal willpower becomes less important when we're really attuned to our body's reactions to what we eat and drink.

Janice, a middle-aged woman on the Spiritual Diet, who laughingly called herself a chocoholic, became aware of her physical being more acutely than ever before, and reported that she could clearly see that eating chocolate gave her very unpleasant symptoms, including a mild shoulder ache, intestinal tenderness, and discomfort in the joints of her fingers. As she became more keenly aware of the link between these problems and chocolate, she began to find her chocolate addiction diminishing. Janice reported being given a box of Godiva truffles and, with little conscious effort, passed them along to a friend (something that would have been impossible before), with almost no twinge of regret (though with some concern for her friend).

Exercise is natural, and it's the healthiest way to lose physical weight. When we become more aware, we realize our body needs to move—to run, walk, dance, stretch, skip, and bend.

The joy so many children feel in the sheer act of moving, running, and jumping is lost to most adults. For adults, moving is a means of achieving some goal, and all the while our mind is busy with hundreds of thoughts and images. Yet, we can get out of our head and come to our senses if we take a few moments to be aware.

When we pay attention to our senses, we discover the need to use our body more often and more vigorously. The result is a healthier, lighter, stronger, and more flexible body, and we lose more of our excess physical weight.

Keeping as physically healthy as we can enables us to live more spiritually, as we're less preoccupied with our physical existence and can more fully relax and rest, alert and aware, where we are.

Beyond the Body

> As we become more and more fully attuned to our senses, we begin to realize that our Spirit expresses itself through the body. We become aware of our physical existence, and through our senses we experience spirituality.

In time, we come to see the spiritual value of more fully inhabiting our body, and see how to do it for our self at any moment.

When sitting, we know we're sitting. We feel the chair's bottom under our bottom, its back against our back. When walking, we know we're walking. When lying down, we know we're lying down. In this simple and direct way, we inhabit our body more fully. And when we do, we lose the weight that comes with being unaware of our senses. When we come to this understanding, we're enriched by all the colors and tastes and sounds and sights and touches that we experience moment after moment throughout our whole life.

We can breathe and be in our body,
Breathing in, breathing out.
Right now, sitting here,
Reading this book.
Seeing the words, touching the paper.
And as each page goes past, I notice myself more and more aware.

And as we come more fully to our senses, we can recall a song of the Navaho Indians:

As I walk, as I walk,
The universe is walking with me
Beautifully—it walks before me
Beautifully—it walks behind me
Beautifully—it walks below me
Beautifully—it walks above me
Beautifully—on every side
As I walk—I walk with beauty.

We are our body and we're more than our body. Even if we believe that our physical existence and our senses are our most basic fact of life, actually our spiritual nature is more encompassing, enduring, and elementary. We're attached to our appearance, our sensations, our pleasures, yet we are also something deeper and vaster than our physical being.

We're alive in a body. It's natural to feel at home in our physical existence. Conscious, present breathing anchors us physically in the present, and as we rest in our body, our senses are awake and alert. We're on solid ground in the midst of everyday life.

When we're aware in the present, acting out of a warm heart of goodness, at home inside our physical self, then the universe is truly beautiful, and wherever we walk, we walk with beauty.

Chapter 6

 ────────────────────────────

Endless Lust

It is painful to be suspended in unfulfilled
desire, continually searching for satisfaction.

CHOGYAM TRUNGPA

Our personality is endlessly desiring and frustrated.
We can find fulfillment and satisfaction when we understand and meet our needs and gain a spiritual
perspective.

More, Bigger, Better

I never seem to have enough. I'll get something new and quickly find myself wanting to go shopping for something else. I'll buy another pair of shoes when I've already got ten in my closet.

I never feel good about what I've accomplished. For years I wanted to be a division manager, and when I made it I wanted to be a vice-president. Now that I'm V.P. I want to be president. No matter how high I climb, *I always have a sense that I haven't made it yet.*

I want so many things, but I can't afford half of what I want. I'm already in debt, so I'm frustrated every time I walk in a store.

Our desires are as natural as life itself. All of us have basic needs for food, shelter, protection, and closeness with others. Our desires are based in our need to survive, succeed, and satisfy ourselves, particularly in ways that give us pleasure and comfort.

We begin desiring as infants, wanting a pleasant sense of comfort (neither too hot nor too cold, too hungry nor too full). At this early stage, we want to feel pleasure and safety all the time. Our desiring and demands know no limits. We expect to get whatever we want, when we want it, without any consideration of wanting less.

As we grow, however, we gradually learn that our ability to actually *have* everything we desire isn't endless. Unfortunately, it is sharply limited by practical reality. We can't have all the toys we want, and we have to go to school, even if we'd like to stay home and play all day. Still, even knowing that we can't have everything we want doesn't mean we want less. Whatever our practical circumstances, our desires virtually always go far beyond our basic needs for survival.

⬡ **Modern Western culture propels us toward limitless desiring by encouraging the pursuit of happiness through buying and consuming.**

From our earliest years we're stimulated to want ever more. Thousands of commercials and ads enchant and entice us to buy endless toys, foods, and other products.

On birthdays and holidays, love is shown by the giving of new things.

If we're sad or hurt, we're often given food or presents to make us "feel better."

Millions of parents are unable to spend time with their children, because they're away earning money to support the family's needs and desires. One thing they often do to deal with their own frustration and guilt is to buy whatever treats and toys they can for their kids.

Children often find their status among their peers linked to their possessions. Children with the "coolest" clothes, toys, or bike have more "friends" who want to play with them.

We also learn that desiring improves our life. Desiring to get a good grade results in studying harder, which leads to increased learning and better grades. In this way, we learn self-discipline and self-restraint, which helps us in the long run. Civilization itself is based on people's desiring to have things be better than before. We call this progress. So we're constantly reinforced for striving to meet our desires, and seldom, if ever, are we asked to consider (1) the obvious and/or hidden costs of our desires, and (2) that we may already have enough. Thus we grow up with love, attention, friendship, comfort, social status, and progress all associated with the consumption of pleasures and the accumulation of things.

Is it any wonder, then, that we learn so early to seek happiness and comfort through eating, and buying new clothes, toys, gadgets, and all the rest? Is it any wonder that we so often end up devoting so much of our life's energy meeting our wants and desires?

⚛ Once we've met a desire, many of us simply up the ante and want it met even more fully or differently. This pattern is pervasive and usually lifelong.

We may have food, but we want more food, better-tasting food, food prepared for us and served on beautiful plates in a restaurant with a nice view.

We have a house, but we want a bigger house, a newer or more prestigious house in a better neighborhood.

We may have money, but we're spending so much on our house and eating out that we need more.

We have a job, but now we want more prestige or status or power or benefits or salary or better office.

We can fulfill our sexual needs, but we want sex more often or longer lasting or with more cuddling or with more variety.

Of course, as we live, we must meet our needs, so we have to modify and mold the world.

⚛ Meeting our basic needs is essential. The problem comes when we're forever wanting reality to be just the way we want, always wanting it to be different than it is right now. For, as the Buddha taught, the root of human dissatisfaction and suffering is endless desiring.

We Want What We Want When We Want

Why does endless desiring cause us so much trouble? There are two primary reasons. The first is: We want life to be the way we want it to be, and we judge the world based on how well it is, or isn't, meeting our desires and wants. By definition, when we desire something different, we reject *what is* or what we already have. This happens so automatically and unconsciously that we don't notice, yet we're constantly evaluating, judging, and rejecting a part of our life.

> **Endless desire means we're always wanting something different than what we have, which dooms us to endless frustration. Rejecting reality as it exists here and now means we can't ever fully settle down into reality. This keeps us from having peace of mind.**

For example, we wake up in the morning and open our eyes. The weather is good. We accept this with passing notice and little joy. We get up remembering we have an appointment we wish we didn't have to keep, and while we resolve to go anyway, we reject the time we'll have to spend there and feel annoyed. It's just part of our day that we have to get through. We dress hurriedly, on automatic pilot, rarely considering the wealth of choices we have at our disposal and the tremendous time and effort that went into producing what we wear.

We go to the kitchen to find our favorite cereal is missing and we must substitute another. We eat the substitute, perhaps focusing on its not being our first choice, maybe missing the good taste and nourishment of what we do have, losing an opportunity to be spiritually and nutritionally fed.

We find the dog panting at the door to go out and we're running late; we barely notice the dog's loving expression and appreciative tail wagging. As we open the door, we don't see the beauty of the cloud formations or the sun slanting through them. We just feel even more annoyed at being made late by that demanding dog and rush off to work.

In similar patterns, millions of us go through life expecting it all to fit our idea of what we should have. We may have a fine dinner, but it's not exactly what we had in mind and we don't enjoy our food. Or we go to a movie and while it may be entertaining, it isn't as great as some other movie we've recently seen and we diminish the enjoyment available through the comparison.

To one degree or another, we put our time and energy into rejecting what we don't like and changing it to meet our desires, and fail to notice all we do have. The result is that we end up in an ongoing cycle of desire and frustration that, to some extent, makes us suffer.

EGO STEW

Besides rejecting and judging reality, the second reason desiring causes us problems springs from a deeper source.

We live with at least a background feeling of existential tension. No matter how we hide from our mortality, on some level, we know our personality is constantly threatened by our ever-aging body that will one day die. Our personality knows that it, too, is impermanent, so our desiring is in part powered by our wish to escape our mortality and impermanence through pursuing personal power and possessions. This is the food that feeds our ego.

This pursuit is doomed to fail, since the more we identify with our personality, the more we're cooking in the juices of our own anxiety and insecurity (our ego stew), and the more fearful we become of our mortality.

As a result, we try to shore up our tenuous hold on life as we know it, through a stew of ego food. Ego food is a mixture of our accumulations (our car, bank account, clothes, stereo, TV), identifications (our job, family, accomplishments), and attachments (our body, possessions, achievements)—all of which give us a sense of being solid and special. We can tell ourselves, "What I want matters," "I'm as solid and real as I imagine myself to be," "My name and memory will go on and on." We throw all this together in a pot called "our life" and we eat it every day.

Ego stew is highly stimulating. Accumulating things is fun. Having power feels good. Feeling attached calms our insecurities and anxieties. Knowing our roles in life makes us comfortable. Feeling as if we'll go on forever is satisfying.

Ego stew can be a hearty meal, but somewhere in the accumulating process, most of us realize that the satisfaction we experience is fleeting. We get something we want—a new suit, car, stereo, promotion, etc. We get it, we enjoy it, but in short order we find ourselves wanting something else. At some point we may discover that, like sugar and caffeine, this highly stimulating ego stew leaves us with a letdown. We're left endlessly craving more, which makes us spend more time seeking more, which leaves us with less time to spend being connected to our family and friends, less time to be conscious and awake here and now, less of a connection with our spirituality—the only part of us that really is immortal. No wonder many people feel an emptiness, a meaninglessness, and a poverty in the midst of plenty.

Western Poverty

Mother Theresa said that those in the West are even "poorer" than the poverty-stricken peoples of the East, because westerners overemphasize material wealth and underemphasize spiritual riches.

Jesus said, "It's easier for a camel to go through the eye of a needle, than for a rich man to enter the kingdom of God."

Buddha said we are "slaves of desire" who are kept poor because of our endless cravings.

The American philosopher William James said, "The exclusive worship of the bitch-goddess 'Success' [is] our national disease."

In the West, money talks. We may be taught that it's nice to share, but we're mostly taught to highly value what we can accumulate materially for ourselves and our families. Our focus is not just on getting "enough," but on getting as much as possible. As the sayings go, "The one who dies with the most toys wins" and "You can never be too rich or too thin."

Andrew was thirty-eight and already the vice-president of a bank. He was an only child, raised in a huge home by a wealthy family that ate a formal dinner promptly at 7:00 P.M. each evening, tie and jacket required. The supper conversation consisted of how successful Andrew had been at school and sports that day, the stock market, and any new purchases. Andrew grew up focused on getting ahead by aggressively demanding and getting his way, accumulating as much wealth as possible, even if it meant bending the rules to achieve a better bottom line.

When Elizabeth, his wife, filed for divorce, she said, "Andrew is his own god and he worships at the altar of money and success. He's always looking out for his own interests and is so busy struggling to get an even bigger home or boat or plane that neither the children nor I ever really see him. And when he is around he's so intensely preoccupied with himself and his wants that we can't relate to him. He has no real friends, only business associates, and he isn't close with any of his family; not that they ever were. This isn't really living as far as I'm concerned and I can't take it anymore. Unless he can change, I want out."

Andrew is an extreme example of individual and material desire gone awry, but many people are to some degree caught up in the pursuit of their own wants and goals. As a result, they carry the weight of the burden of endless frustration with who they are and what they have.

Part of our difficulty lies in our being caught in a cycle of ever-rising expectations and consumption, without fully realizing the heavy costs involved:

One hundred years ago, few had a telephone and no one had a TV; now 95 percent of Americans have both.

Thirty years ago, the average home was twelve hundred square feet and now it's two thousand, yet who doesn't want more living space? We've come to expect the newer, bigger house.

In the 1950s, very few people had two cars, but now two cars are considered a necessity for suburban dwellers who can't get around without personal transportation for each adult. Car payments, gas, repairs, and insurance require many hours of labor each week that take our time and energy away from other pursuits, thus taking a toll on the quality of our life and relationships.

Thirty years ago, one worker in the family (usually male) could buy that smaller home, while the other (usually female) could stay home with the children. It certainly had its good and bad points, but now most men and women feel they have to work full-time to have the bigger home, TV, computer, and all the rest that we've come to expect. The kids are in day care and the divorce rate is around 50 percent.

We keep raising the standards and in so doing sacrifice parts of life that are crucial for our own and our family's health, sanity, and spiritual renewal. Instead, we should ask ourselves, "Are the things I'm working for worth the time and effort? Do I have enough left over to spend on what matters most—family, friends, living out my main purposes in life, having inner experiences that nurture me and help me evolve as a human being?"

⚜ **Our preoccupation with our desires and our material/pleasure attachments gives us a heavy weight of the world, the sense that life isn't good enough as it is, making us unable to deeply relax and be happy here and now.**

This is the modern person's dilemma. We are, after all, just doing what seems natural, and what our society has trained and reinforced us to do. Are we supposed to just stop ourselves from desiring? What are we to do?

Desiring the End of Desire

Not all people in the West subscribe to such materialistic lust. The Amish are a people who live in Western society, but have very different values from the surrounding culture. They live closer to the land with tight-knit families and community, and without much in the way of modern technology. Recently, an Amish woman from Minnesota, Mary Lambright, was killed when a truck hit her horse-drawn buggy. The modern society she and her people shunned had taken her life. Her husband, now a widower, Mahlon Lambright, is a forty-three-year-old carpenter with eleven children to raise. Yet, when he was offered $212,000 from the insurance company as a wrongful-death settlement, he turned it down, saying that he was concerned that the money would threaten his family's way of life, would cause more problems than it was worth, and that other members of the Amish community "would feel bad" if he took the money. It's almost inconceivable to most of us how anyone could feel this way. Yet, while our lifestyle of material and personal desiring may bring us tremendous benefits, it also causes us a great weight that may only be noticed by the few who are dedicated to its avoidance.

In truth, even if we try to make ourselves stop desiring entirely, we can't succeed because the desire to stop desiring is, in itself, a desire. And this desire continues the desiring process by setting our personality—the desirer—against itself, reinforcing personality's rejection of reality. This creates additional frustration and disappointment and a further desire to be rid of these bad feelings, creating an endless, unhappy cycle.

We cannot stop desiring, nor can we get everything we want. So what are we to do?

We begin by understanding what desires we truly need to meet and limiting the rest. When we realize we have met personality's real needs, our personality has the possibility of relaxing its grip and feeling less preoccupied with our self and our desires. Once personality relaxes, it can open more fully to spirituality, and we are able to meet our deeper needs. At the same time, we learn to set limits, to use self-control and strengthen our awareness of the desiring process.

A key element in beginning to understand ourselves is to understand normal and typical human needs and desires.

What's Controlling Us?

The human motivation chart on page 142 can act as a general map to understanding what motivates us. On the left are *Survival and Security* motivations that drive us to reduce or get rid of tension; they're known as "deficiency" motives in which we're trying to avoid something that makes us uncomfortable.

On the right are *Satisfaction and Stimulation* motivations that excite or increase arousal, and are known as "abundancy" motives in which we're trying to attain something that makes us feel good.

Both types of motivations push and pull us in five basic areas of human life: the Body, Mind, Self, Environment, and Society.

The human motivation chart is a useful device that divides life into ten boxes. In spite of the limitations of any chart, this one is helpful in understanding our bodily, mental, personal, environmental, and social drives, wishes, wants, and needs.

Slow down and take a couple of full, even breaths, conscious and content, here and now. Read through at least some of each section so you get the idea. (Notice your physical and emotional reactions as you read.)

SURVIVAL AND SECURITY	SATISFACTION AND STIMULATION

BODY

Avoid pain, thirst, hunger, lack of oxygen, fatigue, excess heat or cold, illness, overfull bladder/colon, muscle tension, discomfort and death . . .

Attain pleasurable sense experiences (good tastes, smells, touches, sights, and sounds), sexual relief/satisfaction, physical comfort, mastery, exercise, safety, and contact . . .

MIND

Avoid boredom, understimulation, confusion, ignorance . . .

Attain alert awareness, challenges, clarity, knowledge and education, mental training, understanding life and how it works and our place in it, variety and novelty of mental stimuli . . .

SELF

Avoid feelings of inferiority, failure, shame, fear, sadness, loss of identity, blame, guilt, shame, failure in relation to others, embarrassment, inferiority, fear and other painful emotions, loss of identity . . .

Attain self-respect, integrity, sense of achievement, moral code, a meaningful place in society, self-worth, self-respect, self-confidence, sense of achievement, express self, have a moral code of values, self-control, integrity, sense of competence, spiritual union . . .

ENVIRONMENT

Avoid danger, ugliness, objects that disgust or make us unsafe, insecure, or unstable . . .

Attain enjoyable objects, understand and master environment, solve problems, invent objects; seek novelty and change, play, beauty, space, order and closure, objects needed for future survival, safety, stability, security . . .

SOCIETY

Avoid interpersonal hostility, isolation, loneliness, being an outcast who loses social status, blame . . .

Attain love, belonging, understanding, acceptance, attention, help, talk to and enjoy others, independence, power, care from others, normal appearance, praise, acceptance, trust, nurturance, success, acknowledgment, affection, help, recognition, intimacy . . .

Adapted from Kreck and Crutchfield, *Elements of Psychology* (New York: Knopf, 1958).

Another map that helps us understand our self is psychologist Abraham Maslow's hierarchy of needs.

Self-Actualization
(realize potentials and abilities, find beauty, knowledge . . .)
Esteem Needs
(prestige, importance, specialness, respect . . .)
Belongings and Love Needs
(contact, attention, care and caring . . .)
Safety Needs
(security and stability . . .)
Physiological Needs
(hunger, thirst, warmth, sexual release . . .)

Maslow arranged these needs in a pyramid from the most basic to the highest, as we evolve as individuals and as a society. The highest, self-actualization, would include autonomy, creativity, expression of one's talents, and growing beyond one's individual self.

If we fail to meet a "lower" need, then our progress up the pyramid is slowed or thwarted. This means that meeting our basic needs is important, if not essential, to continue evolving.

When we're less focused on desiring, we can be more identified with Spirit, and the more we're identified with spirituality, the less we fear our physical and psychological impermanence. This in turn helps us diminish our need for ego food, which allows us to focus more fully on spirituality. All this creates a positive cycle:

Understanding what *drives* us helps us identify our basic needs and important priorities, as well as our superfluous extravagancies. Meeting our basic needs while learning to limit our unnecessary lusts and cravings allows us to relax our grip and slow the endless desire and frustration. This lightens our load, and we can more fully open to Spirit, meeting our "higher" needs.

More Aware to Make Better Choices

Marilyn is a divorced, working mother with two elementary-age girls, Sandi and Tanya. When Marilyn was offered a promotion in the form of a larger sales territory, she was thrilled. Finally, she'd be able to afford many of the things she wanted for the family. Her "wish list" included a bigger home (so the girls could each have their own room), another TV (to avoid conflicts over what to watch), and a new car with a car phone (so she could keep in touch better with the kids). Marilyn figured her new territory would take an extra four hours a week and would be well worth the time and travel.

Six months later: Marilyn realizes her new territory has her out of town at least five nights more each month and takes at least ten hours more each week. The car phone doesn't replace her being at home, Sandi and Tanya aren't being supervised by the baby-sitter the way they need to be, and now they're frequently fighting. And when they argue, without Mom to mediate, each goes to her own bedroom and watches her own TV, and they never resolve their differences. Notes from Sandi and Tanya's teachers indicate the problems are starting to spill over into their schoolwork and relationships with the other children. And when Marilyn's home, she has hours of extra paperwork and is a lot more tired, preoccupied, and stressed-out. Instead of making life better, Marilyn's promotion added to the weight of her world.

Marilyn's promotion had its advantages, but the hidden costs to her and her family were tremendous. When she fully realized what was happening to her and the girls, she gave up the larger territory and went back to the smaller, more manageable job she had before.

This is not to say that we give up all ambition. But we can look carefully at our ambitions, and, through awareness, we can distinguish between our necessary needs and our superfluous cravings. Do I really need this dessert right now? Do I have to have another pair of slacks? Is the bigger house worth the obvious and the hidden costs?

As you become more aware of your desires, ask yourself: **Is the desire a substitute for an unmet basic need?** If, for example, you find yourself wanting another new shirt or a pair of shoes, but you know you already have enough, then it's important to consider why you're desiring something you don't really need.

Try to be aware of what's beneath the desire. What part of your personality is not being fed? Perhaps the shirt or shoes are related to your wanting to be admired for your appearance and you are seeking good feelings for yourself. Maybe your deeper need for self-worth needs to be addressed and satisfied. (See Chapter 4 on basic goodness and the Good Feeling File.)

Maybe we become excessively focused on food, gathering

recipes, going to restaurants, talking about our latest culinary discovery, when in reality we have a hunger for greater intimacy with loved ones. In this case, it would be more valuable to spend the time seeking greater closeness with loved ones or at least aim more accurately at this deeper, unmet social need. Or perhaps we need to realize our inherent spiritual worth as a basic being (see Chapter 3).

Try to see what's driving the desire and take an action that might actually solve the more basic, underlying need, rather than buying or doing something that superficially satisfies the symptom of your frustration, but that you'll have to pay for through time, energy, money, and attention you might have used to solve the real problem.

We Can Appreciate Needs That Are Being Met

It's extremely common to take for granted needs that are already being met, focusing our time, energy, money, and attention on our frustrated desires. Like Marilyn, our focus is on the larger home, new TV, or car phone we'd like to have, feeling a lack and imagining how much nicer life would be if only we had what we crave.

We can more fully extract the nutrients from our life when we appreciate the myriad ways in which we get our needs met. Take a look at the charts on pages 142 and 143 for a minute, realizing all the ways your needs are already satisfied.

Take a beginning and a second breath to become aware and present, and appreciate having a roof over your and your family's heads. Breathe out with an "ahh" of satisfaction. Consciously, presently breathing, acknowledging the food and drink you've consumed today, "ahh." Be aware of having air to breathe, "ahh," aware of having friends and family who meet our social needs, "ahh."

Aware of being healthy enough to appreciate what we have, "ahh." Keep aware of the next experience of satisfaction and relief.

We can expand our experience of appreciation when we realize that there are millions who are less fortunate than ourselves—women, men, boys, and girls around the world who don't have enough food, or meaningful work, or roofs over their heads. We can and should try to be of help to those with less than ourselves, and we can and should appreciate all we have, enriching us personally and spiritually.

We Can Be Awake and Present with Our Desires

We can know and meet our underlying basic needs, see the hidden costs of our desires, and appreciate all that we have. We can also loosen desire's grip.

> When we breathe to be aware and to relax in the moment, settling down here and now, we can see our desires more objectively and discover we're not our desires. As we grow in awareness, we feel the part of us that is deeper than our own desires. We see that our inner spiritual Self is neither the desire nor the desirer. Our personality feels the desire, our personality acts in order to satisfy the desire, but there's more to us than our personal desires.

Ken Wilber, author and consciousness theorist, describes this state of mind when he says, "I have desires, but I am *not* my desires. I can know my desires, and what can be known is not the true Knower. Desires come and go, floating through my awareness, but they do not affect my inward I. I *have* desires but I am *not* my desires."

Again, this is not to say that we must reject or give up desiring (setting up an internal war within our self), but rather that we learn to be more conscious and get a clearer perspective of our desires. Instead of unconsciously letting our wants control us, we can be aware and awake within desiring.

> **We can see the process of desiring as an unsatisfied want, and we can judge whether or not we already have enough. This allows us to focus on *what we really need* as opposed to what we simply crave.**

We Can Identify and Label Our "Desiring"

So you're reading this and realize you're working a sixty-hour week at a promising career and have a family to support and mortgages to pay and lots of plans to spend more whenever you can. Where do you start to turn things around?

Start with being present and awake. Begin to separate yourself from the desiring. When you breathe to bring awareness into the present, see the thoughts that come to you. When they're thoughts of desiring, *see* that they're thoughts of desire—for a new car or dress, a new job, or a trip to Bali. Realize that while you have personal desires, there's much more to you than your desires. It's our personality that is the desirer, not our soul or Spirit.

Become aware of your desires and wants. See the desire for sex or food or drink, the thoughts of desire for achievement and prestige, for activity and pride. Whenever desire arises in your awareness, say "wanting" or "desiring" to yourself. You can be more specific if you like, saying "wanting a new stereo" or "desiring coffee."

I'm sitting in my office and wanting a donut, wishing I could fly off to Rio. I label "fantasy," "sweets," and "bored." I realize I need to take a break and go for a glass of water, taking my time walking to the water cooler and back. Sitting down, resting, I take a full, relaxing breath with awareness and presence, sipping my water with awareness and contentment for a moment. It's not Rio, but moments like this throughout the day, weeks, months, and years can dramatically nourish our life.

American meditation teacher Ram Dass says, "The dialogue between one's deepest self and one's ego is a continuing dialogue . . . One constantly is listening to get the ego and the deeper self integrated into some kind of harmony so that the ego speaks from the deeper self or represents the deeper self. That comes from extricating the self and the ego from identification with desires."

Labeling our needs and desires is like a mental aerobic exercise that energizes us, makes us stronger, and lightens our load. When we take the individual cravings and gather them together under a mental heading, we get a clearer sense of our self and of what drives us. We're less lost in the midst of it all, gain some distance from the individual desires, and have a greater sense of control as we become more conscious of how we operate.

We also learn more about our self. When Andrew (whom we discussed above) started labeling his desires, he discovered that he was much more preoccupied with getting money and security than he'd ever realized. While this was obvious to those who knew him, it wasn't obvious to him. He said he already had enough money to support five families, yet he lived as if he was barely getting by. When he looked more deeply, he realized not only that the pursuit of riches was a habit pattern and an old family tradition but that he had a deep loneliness and emotional insecurity. He said he'd grown up in a wealthy family that was "emotionally bankrupt." There had been no affection or warmth in his childhood, and he was trying to fill up his emptiness with material riches (just as his parents had done), becoming even more isolated and financially addicted. Through labeling, Andrew discovered for himself a perspective and insight he'd never been able to receive from another. And it was only then that he could begin to relax his financial obsession and appreciate all he already had.

If our needs are observed, understood, labeled, met (when worth meeting), and released, we'll continue to naturally evolve.

This evolution will bring forth our basic spirituality—awareness and experiencing what is here and now, wholeness, love, presence with a spiritual force (God, Buddha, Nature, Jesus, Great Spirit...), union of identification with other living things, goodness, truthfulness, altruism, faith, trust, openness, consciousness, self-control, peace of mind, clarity, joy, awe, compassion, generosity, forgiveness, and wisdom.

The direct path, however, is *not* to go directly after these qualities, turning them into goals to be achieved (reinforcing the desiring and the desirer). The direct path is to be conscious and present with what is, as it is, allowing and trusting. This includes meeting our basic needs with awareness in a healthy way and discovering the limits of personal satisfaction.

What Can I Do?
The "Nourished Needs" Recipe

1. Breathe to be conscious and present, aware of our desiring. We can be conscious of our acceptance and rejection of what is, as it is, experiencing the desiring, frustration, and satisfaction that come with the desiring process.

A Nourished Needs Recipe might include taking deep, slow breaths, conscious and present, then saying our current wish or craving to ourself—"wanting ice cream," "wishing that noise would stop," "craving a new computer." We don't need to make a judgment about our self. We're aware, paying attention to our cravings and our actions, seeing the patterns that we repeat over and over.

2. We can use the human motivation chart on page 142 to understand and prioritize our wants and needs, identifying the extent to which our basic desires are unmet, denied, or indulged. We can assess whether or not any particular need is worth meeting.

3. We can learn the limits of need meeting. Seeing that desiring is endless, we must learn that there are limits to meeting our needs, especially when we consider the real cost of our desires in terms of endless frustration and separation from Spirit.

4. We can exercise self-control. It is extremely important that we control our actions and limit how much of our time and energy is spent on superfluous desires. We can save our resources for our highest priorities and our basic needs.

5. We can appreciate and enjoy what we already have. Notice what we usually take for granted, appreciating the myriad ways that our needs are already being met, feeling filled and satisfied so our personality can relax.

6. We can identify and label our "desiring." When we consciously breathe to be present, we can label "desiring a vacation" or "desiring sex" or "desiring candy" and in so doing gain some distance from our cravings and understand ourselves more clearly.

Once we've understood how to appreciate what we have, meet our basic needs, be aware of desire, limit our drivenness, and see through the whole desiring process, the Spiritual Diet shifts focus to the jumping monkeys in our mind.

Chapter 7

Jumping Monkeys

We are what we think. All that we are arises
with our thoughts. With our thoughts we make
the world.

GAUTAMA BUDDHA

**Our mind jumps from one thing to another, making us
scattered, unable to concentrate, forgetful, and confused. We can have greater spiritual awareness when we
learn to watch and understand our thinking process
and use prayer, mantras, and holy thoughts.**

Monkeys in Cages

When I try to meditate or pray, my mind jumps all over the place. <u>I don't really know what "peace of mind" or "quiet mind" means.</u>

<u>My thoughts jump from one thing to another.</u> First I'm thinking about what I'm going to say at the meeting. Then I'm thinking about my car's brake problem, then about a coworker who's causing me problems. <u>I wish I could concentrate better,</u> but my mind is so scattered and unfocused and I don't know what to do about it.

I go in the other room to get something, but when I get there, <u>I can't remember</u> what it was. I'm not old enough to be senile, so it must be all the things on my mind that make me forgetful and preoccupied.

Every day, from the moment we awaken, our mind is busy chattering with thoughts and fantasies.

"Oh—morning. I've got to get going. I've got to run the meeting today and I'd better go over the agenda. And make sure we have coffee to keep everyone going. Boy I could use some now. Oh, the kids need to get going. I wonder what they want for lunch. Oh, lunch. When will I have time to get something for myself today?"

Thoughts, figurings, fantasies, imaginings, rehearsals, reenactments—our mind jumps from cookies to sex, to a fax that must be sent, to a credit card bill, to tonight's dinner, to the phone calls that must be returned.

Like a voice in our brain talking nonstop, our mental chattering goes on all day. When we find our self back in bed at night, our mind might even slow down. If it does, it goes on talking to us in our dreams.

Our mental busyness reflects the busyness of our modern life. Those of us with few responsibilities and demands may have a relatively quieter, calmer mind than those who have more to do. But whatever our level of life activity, all of us manage to fill our mind with a constant flow of brain chatter.

Try an experiment right now. Put this book down for a minute, close your eyes, breathe, and try to be without thoughts.

For most people, our monkeys continue jumping as our incessant mental monologue goes on and on. It's as if we're talking to our self all the time as the voice in our brain chatters about money or food or sex or work or the kids. Thoughts pop out of our mental mouth, chattering and jumping whether we like it or not, whether we want it to stop or not.

Brain Chatter

Obviously, thinking is crucial in a modern world, and because our brain is highly developed, we can't automatically turn it off. But if we're constantly flooded with a rapid flow of thoughts, we can't calm down or focus our mind.

Our endless mental chatter not only hijacks our mental energies but creates a false impression that we are our thoughts.

This false impression is a result of our personality's use of thoughts to accomplish two main purposes:

1. Personality uses thoughts and thinking to control our world to help us survive, succeed, and satisfy ourselves. We live within complex situations that require thousands of decisions every day. Personality uses thinking to make decisions and take actions that help meet our personality's needs and goals.

2. Personality uses our thoughts and thinking to create and maintain our personal identity. So while our thinking gives us the ability to survive and succeed, it also gives us a sense of solidity. Our thinking gets us to identify ourselves through what we acquire in the way of titles, power, personal relationships, and possessions.

For example, we might think of ourselves as a businessperson, a parent, a Ford owner, a club member, a resident of a particular neighborhood/city/state/country. We create a set of roles, a wardrobe, a set of home furnishings, all of which support our personal identity. We label ourselves as a grandmother, apartment renter, middle-ager, government employee, computer novice, extrovert, baby boomer. The more of these labels we identify with, the more we feel we exist as a unique entity who's important and solid. A wealthy student once said, "I wear a Rolex watch and Calvin Klein jeans because that's just who I am." In this case, she believed "I am what I own and wear," actually identifying with her possessions. This was her specific personality and thinking at work, illustrating how we view ourselves and our world with millions of supporting perceptions, choices, reactions, and thoughts.

Personality creates such a complex world that we think of our thoughts and decisions as our self.

We Are What We Think We Are

The Bible says, "As a man thinketh, so will he be." We are what we think we are. Our personality, then, largely creates our world with our thoughts. Our particular thoughts depend in large part on our particular experiences in our family and our culture. The thoughts of each of us are filtered by our experiences and background.

Perhaps we did poorly in school or felt unattractive or our parents fought or we were regularly ridiculed or abused or those around us were unhappy. Any of these childhood experiences could lead to our personality learning a pattern of feeling sad and inadequate. As a result, we'll have thoughts that reinforce this pattern and produce sad and inadequate feelings and thoughts, rather than things that produce more positive emotions. Our sadness "radar" homes in on sad feelings and magnifies them, as other aspects of our existence fade into the background.

If we grew up with experiences that made us angry, and we developed a pattern of being easily angered, then we'll look at the world with a filter that selects things that frustrate and irritate us, and we'll readily think angry thoughts. Our filter will let through and highlight those aspects of life that annoy or irritate us, and our thoughts will be filled with the problems that anger us.

These personality or thinking patterns are an integral part of our self-identity, of who we think we are, and if we observe our thoughts, we'll often notice these mental patterns.

Waves in an Endless Ocean

Buddhists speak of Big Mind and small minds. Big Mind is the vast and endless ocean of consciousness shared by all living things. Small minds are our individual, mental personalities. We are waves in the ocean, each of us a particular, individual portion of vast consciousness.

Our small mind churns the waters through its own thoughts, picking and choosing, dividing the world by its likes and dislikes. Small mind falsely thinks it's separate from Big Mind. But small mind is always part of Big Mind, whether we realize it or not, just as each small wave is always a part of the vast ocean. As Shunryu

Suzuki explained, "That everything is included within your mind is the essence of mind. To experience this is to have religious feeling."

Imagine the billions of people around the world all thinking. Each of us is in the same ocean of consciousness and thought. Now realize that your personal thoughts are variations on the same themes as the rest of humanity (work survival and success, family and friends, breakfast, lunch, and dinner, aches and illness, closeness and sex), variations of the waves on the ocean of consciousness.

Suzuki continues, "Even though waves arise, the essence of your mind is pure; it is just like clear water with a few waves. Actually water always has waves." The nature of the human mind is to have thoughts. "Waves are the practice of water. To speak of waves apart from water or water apart from waves is delusion. Water and waves are one. Big mind and small mind are one."

Our personal consciousness is actually a manifestation of divine consciousness; our everyday mind is God's mind. To see divine consciousness, we need only look behind the thoughts, to the power of consciousness itself, the ultimate source of our awareness. Yet, we're unaware of this divine connection because we're so caught up in, lost within, and identified with our personal thinking.

We are walking along a path, bordered by a series of trees. From outside, the sun is visible between the trees. The sun is the source of consciousness, the trees are like our thoughts, blocking it out. When we slow down, we can see the light shining in between the trees. Deep, slow breaths focus our awareness in the moment, enabling us to see the light. In time, we realize that the trees are also a result of the sun's light, as our thoughts are ultimately the result of spiritual consciousness.

While the world's religious traditions agree that the personal is a manifestation of Spirit, their language is different. Buddhists call it small mind and Big Mind; Hindus say Brahman (the ultimate reality) and Atman (the individual self or soul); Christians say "the Spirit of God dwelleth in you" and refer to the Godhead and the trinity of Father, Son, and Holy Spirit manifesting in our life. The Sufi Pir Vilayat Khan says, "We think the way the Universe thinks, except that the thinking of the Universe gets funneled in our thinking and gets distorted in our thinking." Nevertheless, "we are the Divine thinking." We may have divine mind, but we can't realize it because we have a divided mind that's lost in mental chatter, and distracted by a thousand thoughts and flights of fantasy."

"What is the Tao [the Way, the Truth]?" asks the disciple. "Your everyday mind," replies the master, who goes on to say, "When I'm hungry I eat; when I'm tired I sleep." The disciple is puzzled and says, "Isn't this what everyone does?" "No," says the master. "Most people are never wholly in what they're doing. When they're eating they're preoccupied with a thousand thoughts and fantasies; when sleeping they don't fully rest. The supreme mark of the mature person is to be without a divided mind."

> As we devote ourselves to maintaining our personal world with our mental patterns, thoughts are one way our personality eclipses our spirituality. We're so busy *doing* and *thinking* that we've little space left for *being*.

Monkeys on a Sugar High

Our patterns of personality promote our survival, satisfaction, and sense of solidity. They take such a tremendous amount of time and thought that our mind is usually filled with them. Indeed, most of the time we're not only thinking but thinking so rapidly and covering so many subjects that our mind is like a caged monkey on a sugar high. Our thoughts, these mental monkeys, are jumping from one branch to another so fast we're often forgetful, preoccupied, and unable to concentrate.

For some, the monkeys are so crowded together they're climbing over each other. They're so thick and jabbering and jumpy that we can't see beyond the cage to the sunlight, maybe doubting, or even denying, the light exists.

How do we get beyond the mental chatter, distraction, and division? How do we focus our jumpy monkey mind? We may want to stand on some mental mountaintop above our monkey mind and scream, "SHUT UP!"

But it won't do us any good. We can't simply stop thinking. Nor do we need to. Our inner mental chattering is useful for our survival and satisfaction, and thinking continues to some degree regardless of what we do. But we can practice techniques that help our personal thoughts become calmer and clearer.

When we calm our mind and focus our thinking, the monkeys slow down and begin to sit quietly. Many return to their den. As the crowd thins out, the sun (our natural light of consciousness) shines through.

A spiritually developed person has calmer mental monkeys, because his or her thinking is aimed in the here and now. The Basic Spiritual Diet helps us spiritually by using breathing to develop focused awareness and presence. In addition to the Basic Spiritual Diet, there are other ways to calm our mental monkeys. These ways include paying attention to our thinking process, labeling our thoughts, understanding our mental patterns, seeing through our thoughts, counterbalancing excessively negative thoughts, and using holy thoughts, prayers, and mantras. Each of these is covered in the following pages.

Pay Attention
to Our Thinking Process

Actively fighting against our thoughts is like running at the monkeys; they'd jump and jabber all the more. A smarter strategy is to be more conscious. Awareness of our thoughts frees us from being caught in them and gradually changes our patterns.

We can, in effect, feed the monkeys a spiritually nutritious diet of calm awareness and acceptance. We can apply our Basic Spiritual Diet (breathing to be conscious in the present moment) to our thinking process. We don't try to stop thinking. We simply breathe with awareness in and out and watch our mental monkeys jump and jabber.

Do it now for a moment. Breathe in and out with awareness of the air entering and leaving your body. Now rest where you are, a conscious breath in and out. Continue breathing and notice where your mind is going. Whether you think of it as monkey chatter, waves in an ocean, trees along a path, or an inner movie, be aware of the thoughts that appear. Be like a moviegoer or someone sitting on a bench at the zoo. Your thoughts feel more separate from you as you watch them on a screen or as if they're in a cage. As we sit back from our thoughts and watch them, instead of being so caught up in them, we begin to realize we have a part of us that is not the thought.

We cannot control the speed of our thoughts, but awareness of them in the present will, in time, calm the monkeys in our mind. The Upanishads says, "When the mind is at rest, then the intellect wavers not—then, say the wise, the highest state is reached."

Our personality can barely conceive of what it would mean for our monkeys to be at rest.

Giving nonjudgmental, calm attention to our thoughts feeds

our mental monkeys nutritious food instead of a rush of sugar, and they begin to calm down if we allow ourselves to slow down awareness and presence. Krishnamurti asks:

> Have you ever sat quietly without any movement? You try it. Sit really still, with your back straight, and observe what your mind is doing. Don't try to control it, don't say it should not jump from one thought to another, from one interest to another, but just be aware of how your mind is jumping. Don't do anything about it, but watch it as from the banks of a river you watch the river flow by. In the flowing river there are so many things—fishes, leaves, dead animals—but it is always living, moving, and your mind is like that. It is everlastingly restless, flitting from one thing to another like a butterfly . . . just watch your mind. It is great fun. If you try it as fun, as an amusing thing, you will find that the mind begins to settle down without any effort on your part to control it. There is then no censor, no judge, no evaluator; and when the mind is thus very quiet of itself, spontaneously still, you will know what it is to be gay. Do you know what gaiety is? It is just to laugh, to take delight in any thing or nothing, to know the joy of living, smiling, looking straight into the face of another without any sense of fear.

We can let ourselves sit and breathe and be where we are with awareness. We can watch the movie in our mind, seeing the monkeys jumping and jabbering. It's natural. Just trust in our spiritual nature, whatever we like to call it or in whatever form we think of it. Then we no longer try to make our self change (a personality-based effort), but instead bring awareness to what is (a spiritually based state).

This means that when the monkeys are jumping, we enjoy the

playfulness and productivity, and don't try to force the thoughts to stop, but rather become aware of the thought, the daydream, the fear, the fantasy, or whatever goes on in our mental jungle. Over and over again, we simply, gently, trustingly bring awareness back to the jabbering monkey, the mental movie, treelined path, or the churning waves.

Once we stand back from our thinking, we may suddenly realize just how fast and how much thinking is going on. When we really look, we see that basically our minds are out of control.

AM I CRAZY OR WHAT?

When we begin to be aware of our thinking process, problems arise. The Sri Lankan philosopher Henepola Gunaratana says:

> Somewhere in this process, you will come face to face with the sudden and shocking realization that you are completely crazy. Your mind is a shrieking, gibbering madhouse on wheels barreling pell-mell down the hill, utterly out of control and hopeless. No problem. You are not crazier than you were yesterday. It has always been this way, and you just never noticed. You are also no crazier than everybody else around you. The only real difference is that you have confronted the situation; they have not ... don't let this realization unsettle you. It is a milestone actually, a sign of real progress. The very fact that you have looked at the problem straight in the eye means that you are on your way up and out of it.

When we see ourselves from a quieter, more centered perspective, we're bound to discover many things inside us we never noticed before: an old sadness over a long-lost friend, an embarrassing moment from high school, a hysterically funny time with a loved one, a red rage over a recent wrong.

We don't want to turn against our self, but rather to be kind and compassionate with our self. We can express basic goodness in our attitude toward our thinking. Let our self be here now with what is, with our thinking as it is, simply being aware.

When we're free from the cage, our thoughts are like birds flying through the open sky of our mind. Our spiritual awareness, our *inward I*, our inner eye, shines forth more fully. As we go through our day, we can be aware of our thinking in the midst of working, driving, talking, waiting in line, or watching TV. Let a breath or a thought be our reminder to attune to our mental monologue.

Label Our Thoughts as "Thinking" or "Jabbering" or "Monkeys"

Labeling our thoughts can help us to be aware of them, detach from them, and calm them down. When we mentally label a mental process, we develop the witness within. Then this inner observer can watch with greater clarity and calmness. Over and over, we can label and return our attention to our breath.

As we slow down, we can be

Aware
of the air
entering our nose or mouth
"thinking, thinking."
Aware of the air
leaving our nose or mouth,
"monkey jabber, monkey jabber."

Understand the Patterns
and Content of Our Mind

As we attune to our mind, we discover patterns that are integral to our personality's strivings for survival, success, and solidity. We have thousands of thoughts every day, and most of them are variations on the same old themes we've thought before. Neutral thoughts ("Put cereal on the shopping list," "Turn off the TV," "Lock the back door") contain basic information that make our life functional and orderly, and are the most common. "Negative" thoughts ("I'm such a dope," "I hate those shoes," "Yech, another Monday morning") are like junk food for our personality. "Positive" thoughts ("I'm doing my best," "That plan worked well," "I can't wait to see my grandchild") make our personality feel good. Regardless of their charge and purpose, we can be aware of the content and patterns of our usual thoughts.

Some people find it gives them a better grip on their mental processes if they combine the Basic Spiritual Diet with the category of thought. Breathing consciously: "thinking about work" or "Now I'm thinking about shopping," "thinking about a bath," "thinking about Aunt Sis," "thinking about Mom," "Now I'm rehearsing," "Now I'm reliving a good time," "Now I'm worrying."

In general: breathing to be aware and present, "Now I'm thinking about _____."

Although most spiritual teachings say to ignore the content of our thoughts (simply noting that thoughts are operating and letting them go), if we pay attention to the pattern of our thinking, we discover that most of the time we're trying to meet one or more of our normal and necessary needs (see the human motivation chart in Chapter 6). We may want to make note of an unmet need and come up with a plan of action, set it aside for a while, then return to paying attention. As we're breathing and "thinking about being success-ful," perhaps we make a note to make an important work call, then we go back to: breathing, thinking about something else.

When we understand the content of our thoughts, we notice that, in addition to our needs, our thinking is often driven by our emotions. If we're depressed, then our thoughts tend toward the negative and pessimistic; if we're happy, then our thoughts tend to be optimistic and positive. In Chapter 8, we'll look at five basic emotions and learn to be aware of them, but here we can see that our thoughts are often related to our feelings, and we can breathe con-sciously and label our thoughts according to our feeling: consciously breathing in the present, thinking about something sad, aware and present, thinking about something scary, thinking about an annoy-ance. In doing this more sophisticated technique, we feel closer to our personality, while at the same time we're taking a step back by observing what is happening. As we come to know our self well enough to do this, we feel comforted as we understand the patterns of our mind.

See Through Our Thoughts

Inevitably, we all find ourselves lost in thought. But if we recognize those times when we've been swept away by our thoughts, we'll be able to become conscious once again, back to comfortable and con-tented breathing awareness. In this way, spirituality embraces per-sonality. Big Mind, the ocean of consciousness, is awake to small mind, our personality. In time, personality can attune to Spirit as it sees through our thoughts, becoming less identified and attached to them. Ken Wilber, a foremost consciousness theorist, writes, "I *have* thoughts, but I am *not* my thoughts . . . Thoughts come to me and thoughts leave me, but they do not affect my inward I. I *have* thoughts but I am *not* my thoughts."

This is even true of boredom and other "negative" thoughts. As we pay attention to our breathing and thinking, we may find ourselves feeling bored, irritated, or restless. These are natural personal reactions, since personality feeds off the drama of daily life. It's like being used to a lot of salt in our food and then cutting back. At first, food seems more bland, but in time we taste even more clearly and strongly. After a while, even a little mental drama seems intense.

So when our mind begins to calm down, personality seeks out more stimulation. But just as boredom comes, boredom goes. Continue the presence and awareness exercises. Just the same predictable breath in and out. It's calming, but not exciting, like thinking about love or money or sex or ice cream or our next vacation. Personality's intensity is gradually calmed by conscious breathing and resting in the here and now. Through it all, just go on being aware.

Counterbalance Excessively Negative or Positive Thoughts

Some people practice the power of positive thinking, wear rose-colored glasses, and always think the glass is half-full, no matter what the reality. Being a positive person is valuable, but even positivity can be taken too far, posing the danger of making our personality artificial, brittle, and unable to digest and deal with the negative aspects of life. If we avoid or deny difficulties and painfulness, we are fighting against what needs to be seen and dealt with, failing to properly digest important aspects of real life. In this case, we may have to be more conscious of our true reality—the difficulty and suffering in need of help and healing.

If we find our self being excessively negative or pessimistic, we can, for example, use our Good Feeling File (see Chapters 4 and 8) and focus on basic goodness (see Chapter 4).

Or we can use holy thoughts that bring us closer with Spirit— prayers and mantras. In which case, we might want to regularly take a slow, full breath in the present and be aware of a particular prayer or mantra which personally suits us. If we did this for just five or ten moments a day, in time our life would be spiritually transformed.

Holy Thoughts, Prayers, and Mantras

Most major religions calm and focus the mind through prayer or mantra. In this way our thinking is aimed toward Spirit using holy thoughts, a counterbalance to our usual personality-dominated thinking.

Prayers focus our thoughts and aim them toward the spiritual. Mantras are words or phrases that are repeated over and over, focusing the mind on the divine. A meaningful mantra is done consciously, not mindlessly repeated.

Prayer and mantra can be done either silently to oneself or out loud. Regardless of how it's done, it's designed to make the spiritual and the sacred an ongoing part of daily life. Prayers and mantras are personality's way of reaching toward Spirit, and Spirit's way of reaching out through us.

Millions pray each day, including people with no attachments to any particular religion. Around the world, it's especially common for people to pray when they sit down to meals and when they go to bed at night.

Praying has been shown to have great health benefits—reducing stress and speeding the healing process.

Prayers can be in the form of either *receptive awareness* or *concentrated effort*. Either way, our aim is to come closer to the spiritual through sustained alertness, the aim of the Basic Spiritual Diet.

When we're *receptively aware*, we're like a living mirror that's relaxed and open to what comes, and then our mental monologue stands out more clearly. When we focus on our thoughts, they lose speed and intensity, and we become calmer and clearer. It's the view of some scientists that prayer travels the same biochemical pathways as relaxation, leading to slower heart and respiration rates, which reduces stress chemicals and empowers our immune system. Whatever the specific reasons, awareness itself feeds our mental monkeys sustained spiritual sustenance.

When we use *concentrated effort*, we purposely aim toward a particular prayer or mantra, so that our internal monologue of thoughts can be temporarily overridden. Our jumping monkey mind can be replaced with our chosen spiritual prayer or mantra.

People tend to use prayer to get Spirit to serve personality, but spiritual prayer is a way for personality to serve Spirit. Jesus said, "Not what I will, but what Thou wilt." Rather than asking God to help me win the game or the lottery (fulfilling my personal desires), it's of greater spiritual value to pray that we can live with the facts of life that God brings to us (including a lost game or a losing lottery ticket).

This does not mean we stop trying to affect the outcome. I may try as hard as I can to win the game and I may choose to buy a lottery ticket which I hope will take away my financial pressures, but God grant me the ability to consciously and successfully live with whatever happens (including my disappointment).

⊛ Instead of "God grant me my wish so I feel satisfied," "God grant me awareness and presence and the ability to work with whatever is set before me."

I feel disappointed about losing the game or the lottery, but I appreciate the playing and fully digest the emotions (see Chapter 8). Curious, I wonder why I'm so disappointed about not winning money I never had in the first place. Taking a conscious breath in, I see my thinking pattern, a preoccupation with wanting money for the bills; taking a present breath out, I see my desire for financial relief. Taking a breath out, I see my desire to feel like a winner. Little by little, I come to know myself more intimately and open to a larger reality beyond the confines of my personal needs and desires.

In personal prayers, we ask for something for our personality. In spiritual prayer, we listen to the deep spiritual voice within. We listen for the secret sound, the quiet voice that grows louder, leading us to greater understanding and connectedness, helping us feel less alone, lighter, losing the weight of the world.

My personality-based prayer may be answered by a new TV. But this doesn't necessarily answer my spiritual prayer. Rather, spiritual prayers are answered when we feel a closeness with the spiritual element in life, when we feel greater peace of mind, when we see the divine in the daily details, when we're more awake and present in the midst of it all.

⊛ The Spiritual Diet suggests combining breathing to be aware and present with holy thoughts—prayers or mantras—each day.

Time and patience are needed to feel the effects of both prayer and mantra. Whatever we're used to doing has momentum and we tend to continue it in the future, so it's extremely valuable to create a simple, achievable daily routine. If our daily actions include aiming toward Spirit, we can add great momentum to our spiritual growth through holy thoughts. When I awake in the morning, or when I sit down to eat, or when I take a shower, or when I lie in bed each night, I can build spiritual power by using the Basic Spiritual Diet with my prayer or mantra.

It's valuable to keep the Oglala Sioux holy man Black Elk's words in mind: "Great Spirit is everywhere; He hears whatever is in our minds and hearts, so it is not necessary to speak to Him in a loud voice." And while we're opening the communication lines with Spirit, Rabbi Harold Kushner reminds us that "the *best* part of prayer is listening, an opening up to messages we would not get if we weren't praying." We can speak softly and be open to what comes.

The Way of a Pilgrim suggests, "Everywhere, wherever you may find yourself, you can set up an altar to God in your mind by means of prayer." Whether we choose an organized religion's prayer or one of our own, we create an altar to the spiritual force within and around us.

Following are a few of the endless possibilities. We can learn a great deal from traditions other than our own. When we read other traditions' holy thoughts, we foster our openness and enlarge our connectedness.

CHRISTIAN PRAYERS AND MANTRAS

John of Damascus said, "The ascent of the mind to God" is what prayer is about, and Paul instructed the Thessalonians to "pray constantly" (1 Thess. 5:17). Contemplative prayer entails silently allowing simple awareness of the divine presence. The fact that we breathe constantly can serve to help us pray. Use your breathing to remind yourself and to empower your prayer: "Jesus" (on the in-breath) "loves me" (on the out-breath). "Hail" (on the in-breath) "Mary" (on the out-breath).

The fourteenth century's *The Cloud of Unknowing* instructs Christians:

> Lift up your heart to God with a meek stirring of love; and intend God himself and none of his created things. And be sure not to think of anything but himself, so that nothing may work in your mind or in your will but only himself . . .
>
> When you first begin, find a darkness and, as it were, a cloud of unknowing, you don't know what, except that you feel in your will an intent toward God. This darkness and this cloud, no matter what you do, is between you and your God, and hinders you . . . prepare to abide in this darkness as long as you must . . . By love he may be gotten and held, but by thinking, never.

The most common Christian prayer is the Lord's Prayer, which Jesus taught his disciples and which is found in his Sermon on the Mount (Matt. 6:9–13):

> Our Father, who art in heaven, hallowed be thy name; Thy Kingdom come; thy will be done on earth as it is in heaven. Give us this day our daily bread; and forgive us our wrongs as we forgive those who have wronged against us. And lead us not into temptation, but deliver us from evil. Amen.

The Jesus prayer is also widely used among Christians: "Lord Jesus Christ, Son of God, have mercy on me a sinner." Benedictine Brother Stendl-Rast says he uses a short version as a mantra or prayer, coordinating it with the rhythm of his breathing: "Lord Jesus, Mercy, Lord Jesus, Mercy." Breathe in "Lord Jesus," breathe out "Mercy," breathe in "Lord Jesus," breathe out "Mercy."

First-century church patriarch Callisotas said, "We breathe the air in and out. On this is based the life of the body, and on this depends its warmth. So, sitting in your room, collect your mind, lead it into the path of the breath, along which air enters in, constrain it to enter the heart together with the inhaled air, and keep it there . . . give it the following prayer: Lord Jesus Christ, Son of God, have mercy upon me. Let this be its constant occupation, never to be abandoned."

St. Simeon was an early church father who said that "attention should be linked to prayer as inseparably as body is linked to soul," and suggested that "the mind should be in the heart, and thence from the depths of the heart, offer up prayers to God . . . By keeping your mind attentive and in your heart holding Jesus, that is His prayer—Lord Jesus Christ, have mercy on me! One of the holy fathers says: 'Sit in your room and this prayer will teach you everything.' "

"In the beginning was the Word, and the Word was with God, and the Word was God" (John 1:1).

> O divine Master, grant that I may not so much seek
> To be consoled as to console,
> To be understood as to understand,
> To be loved as to love;
> For it is in giving that we receive;
> It is in pardoning that we are pardoned;
> It is in dying to self that we are born to eternal life.
> (St. Francis of Assisi)

"That which I am I offer to you, O Lord, for you are it entirely. Go no further, but rest in this naked, stark, elemental awareness that you are as you are" (St. John of the Cross).

JEWISH PRAYERS AND MANTRAS

Jews have a history of meditation and prayer many thousands of years old. Traditionally, Jews worship (or *davens*) three times a day. Prayer can be done in a temple or synagogue or at home. Sit in a comfortable position, hands resting comfortably in your lap, eyes closed or unfocused. Allow yourself to settle in the place, making yourself at ease. Many Jews find it quite helpful to sway forward and back. Breathe comfortably and allow yourself to be present, letting stray thoughts be replaced by the prayer, which may be memorized or read.

The main Jewish prayer is the Amidah, dating back to the first century, the first blessing of which is:

> *Blessed are You, Adonoy,*
>   *our God and God of our fathers,*
> *God of Abraham, God of Isaac and God of Jacob,*
> *Great, mighty, revered and awesome God,*
>   *Highest God,*
> *Doer of good, kind deeds,*
>   *Master of all,*
> *Who remembers the love of the Patriarchs*
>   *and brings a redeemer to their children's children*
>   *for his name's sake,*
>   *with love.*
> *King, Helper, Rescuer,*
> *Blessed are You, Adonoy, Shield of Abraham.*

Perhaps the oldest Jewish prayer and the core declaration of Judaism is the Shema (literally "hear"), taken from the Torah (Deut. 6:4–7): *Shema Yisrael, Adonoy Elohenu, Adonoy Echad* (Hear, O Israel, the Lord our God, the Lord is One!).

The word "Israel" means "he who contends with the divine" (Gen. 32:29), so Jews, who are supposed to be making God a central focus of their life, are told to be aware of the unity or oneness of God. This is the root of monotheism and why one of the Ten Commandments is not to worship other gods or idols. The Torah says that the Shema should be recited twice a day, morning and evening, telling Jews to pay attention to God's unity. Many Jews simply say *"Sh'ma Yisrael."*

The Shema continues: "And thou shalt love the Lord thy God with all thy heart, and with all thy soul, and with all thy might. And these words, which I command thee this day, shall be upon thy heart, and thou shalt teach them diligently unto thy children, and thou shalt talk of them when thou sittest in thy house, and when thou walkest by the way, and when thou liest down, and when thou risest up." The message loud and clear is to make the spiritual dimension of life ever present and central, and prayer helps us do exactly that.

"Holy, holy, holy is the Lord of Hosts, the whole world is filled with His glory" (Isa. 6:3) is another ancient Jewish prayer.

Rabbi Aryeh Kaplan suggests using *Ribbono shel Olam*—"Lord of the Universe"—as a mantra. This has been used for over two thousand years and is to be repeated out loud (or at least mouthed) twenty to thirty minutes a day for at least a month, before expecting results—the result being greater closeness with God, not necessarily getting our own wishes and ways.

"Blessed be the Lord" (Gen. 24:27) is common to both Jews and Christians, and the Dead Sea Scrolls offers "Blessed art Thou, O Lord, who has given unto humanity the insight of knowledge to understand thy wonders."

A nice way to begin the meal is with an attitude of gratitude and the prayer "Blessed art Thou, O Lord, King of the Universe, who brings forth bread from the earth."

BUDDHIST PRAYERS AND MANTRAS

The Heart Sutra says, "The great mantra, the mantra of great knowledge, the utmost mantra, the unequaled mantra ... goes like this: *'Gate gate paragate parasamgate bodhi svaha,'* Gone, Gone Gone Beyond, Gone Beyond Even the Beyond to Full Awakening! All hail!"

The Lotus Sutra says, *"Nam myoho renge kyo",* veneration to the Sutra of the Lotus of the Good Law. Our life is Buddha's life, and the mantra itself is the sound of Buddha wisdom.

The Pure Land Buddhist practice of *Nembutsu* consists of meditation on the Buddha through repeating *"Namo Amida Butsu"* (Praise to Buddha of infinite light and life). You don't see Buddha with your eyes, but feel Buddha with the heart, being enveloped by a warm, loving, and glowing light.

Zen's *Mu* can be repeated, too, as a mantra of consciousness, usually translated as "nothingness" or "emptiness."

The fourteenth-century Zen monk Shataku wrote:

Mind set free in the Dharma realm,
I sit at the moon-filled window
Watching the mountains with my ears,
Hearing the stream with open eyes.
Each molecule preaches perfect law,
Each moment chants true sutra:
The most fleeting thought is timeless,
A single hair's enough to stir the sea.

The Bodhisattva vows:

However innumerable sentient beings are, I vow to save them.
However inexhaustible the defilements are, I vow to extinguish them.

However immeasurable the dharmas are, I vow to master them.
However incomparable enlightenment is, I vow to attain it.

HINDU PRAYERS AND MANTRAS

Aditya Hridayam Punyam, Sarva Shatru Bina Shanam means "When the sun is in the heart all evil vanishes from life." When using this as a mantra, visualize the sun warming everything and shining from the heart.

Upanishad invocation:

Lead me from the unreal to the real.
Lead me from the darkness to light.
Lead me from death to immortality.

From the Chandogya Upanishad:

Out of himself he brought forth the cosmos
And entered into everything in it.
There is nothing that does not come from him.
Of everything, he is the inmost Self.
He is the truth; he is the Self supreme.
You are that, Shvetaketu; you are that.

Ramana Maharshi suggests constantly asking the question "Who am I?" so there is an endless seeing through our personal identifications with thoughts, feelings, sensations, etc., until we eventually come to the root of our being.

The Isa Upanishad says: "Behold the universe in the glory of God; and all that lives and moves on earth. Leaving the transient, find joy in the Eternal."

Aurobindo:

O mind, grow full of the eternal peace;
O word, cry out the immortal litany:
Built is the golden tower, the flame-child born.

ISLAMIC PRAYERS AND MANTRAS

Muslims pray five times a day, thus making their spirituality an integrated focus in their daily lives. Bowing toward Mecca, with no other thoughts or interruptions, say four times *"Allahu akbar"* (God is most great).

"Sami'a allahu li-man hamida, rabbana la-kum al-hamd" (God hears the one who praises him, Our Lord, praise is due to you).

"Subhana rabbiya al-a'la" (Glory be to my Lord, the Most High).

"La ilaha illa Allah" (There is no God but God). Repeat with the energy flowing from the navel into the heart, telling oneself: I want nothing, seek nothing, love nothing *illa Allah*—but God.

O My servants who believe!
Surely My earth is vast,
Therefore Me alone would you serve. (The Koran)

Rumi:

Glorious is the moment we sit in the palace, you and I
Two forms, two faces, but a single soul, you and I
The flowers will blaze and bird cries shower us with immortality
The moment we enter the garden, you and I
All the stars of heaven will rage with envy
In that place we laugh ecstatically, you and I
What a miracle, you and I, entwined in the same nest

What a miracle, you and I, one love, one lover, one Fire
In this world and the next, in an ecstasy without end.

NONDENOMINATIONAL PRAYERS AND MANTRAS

Other prayers and mantras can be used by anyone, regardless of religious affiliation, if any.

The American Indian Lakota daily prayer:

Let us give thanks for this beautiful day. Let us give thanks for this life. Let us give thanks for the water without which life would not be possible. Let us give thanks for Grandmother Earth who protects and nourishes us.

An American Indian Chinook blessing:

We call upon all those who have lived on this earth, our ancestors and our friends,
Who dreamed the best for future generations, and upon whose lives our lives are
built, and with thanksgiving, we call upon them to
Teach us and show us the Way.
And we call upon all that we hold most sacred, the presence and power of
The Great Spirit of love and truth which flows through all the Universe, to be with us to
Teach us, and show us the Way.

Vietnamese Zen monk Thich Nhat Hanh suggests:

Waking up this morning, I smile,
Twenty-four brand-new hours are before me
I vow to live fully in each moment
And to look at all beings with eyes of compassion.

A Unitarian prayer says:

From all that dwells below the skies,
Let faith and hope with joy arise,
Let beauty, truth and good be sung
Through every land, by every tongue.

And Samuel Taylor Coleridge wrote:

He prayeth well
*   Who loveth well*
Both man and bird and beast,
He prayeth best
*   Who loveth best*
All things both great and small;
For the dear God
*   Who loveth us,*
He made and loveth all.

Perhaps we can simply say "God" with the out-breath and "love" with the in-breath.

The point is to aim our thinking toward spiritual awareness, presence, goodness, and loving kindness.

What Can I Do?
The "Monkey Calming" Recipe

1. Combine the Basic Spiritual Diet with our thinking. Breathe to be awake here and now and pay attention to the thinking process. A "monkey calming" recipe might include breathing consciously, aware of my jabbering jumping monkeys, hearing my chattering inner monologue.

2. Label "thinking" and see patterns and content of thought. Consciously resting here now, "thinking about work," "thinking about a snack . . ."

3. See through the thoughts. I have thoughts, but there's much more to me than my thinking.

4. Counterbalance excessively negative or positive thoughts. Excessive gloom and doom doesn't bring forth light and health, but loving goodness does and we can focus our thoughts on the positive to counteract excessive negativity. Excessive positivity, on the other hand, may call for facing life's harsher realities.

5. We can combine the Basic Spiritual Diet with a daily prayer or mantra to supercharge the spiritual power in our life. Once we've decided on a prayer or mantra, we can write it down and keep it in our wallet and appointment book—where we will see it and be reminded to say it each day.

Once we've learned about breathing with awareness and presence while focusing on thinking, and using holy thoughts, prayers, and mantras to bring personality closer with spirituality, the Spiritual Diet calls for us to turn our attention to the next course—our inner streams of emotion.

Chapter 8

 ───────────────────────────────

Inner Streams

We human beings are completely vulnerable
emotionally. We are probably the most
emotionally vulnerable creatures on earth. Our
vulnerability is a total openness to any
possibility.

A. H. ALMAAS

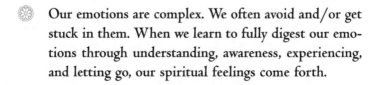

Our emotions are complex. We often avoid and/or get
stuck in them. When we learn to fully digest our emotions through understanding, awareness, experiencing,
and letting go, our spiritual feelings come forth.

Crosscurrents
and Rocky Rapids

Getting out of bed in the morning is hard. Even by lunch I often still feel sluggish.

My anger and irritability can really be a problem. Sometimes I'll erupt over small things. I feel bad about it, but I still get really annoyed and impatient.

I can dwell on things too long. If someone makes me mad, I have a hard time forgiving them.

I find myself feeling jittery and worried. My bills are getting paid, but I'm still preoccupied. I'm nervous and scared, but I'm not really sure why. It can't just be the coffee.

I don't seem to let myself feel really good, even though I've got a lot to feel good about. I guess I see the glass as half-empty. I just wish there was a way I could feel happier.

Like the ocean, we may appear fairly calm on the surface, but underneath, we have currents of emotion flowing through us with differing temperatures and intensities. Feelings can bubble up to the surface. They can capture us, sucking us into a whirlpool. They can be like an iceberg, cold, frozen, and mostly concealed beneath our awareness. They can sap our energy, make us ill, and appear when we wish they wouldn't. Feelings can also be like free-flowing streams, quenching and nourishing us.

These emotional currents are so complex that at times we may even baffle ourselves. We'll be in a particularly good or bad mood and not really know why we feel that way. How we feel is influenced by many factors—genetic predispositions, brain chemistry, hormones, amount of light, general health, social, financial, and psychological forces, to name a few.

Emotions matter, and they can be difficult to sort out. They play a central role in making us feel light and up, or down and carrying the weight of the world.

The word "emotion" comes from the Latin *motere*, meaning "to move." Centered deep within our brain, human emotion developed long before our ability to think. Emotions provide us with immediate impulses to act. Fear puts us on alert and readies us to run or otherwise handle a danger; anger pumps us up with the power to fight an enemy; sadness makes us quiet down and pull inside to deal with disappointment, death, and other losses; love fosters life as it pulls us toward others in caring, nurturing ways; happiness lifts our energy and gives us the drive to positively go forward in life.

While all human beings feel emotions, our individual personality can experience and react to our own emotions in a multitude of ways, depending on our biological predispositions, life experience, habit patterns, and whim. Some of us might feel fear, but because of our personal pattern, we decide to stand and fight. Others feel fear and because of their personal pattern, run away. Still others might meditate on the emotion. This means not only that our emotions help create and mold our personality but also that they're created and molded by personality.

Because of the complexity of our emotions and the difficulties in both knowing what they are and what to do with them, we often fail to handle our feelings in the healthiest ways. Yet, what we do with our emotions affects every aspect of our life, including our spirituality.

Mishandling Emotion

Emotional intelligence (knowing our own feelings, empathy for others' feelings, making good use of our emotions, and fully digesting them)* is related to being successful, not only in our outer personal life of careers and chores but also in the inner world of spirituality. Yet most of us mishandle at least some of our emotions in two basic ways.

1. We avoid our emotions.

Keeping a stiff upper lip is considered admirable in many societies, because emotions can interfere with our accomplishing our goals and doing what we have to do in daily life. We especially see emotional denial and avoidance in business, sports, and war—where emotional control is valuable in surviving and winning. Such popular sayings as "Play injured" and "Don't wimp out" encourage us to deny our feelings in order to win and succeed.

While emotional control is obviously important and a sign of maturity, we too often feel that our emotions are embarrassing, shameful, or a sign of vulnerability and weakness. Parents often react to children's feelings by trying to get them to avoid their emotions or to have them feel something different. Parents, teachers, and other role models will say things like, "You don't really feel that way, do you?" or "You're not really angry at Aunt Margie, are you, after all she's done for you? You really love Aunt Margie," or "How dare you feel that way?" or "You have no right to be upset."

It's very common for children to be scolded, sent to their rooms, or otherwise punished for showing negative emotions such as anger or for crying out of sadness or fear. So, millions grow up with the sense that it's not safe to feel their feelings, that many of their

* See Daniel Goleman's *Emotional Intelligence* for further information.

feelings are unacceptable, and they shouldn't fully feel them, or feel them only in an acceptable way.

Instead of being aware of our emotions and handling them effectively, many learn emotional avoidance and overcontrol. We learn to ignore and suppress our emotions so we may have little idea of what we actually feel, or our feelings may be confused or ambiguous.

🌸 **Unfortunately, ignoring or suppressing emotions often leads to depression, anxiety, sexual dysfunction, overuse of food/drugs/alcohol/shopping, or many other difficulties symptomatic of being unaware of, and improperly processing, our real feelings.**

People who have their feelings under tight control may find that getting out of bed in the morning is hard. They may feel sluggish during the day. This is because it takes enormous energy for the personality to ward off powerful feelings and keep them from coming to consciousness. This effort (though most of us hardly know we're making it) saps our energy and makes everything in our life more difficult. For example, a child may be furious at a parent, but if she fears expressing (or often even thinking about) her anger, she holds the anger in and may turn it against herself, becoming excessively self-critical, emotionally wounded, or even depressed. (Suicide is often internalized homicide plus hopelessness about changing the situation—we can't kill the one we're angry with, so we turn the anger on our self.) Sometimes it's not a particular person, but a circumstance, that we're angry with, or even with life itself (how can bad things happen to good people?).

🌸 **Emotions are often difficult, painful, or inconvenient to feel, and denying them is simply easier.**

We hate our boss, but know we have to work for him/her, so we suppress our anger to keep from feeling angry every time we're at work. Perhaps we fear that if we feel our anger, it might somehow leak out in our behavior or attitude, threatening our work security. Our teenager has symptoms of taking drugs, but we don't know what to do about it. So we avoid our fears by ignoring the symptoms (maybe he'll outgrow it and it'll take care of itself).

Another way that we ignore feelings is to overemphasize another feeling. For example, a person is angry or sad but doesn't acknowledge this to himself that and instead becomes dedicated to love or service to others. This sounds like a constructive path, and to a point it is. But denial and avoidance of strong emotions—no matter what form it takes—frequently backfires. We're shocked to hear that a presumably religious person is guilty of a crime (such as child molestation or of violating one of the person's own vows, such as committing adultery) and wonder why. Commonly, it's the result of suppressed anger, denied sexual needs, or starvation for love. Emotions that are ignored don't just go away; they bubble beneath the surface and may boil over in ways that horrify even the person himself. In this way, people might become unable to control the power and destructiveness of their actions because of the buildup from suppressed feelings, as they have a big reaction to a trivial incident.

So we tend to avoid our feelings, but the results are burdensome.

The second way people mishandle emotions is the opposite of emotional avoidance.

2. We get "stuck" in our feelings.

Like a default position on a computer that automatically returns to the same setting, we tend to specialize in one or another feeling, spontaneously returning to the same primary emotion over and over again.

We've all known people who are irritable. Even if they aren't sick or in pain, they're simply easily annoyed for little or no apparent reason. Others are sad and depressed even at times when it would seem they'd be happy. Still others seem endlessly nervous, no matter how hard people around them may try to make them calm and comfortable.

It's often true that earlier in life these people were legitimately annoyed or wounded or scared, and perhaps their temperament predisposes them in one emotional direction or another. But over time their primary emotion became a habit. In fact, continuously having an emotion actually changes our biochemistry, so in time the emotional habit becomes a bio-electro-chemical pattern.

For example, a person may have had great difficulty during childhood. Perhaps she was physically unattractive or without friends. Or she may have lost a parent or been in an unhappy home-life where those around her were also sad. Perhaps she did poorly in school and felt badly about herself. Once she grew up, her circumstances may have completely changed. She may no longer have any strong reason for her sadness, yet her pattern of pain persists. Perhaps, deep inside, her emotional heart is still bruised or broken, and she's never fully healed. Perhaps she's developed a pattern of not meeting some important need and constantly generates more bad feeling. Or perhaps there's something comforting in being sad, since the emotion is so familiar and makes her feel secure.

Such people may even unconsciously construct their lives to produce sadness so they continue feeling sad. Miriam, one of Jonathan's therapy clients, came from a home in which her parents were Holocaust survivors. Miriam had spent her entire life with people who had tremendous, traumatic sadness. Grief and suffering were normal to her, and while she complained of this in therapy, she'd also engineered her life to be sad. At the time she entered therapy, Miriam had been working for seven years in a hospice for dying patients. Pain, loss, and mourning of both terminally ill patients and their families was the daily fare. Her habitual sadness was valuable to

her in her job, because it helped her relate more closely and comfortably to her patients, but it also perpetuated her own pattern of
constantly carrying grief—Miriam's weight of the world.

People also get stuck in newly discovered emotions. A person
may enter therapy not acknowledging his sadness or anger, but once
in therapy he becomes aware of it. Rather than experiencing it and
letting it go, he gets stuck in the emotion and generates even more
of it by endlessly dwelling on it. Then, unable to empty himself of
his endless sadness or anger, he goes deeper into it, generating ever
more of the bad feeling and never moving on.

People can get stuck in positive emotions as well. For example,
we can get stuck in "love." This can be love for a particular person,
no matter what that person did that in most relationships would un-
dermine that love. A close friend of our family was a very religious
and loving person who was almost never angry. She felt anger was an
unholy emotion and forgiveness was the only way to deal with people that made her mad. She was married to an abusive alcoholic for
over fifty years, and at the end of her life she said she thought if she
just loved him enough, he'd eventually change. But he never did and
she put up with a great deal of pain. She was stuck in love and therefore lost the potentially positive power of her anger that might have
motivated her to change her situation.

Getting stuck in emotion acts as a logjam, slowing or limiting
the free flow of other feelings. For example, we can be so fearful
about losing a loved one that we have trouble feeling our genuine
caring, or so sad that we have trouble feeling happy.

Aside from avoiding and getting stuck in emotion, our life and
our personality are constantly generating more emotion, so there's
the ongoing challenge of constructively dealing with these ever-
flowing streams.

In addition, we have feelings about our feelings. Being scared
can make us angry, and anger can make us feel ashamed or fearful

we'll lose control. The constant complexity of our emotions often results in confusion and complication that can drag us down, causing physical, emotional, and behavioral problems. Indeed, emotional burdens are most people's main weight of the world.

Five Basic Feelings

As we've seen, we often deny and get stuck in one or more feelings, we're constantly churning out more feeling, and our emotions generate other feelings. In addition, as we can see from the chart on page 190, we have many different moods and emotions.

While it's important to see and understand all our emotions, they are so varied that for our purposes here, it's best to concentrate on understanding and processing five fundamental ones: love, happiness, sadness, fear, and anger. If we can understand and fully digest these five basic inner streams of emotion, we'll more easily understand the others. As we better understand our feelings, we can more easily experience them fully and let them go. The more we experience them and let them go, the more we connect with our spirituality, conscious and present with the flow of feelings within. Let's begin with love.

LOVE

Love ranges from mildly liking, accepting, feeling friendly, kindly, and caring, to loving, devotion, and trusting, to intense passion, infatuation, and adoration, to universal, spiritual love.

Love fosters life.

aggressive	alienated	angry	annoyed	anxious	apathetic	bashful
bored	cautious	confident	confused	curious	depressed	determined
disappointed	discouraged	disgusted	embarrassed	enthusiastic	envious	ecstatic
excited	exhausted	fearful	frightened	frustrated	guilty	happy
helpless	hopeful	hostile	humiliated	hurt	hysterical	innocent
interested	jealous	lonely	loved	lovestruck	mischievous	miserable
negative	optimistic	pained	paranoid	peaceful	proud	puzzled
regretful	relieved	sad	satisfied	shocked	shy	sorry
stubborn	sure	surprised	suspicious	thoughtful	undecided	withdrawn

In the classic children's story *The Velveteen Rabbit,* the stuffed bunny comes to life when a child loves it. In essence, love made the bunny real.

In the real world, love can't literally bring an inanimate object to life, but love's magic is powerful and real. Love can be felt within us so profoundly and so deeply that it seems miraculous. It brings an entire dimension outside ourselves, whether our love is focused on one individual, our family and friends, a pet, a cause, or humanity as a whole. Love is the emotion that most pulls us toward others, creating a warm, intimate, interconnected life.

The poet Robert Browning wrote, "Take away love and our earth is a tomb." The Bible says that "God is love." Spiritual love is acceptance and compassion for whatever is, an eternally welcoming fire that warms whoever or whatever experiences its glow. Love is the essence of Christ's message, the heart of Christianity—Jesus said, "I give you a new commandment, that you love one another."

Spirituality is without boundaries, open, loving. Almaas describes spiritual love when he says, "A loving person is love. Love isn't given. It overflows. It's not even your love—it's everyone's love interacting. Love emanates from us like the scent from a rose."

Ultimately, divine love wraps loving arms around us and helps us feel safe enough to relax.

But first, most of us must learn to have a loving relationship with our self, because, unfortunately, we grow up feeling conditional love. We're loved on condition that we get good grades, get along with others, and live up to others' expectations. And when we're loved conditionally, self-love is lost or never developed, and then we're cut off from, and we feel unworthy of, spiritual love.

But we can change our relationship with our self. Self-love, self-understanding, self-acceptance, and self-compassion calm, nourish, and heal us. To love and care for our self enables us to relax our personal grip on life and opens us to a deeper love and caring. The more we relax and care about our self, the more we can feel the fountain within us that expresses love regardless of who or what appears. As we find this part of our self, our love becomes less conditional, less self-focused, and more universal. This unconditional love is a bridge between the personal and the spiritual and, by its essence, heals us and makes us whole. We can feel empathy for all that we and our fellow creatures endure, and with this understanding we can sense the weight of the world being lifted off us, as we more fully find our self in a warm, loving embrace.

HAPPINESS

Happiness ranges from mild enjoyment, contentment, relief, and satisfaction, to being happy, cheerful, and delighted, to being elated, ecstatic, thrilled, and joyful.

Happiness brings positive feelings that encourage us to go forward in life, and can be both personal and spiritual. Personality feels happy when it achieves a goal, as when we graduate from school, win a game, or get a promotion. We feel happily relieved when something we fear doesn't happen, or when our child gets better after being sick. So personality feels good when it gets pleasure and satisfaction and avoids pain, frustration, and disappointment. But personal happiness is fleeting.

Spiritual happiness brings the contentment and peace of mind inherent in our basic being, a sense of joy from the sheer fact of being awake and alive in the moment. Rajneesh describes this when he says, "Why am I happy? What have I got that you have not got? Why am I serene and quiet? Have I achieved something that you have to achieve? No. I have simply relaxed into the suchness of it." Spiritual happiness comes with a deep relaxation in the present with life as it actually is.

ANGER

Anger ranges from minor frustration, irritability, upsetness, impatience, resentment, and annoyance, to hostility, outrage, and animosity, to intense hatred, rage, and fury.

Anger comes primarily from our personality. For example, when we don't get what we want, we may feel frustrated and annoyed. Or when our feelings are hurt and we suppress our vulnerability, we may become irritable and tense. Anger also comes when we feel afraid, as when we're wounded, under attack, or in physical or emotional danger. When we fear pain or death, we may cover our existential anxiety with irritability or even rage.

Anger can serve as a powerful energizer that prepares us to use our physical and mental resources to protect ourselves by defeating and warding off anything we experience as a threat.

We all experience anger to some degree. The Dalai Lama admits, "Sometimes I get angry . . . small, small things create anger . . . when staff members do a small thing, such as incomplete work or insufficient work, then I feel very irritated. Then I use harsh words! *[Laughs]* But, one good thing is that it never stays long. It comes and it goes."

The problem isn't so much in the anger itself as in our relationship with the anger. If we suppress and deny it, it lasts longer, may build in intensity (making it more difficult to deal with), and acts as a barrier to peace of mind.

On the other hand, if we get stuck in anger, feeding it and keeping it alive, we can end up depressed (when it's turned against our self) or having outbursts (when it's turned against others and the outside world). And both depression and outbursts are bad for our health, happiness, and relationships.

If, however, we understand our anger, we may be able to meet the unmet need that's causing the frustration or allay the underlying anxiety behind the rage. If we recognize it, we can know it at the low level of irritation or annoyance, when we can much more easily digest it and let it go. (We'll soon learn to use the "digestion process with emotion.")

While anger is most often personal, it can also come from Spirit. For example, we might feel righteous indignation when we see a child being harmed or an animal being neglected or abused. Empathy, compassion, and our connectedness with other living things can make us share others' pain, and an impersonal anger can naturally arise. The writer Robert Louis Stevenson was out walking one day when he came upon a man hitting a dog with a stick and yelled, "Stop that immediately."

The man said, "How dare you, sir. It's my dog and I can do what I want to it."

"No, sir," cried Stevenson. "It's God's dog and I'm here to protect it!" Stevenson felt a natural anger and was automatically moved by it.

Perhaps Jesus' anger at the money changers in the temple and Moses' rage at the children of Israel's worshiping a golden calf are other examples of righteous or spiritual anger. Indeed, who among us has not been moved to action by our outrage over someone abusing another person, animal, or the natural world?

In spite of its naturalness, most religions teach us to avoid anger and instead find love, compassion, understanding, and forgiveness.

Hinduism: He who gives up anger reaches God.

Judaism: He who is slow to anger has great understanding.

Christianity: Let not the sun go down upon your wrath.

Shinto: Let us cease from anger and angry gestures.

Islam: Repay evil with good.

Buddhism: Conquer by love.

Taoism: Love is sure to be victorious.

Anger creates separation; love and forgiveness create closeness. One of the big problems that plague the emotional life of many adherents of organized religion, however, is premature forgiveness, the attempt to never be angry. In an effort to spiritually do the "right thing," millions turn the other cheek, forgiving and forgetting without having allowed their anger to be flushed from their system. The result is compromise forgiveness, halfhearted and incomplete, the anger lurking in the background. Turned inward, it becomes self-criticalness and suppression of self. Turned outward, it becomes resentment, cynicism, impatience, and irritability. Their aim is obviously correct, but their method is faulty and the results are unfortunate.

Rather than suppressing anger, it's better to accept that life makes us frustrated, irritated, even furious. What is important is to recognize it at a low level, control our behavior, accurately understand, properly process, and counterbalance the feeling so as to move beyond it.

Of course, if we're angry over a situation that cries out for action, then we act. We protect an endangered child or pet or stand of ancient sequoias. And when we allow our anger to be processed and used for good, then we lose a great weight and our spirituality can come forth more powerfully.

SADNESS

Sadness ranges from feeling mildly low, down, disappointed, or blue, to being somber, unhappy, grieved, or sorrowed, to being intensely depressed, hopeless, miserable, in despair, or suicidal. Sadness can also come from spiritual sensitivity to human and nature's suffering.

We humans are vulnerable creatures, and all of us, at one time and to some degree or another, feel sad. Life is impermanent and ever changing. Inevitably, it's not all to our liking, so we usually feel at least somewhat disappointed. Personally, we all experience disappointment, defeat, failure, criticism, and the deaths of loved ones and our self—all part of the human condition. In fact, many millions are deeply wounded, despairing, and depressed.

At the same time, our spiritual heart of caring and compassion goes out to the world's suffering as every day the media serves up big helpings of others' pain and desperation.

As if that weren't enough, there's also what Almaas describes as the "hole of love" and the "deep wound." This sadness comes from the loss of our own self-love, usually a result of being measured against external standards or ideals, from feeling we're inadequate or unacceptable, from not fully realizing our potential, and from failing to realize and manifest our inherent spiritual nature.

Sadness is a natural and universal feeling. A woman came to the Buddha saying her child had died and she was in deep despair. Was there anything he could do for her? He instructed her to go from house to house to find one who had not been touched by a painful loss. As the woman went from one home to another, she heard one sad story after another, and came to realize that sadness is a shared, universal emotion.

Because sadness is often so uncomfortable, it's also natural to try to avoid it. But suppressing and denying sadness keeps the pain and the weight of the world going. Sadness can fester like an infection, sapping our energies as we control the pain and do what we can to keep it at bay. Maybe we work more to keep busy, or eat more food, or use medicine, shopping, drugs, or alcohol to cope. Maybe our sadness turns into irritability or we create a whirlwind of activities that keeps us from feeling the sadness and blocks our spiritual awareness, presence, and growth.

By learning to be strong enough to be vulnerable to our sadness, we can properly process the feelings, so that opening to our sadness and letting it go brings a sense of aliveness, caring, and intimacy with life.

FEAR

Fear ranges from being mildly concerned, on edge, apprehensive, cautious, uneasy, and wary, to tense, nervous, fearful, jittery, scared, uptight, and worried, to terror, dread, fright, panic, and hysteria.

Accidents happen, criminals are real, bodies get old and ill, and none of us gets out of life alive. Of course, the news media constantly remind us of all the nasty possibilities, and we all live with some degree of tension about our own and our loved ones' physical and personal safety.

We also get ego wounds from errors, embarrassments, disappointments, and failures, causing us tension about a possible next faux pas, failure, setback, or limitation.

The result of all these worries, fears, and insecurities is an existential anxiety in the background of our life, dividing us from Spirit, and creating insecurity and separateness, whether we're conscious of it or not.

We can face our fears or we can fail to feel them. We can cover over our anxieties, hiding from them in excessive work, alcohol, entertainment, or materialism, or we can deal with the situation as best we can, learning to properly process our fears so they can come and go.

Religious teachings tell us to calm our fears by relying on God, Jesus, Buddha, Muhammad, Great Spirit ... We are made of Spirit so we can always be helped and supported by Spirit. The biblical Psalms says,

"Yea, though I walk through the valley of the shadow of death, I will fear no evil; for thou art with me; thy rod and thy staff they

comfort me." If personality can find its way to Spirit, then our fears
can be calmed in a deep and genuine way, and we find comfort and
contentment in the midst of it all.

My Basic Feelings

In order to properly handle our emotions and have them lead us to
greater spiritual awakening, we begin by understanding our relationship with our basic feelings.

We can begin to understand our feelings by thinking about our
five basic emotions. Think or write about two or three things that
make you:

Happy_____

_____

Loving_____

_____

Sad_____

_____

Scared_____

_____

Mad_____

_____

Once we've thought a little about our emotions, we can focus
on what it means to properly handle our feelings.

The Positive Power
of Uncomfortable Emotions

The uncomfortable feelings of sadness, fear, and anger are usually more difficult to handle well than are the more pleasant ones like love and happiness. Unpleasant emotions are often seen as *bad* feelings. We may be afraid of these feelings, they may embarrass or frustrate us. Few of us welcome our bad feelings. Yet, when we control our actions and properly process them, there's a positive power even to negative emotion.

Feeling our anger can mobilize our energies to confront a danger, as when anger empowers us to leave an abusive relationship.

Our fears alert us to threatening situations so we can focus our thinking and effectively handle the potential problems.

Sadness can heal our pain and enable us to feel kinship with others who've suffered, helping us go forward and live more fully and happily.

Crying washes away oils, salts, and stress hormones produced by intense emotion; tears flush and clean our system.

When we use uncomfortable emotions in a constructive way, we find a positive power. In essence, then, by learning to fully digest our uncomfortable feelings, we open another way to the growth and relaxation of our personality, which in turn leads to the flowering of Spirit.

Many religious people, however, avoid and deny any negativity or unpleasantness, trying to rise above it all, as if all we are is spiritual. But denial blocks our having a constructive relationship with comfortable emotion, which inhibits spirituality. Denial or suppression just creates a barrier to the fullness of our being by allowing us to only experience part of what we are. Rejecting unpleasantness creates a division within our self that strengthens our personality and suppresses Spirit.

As we'll see, there are many ways to cope with and process uncomfortable emotion that don't create a barrier within.

Fully Digesting Our Emotions

The Spiritual Diet's method for properly processing—"digesting"—emotions includes the following:

* As we may recall from Chapter 5, the "digestion" process consists of the five steps of (1) awareness, (2) presence, (3) experiencing, (4) letting go, and (5) opening to whatever comes next.

In order to fully digest our feelings, we need to (1) know our feeling(s) at the moment (the sooner we realize we're having an emotion and the earlier we begin processing it, the better), (2) allow our self to be present with the emotion, (3) feel it in our body, then (4) let it go and (5) open to the emotion (the same or others) that next appears.

While personality craves good feelings and rejects the bad, from a spiritual viewpoint, whether a feeling is "good" or "bad" isn't as important as our relationship with our feelings. With practice, the digestion process becomes a natural flow of feeling that allows personality to loosen its grip, enabling spirituality to come more fully to the fore.

Right now as I take a breath, I'm aware that I'm feeling excited and happy about getting a new puppy, and I let myself have the excitement in my body as my energy feels charged, my face has a little smile, and my mind jumps around excitedly, with mental images of past puppies I've known and imagined puppies that might exist. I take a breath and feel the electrical excitement within. Breathing with the feeling, I can then let it go, opening to the next feeling.

Our spirit is lightened when we let go of negative moods and move on. But we can't let go until we know the "bad" feelings in the first place.

A touch of fear appears in my awareness when I think about the puppy chewing on my new shoes and scratching the good table. I breathe in and out as I feel it in my tense neck muscles, constricted chest and breath, and my worried thoughts, rehearsing how I'll handle the dog's destructive behavior. I physically feel the concern and let it go, opening to whatever feeling next bubbles up (including the same excitement or worry).

Whether feelings are positive, neutral, or negative, we allow our self to be aware, experiencing them, and then we avoid clinging to them, as we let go and open to whatever comes next. We feel and let go, staying open and available. Of course, the exact same feeling(s) may immediately be present once again in the next moment, but regardless of what's there, we avoid either rejecting or grasping. Spirituality welcomes and mirrors what is, letting feelings come and letting feelings go.

Properly digest emotion by counterbalancing the overweighted with the overlooked.

It often happens that because of personal predisposition and life experience, we become more familiar with one or another emotion, while avoiding or overlooking others. Some people always seem angry, others fearful, still others sad. People who have a lot of anger tend to be unfamiliar with happiness, while the scared overlook safety and the sad overlook happiness.

We can think about our typical relationship with each of these basic feelings along a continuum from overlooked (that which we avoid and fail to feel) to overweighted (that which we feel frequently or even habitually). Think about or mark where you'd put yourself on the following continuums:

My HAPPINESS is usually

---

overlooked   handled comfortably   overweighted

My LOVE is usually

overlooked	handled comfortably	overweighted

My ANGER is usually

overlooked	handled comfortably	overweighted

My FEAR is usually

overlooked	handled comfortably	overweighted

My SADNESS is usually

overlooked	handled comfortably	overweighted

As we've seen, sometimes we specialize in one or more emotions and habitually avoid others. When our emotional "default" position is set on "sad," "scared," or "mad," we feel emotionally out of balance and are left with a portion of undigested feeling. But we can correct the problem by *counterbalancing the overweighted with the overlooked.*

For example, if we overemphasize sadness (out of painful and scary experience, genetic predisposition, or habit and training, as with Miriam, mentioned earlier, who was raised by Holocaust survivors and a daily diet of sadness), then in addition to using the digestion process with sadness as it arises (aware, present, experiencing, letting go, and opening to whatever comes next), we can also counterbalance our excessive sadness with happiness as well as physically exercising to lift our energy and mood (or whatever the opposite feeling is from the one in which we're stuck).

Miriam decided she needed to counterbalance her excessive grief with better emotion, and she started to focus on the fact that in spite of the horror and tragedy of millions, World War II ended successfully and she was not in danger as her parents had been. She started to look around for real reasons she deserved to feel happier, and she discovered quite a few: her husband, Norman, and her six-year-old son, Noah, both of whom she loved dearly; that they were all in good health; that they had enough to eat every day . . .

If we're stuck in fear, we can build safe and secure feelings by noticing truly safe aspects of life that our personality usually takes for granted and overlooks: noticing how many times we've been needlessly worried in the past when our fears didn't turn out to be warranted (probably 99 percent of the time), noticing what good locks we have on our doors, avoiding the local news or movies that are designed to create anxiety, insecurity, and fear.

We're *not* suggesting to ignore reality (the digestion process fully immerses us in it), but to counteract feelings that we exaggerate and to pay more attention to those we avoid.

So if, like Miriam, we tend to feel excessively sad or our "default" is set for "depression," we can look for genuine reasons, big and small, to feel happy. If a feeling feels foreign to you, then it's especially important to pay attention to it. So start off looking for mildly happy feelings, such as contentment, satisfaction, relief. Look for the good feelings usually taken for granted: that your health is good, that you have a close friend, that your child is doing well in school, that you have a job that pays the basic bills and puts food on the table.

Or take action that produces pleasure and satisfaction, which cools the fires of excessive discomfort: visits with friends and family, upbeat music, helping another, reading a good book, watching a funny movie, finishing a chore, getting dressed and cleaned up, going for a long walk in the park. Physical exercise is probably the single best means to lift our mood and energy level.

If we find ourselves overemphasizing anger (in addition to properly digesting the anger that's there), we can look for love, caring, warmth, and closeness that we have, but take for granted. And we can go out of our way to foster close relationships and feelings.

Andrew (whom we discussed earlier) grew up in a cold, materialistic home, and when his wife filed for divorce, he said he'd go for help to deal with his anger and irritability. After first having Andrew identify his anger when it was at a lower level and then learning to digest it and let it go, we discussed the need to counterbalance his habit of anger with better feelings. Andrew confessed that he loved his wife and children a great deal, but couldn't feel it very easily, let alone show it (except by being a good provider).

So he went on a Spiritual Diet. For Andrew, it was unrealistic for him to try to attune to intense love. He needed to begin with what he really could feel—liking, caring, and enjoying. So he created a recipe of conscious present breathing with low intensity, warm feelings for those few he generally cared about. He started becoming more aware of liking, needing, and enjoying his wife, kids, and dog. In three months, he had made dramatic strides forward in becoming comfortable with these more positive and closer emotions, and his wife (while saying he needed to continue his progress) decided to give him a chance and canceled the divorce.

If we overemphasize guilt and shame, we can look for ways to be self-supporting and act in keeping with our basic goodness by knowing our values and living accordingly. We can find ways to make amends for past wrongs, so we can find forgiveness in our own eyes. Then we have more self-respect, and feel better as we lose some of the weight of the world we've been lugging around.

We've seen that we can also overemphasize positive feelings. Excessive love and excessive happiness can feel fake or artificial to ourselves and others if we're too sweet or too nice. If a person seems unreal, it may mean he/she is overlooking an uncomfortable emotion he or she wants to avoid (such as anger, sadness, or fear). If we see this in ourselves or others, we can use these excessive positive feelings to remind us to look for the unpleasant ones we might be avoiding.

Keep in mind that if we've been excessively overweighted toward one feeling or another, it may take great effort on a daily basis for a long time before it loosens its grip and new ones have become comfortably familiar. Andrew was so determined to save his marriage and family that he used his Spiritual Diet Recipe a minimum of ten times every day.

Properly digest emotion through identifying the feeling.

Breathe in the present, allowing the basic feelings to bubble to the surface of awareness.

Labeling helps: Anytime Sandi spoke with another guy, her husband, Dave, felt tremendous jealousy and anger. When Dave started labeling his jealousy and irritability, he became increasingly aware of how much he loved Sandi and how much he depended on her. He felt other men posed a threat to their relationship and reacted with fear and anger. When he saw this, he realized his feelings were unfounded, as Sandi was an honorable person with loyalty and self-control. He realized his many past hurts were the basis for his insecurity and jealousy.

He found that he could more easily digest his fear and anger and let it go. Dave's Spiritual Diet Recipe included taking a beginning breath to be aware and a second breath to be present. Then, watching his anger bubble up, he'd be aware of it and watch it flow away. He'd say to himself, "anger comes, anger goes" and "fear bubbling up and flowing away . . ."

At some point, Dave became increasingly aware of his caring for Sandi and processed these emotions as well. An ancient spiritual technique to feel love is to imagine yourself breathing in and out through your heart. Imagine the center of your chest opening for warm, caring feelings to go in and out with each breath. Dave said to himself "loving Sandi" with each in-breath, sending the feeling of caring out through his heart with his out-breath.

Along the way his recipes got simpler, and he'd breathe in, saying to himself "anger comes," breathing out, "anger goes," breathing in, "anger comes," breathing out, "anger goes"; "fear comes, fear goes," "love, love . . ."

Try this: breathing (awake, alert, conscious) and being (present, here and now), now I'm (happy, loving, sad, scared, mad...). Continue being aware of the emotion, allowing whatever feeling (the same or another) that comes next to bubble to the surface of awareness. Breathing (aware) and being (present), now I'm (sad, scared, mad, happy, loving), breathe and be, and let it go.

Properly digest emotion through seeing its physical and mental effects.

Pay attention to the body and mind that go with each emotion. When we settle down with our feelings, physically sensing their living quality, we find that there's a fundamental energy in them. By allowing our self to stay with the emotions, we can feel they are like inner rivers running through us and stimulating physical and mental reactions.

If I feel fat and ugly, then my thoughts are filled with self-criticism, I hear criticism from others where none may be intended, and my body feels heavy and less attractive than it is. If I feel content and complete, then my thoughts are clearer, I hear things the way they're intended, and my body is more relaxed.

Happiness brings a smile, an opening and relaxing of the chest, a sense of strength and well-being, more optimistic and positive thoughts; sadness brings shallower breath, slumped posture, and pessimistic thinking. Happy bodily feelings and happier thoughts, sadder bodily sensations and sadder thoughts. We can do the same for the five basic feelings, knowing and experiencing the angry body and mind, the scared body and mind, the sad body and mind, the happy body and mind, the loving body and mind. Aware and present, now I'm...

We can *challenge the thoughts* that accompany excessively uncomfortable emotions. When we're starting to get very upset, we can question the foundation of our feeling: Do I really need to be as angry about an insult as I'm starting to get? Do I really have a good reason for getting as scared as I'm starting to feel? Does it really matter that someone cut in front of me in traffic? In this way, we can reappraise the situation and perhaps come to view and feel it in a less negative fashion (making whatever negativity remains more easily digestible).

We can exercise, even if only for a short walk or a brief workout. Physical activity reduces tension and unpleasant emotion, lifting our mood and energy level. If you're a beginner, make exercise easy and enjoyable until you develop a pattern of healthful activity.

Often we can *reframe* our excessively strong emotions so they're not as intense.

We can think about whether our "negative" feelings might be an avoidance of more "positive" ones (out of habit, familiarity, predisposition, family tradition).

We can realize that while the feelings may be unpleasant, they're not really acute or life-threatening. (If they are, we need professional help.)

We can also realize that our emotions change, so that when we're feeling especially bad, we can keep in mind that "this, too, shall pass."

We can put our problems in perspective by realizing that others carry even heavier burdens and are even less fortunate, and/or by considering how much this really matters in the big scheme of things and in the long run. By challenging the foundations of our emotions, we can avoid becoming overly emotional and more easily maintain our peace of mind.

Properly digest emotion through self-control.

We must act responsibly. While we feel our feelings, it's extremely important that we exercise self-control over our actions. As psychologist Daniel Goleman says, "There is perhaps no psychological skill more fundamental than resisting impulse." When we know we have good self-control and we can trust our self to not act impulsively, we can do the Basic Spiritual Diet with anger or any other emotion. For then we know we're *not* going to be out of control and *do* anything destructive. This makes it safe to go toward our feelings and more fully feel them.

We can exercise self-control by cooling down through physical exercise and relaxation. Exercise and relaxation are keys to calming down and good health, enabling us to stay with the feelings we have. When we do the Basic Spiritual Diet, we can breathe more slowly and fully to cool our self down.

Fully digest emotions by seeing through them.

We can be less identified with our feelings and realize, as Ken Wilber put it, that "I *have* emotions, but I am *not* my emotions. I can feel and sense my emotions, and what can be felt and sensed is not the true Feeler. Emotions pass through me, but they do not affect my inward I. I *have* emotions but I am *not* emotions."

After using the Spiritual Diet methods for fully digesting feelings, in time we'll become less identified with our emotions. As a result, we lose the many burdens associated with unprocessed feelings. We have less worry, less irritability, more energy, greater ability to let things go, and better feelings about ourselves and the world.

What Can I Do?
The "Inner Streams" Recipe

1. **Do the Basic Spiritual Diet (breathing with attention and presence) while being aware of five basic feelings—happy, loving, scared, sad, and mad.**

2. **Properly process feelings.** Use:

The **"digestion" process**—aware, present, experiencing, letting go, and opening to whatever basic feeling comes next.

Counterbalance the overweighted with the overlooked. Look for ignored emotions while processing the habitually overemphasized ones. Keep in mind that habitually felt feelings may take a great deal of time and effort before they lighten up and others have become comfortably familiar.

Identify and rate feelings. Labeling and rating helps give us distance and makes feelings available to be processed at milder, more manageable levels.

Notice their mental and physical effects. See them in body and thought, reframing and reappraising to make them manageable.

Use self-control. Act responsibly, cool down, shape up.

See through emotions. I have emotion, but I'm more than my emotions.

In time, we can become emotional experts, as we work with our endless inner rivers of feeling. Awareness and experiencing of our feelings is an endless part of the Spiritual Diet, helping us to lose the weight of the world.

Chapter 9

Why Am I Here?

Calmness of mind does not mean you should
stop your activity.
Real calmness should be found in activity itself.

SHUNRYU SUZUKI

Modern people race from one chore and responsibility
to another. But we find peace of mind in the midst of
this activity when we discover our purpose in living
and use it to guide our daily life.

Nose to the Grindstone

I'm so busy and lost in what I'm doing that it often seems like I just get through the day instead of really living or enjoying it.

I'm not always sure why I'm doing what I'm doing. Sometimes it seems like I'm on a conveyor belt just being moved along without a real sense of direction or meaning.

Everything has gotten so boring and routine. I'm more than halfway through my life and I realize I haven't done the things I always wanted to do.

Every day we focus on what's ahead of us, finishing one task and going on to the next, in an endless flow of chores and responsibilities. By working like this we can be very productive and very successful. But we can also get so caught up in our activities that we don't pay attention to how we feel about what we're doing, or if we find it meaningful.

Meaning is something we don't generally think about. We're usually focused on more immediate or tangible goals: finishing the report, learning the software, getting the kids to soccer, paying the taxes, fixing the car, trying to get a vacation, or just getting through the day.

Perhaps, once in a while, we do stop and sigh, and contemplate questions like: *Why am I here? What am I meant to do? Is my life fulfilling? What's it all for?*

We may actually give it some real thought, particularly on birthdays or at the New Year as we consider our resolutions. But this contemplation is inevitably interrupted by our ongoing routine. Once again, we're caught up doing one task and then the next.

In the midst of daily life, we just keep waiting for *later*, in the hope that these questions will be answered then. Later we'll do what we're "meant" to do. Later we'll have time to settle down and think about our life. Later we'll understand what it's all for. But later never really comes, and we eventually realize that all of humanity has one thing in common—our personality and our body are going to die. Indeed, many of us never take a real look at our life until we're finished living it.

We may have thought about death in the abstract. We may have even drawn up our will and living trust. But few of us ever really imagine what it'll be like when one day we're dying.

Imagine for a moment that **you** *are on your deathbed, and it is the last day of your life:*

You're lying quietly by yourself. You're not in pain. You're calm and aware the end is near. It no longer matters if you're on satin sheets or a mud floor. Neither makes much of a difference, since you know you're going to die soon anyway. All titles and degrees, all property and possessions, shrink into insignificance.

Lying here, facing a journey into the Great Mystery whose total reality none of us fully comprehends, we look back on our life. What stands out as the most important?

Is it the number of widgets we sold, the promotions we received, our adjusted gross income for 1996, the houses we lived in, the clothes we wore, or the car we drove? When looking deeply into the essence of our life, the triviality of what we've spent so much of our life's energy on becomes evident.

As we lie here looking back over our life, what matters is the sense of meaning our life has had for us and for others. Have we lived unconsciously, rushing from one thing to another without considering the meaning of our activities or a mission these activities support? Or have we lived consciously aware of our actions and the purposes they serve? Have we spent our time involved in meaningful activities that support a sense of mission that is larger than our self and fulfills our deepest talents? Have we loved and given to others and been loved in return? And finally, have we lived spiritually so we're consciously and experientially linked with the immortal essence that is the only part of us that is **not** *going to die?*

The **lack of meaning** in our lives and a **lack of mission** are two of the heaviest weights we carry.

While in previous chapters we've focused on getting personality to be less active so spiritual consciousness can more fully emerge, this chapter charges personality with the task of (1) waking up within everyday life, (2) finding what gives our life meaning, (3) finding our life's mission(s), and (4) living so that we create a meaningful life and fulfill our life's mission.

What's It All For?

The purpose of life is a life of purpose.

ROBERT BYRNE

Does our life have meaning? Do our activities feel valuable? There are different ways to give meaning to our life. One way to feel that our activities have meaning is by doing actions that are ends in themselves. Doing acts that feel good, even when we're not getting any tangible reward other than the doing of the activity itself, feels meaningful. These acts are fun, interesting, exciting, enjoyable, or satisfying.

Some activities are meaningful for many people, while others hold meaning only for a few. For example, some people find meaning in playing chess or riding a motorcycle or gardening, while others wouldn't find these interesting or meaningful at all.

The more meaning we have in our life, the happier and the more contented and complete we feel.

But while many of us are aware of those activities that give us meaning, we may not be able to spend as much of our time doing them as we'd like. Most of us find ourselves caught in activities that bore us and give us little meaning—standing in line, doing laundry, filing reports, repairing something broken. Even professionals in "challenging" careers (such as doctors, dentists, and lawyers) report being bored by repeatedly seeing the same illness, doing the same procedure, dispensing the same advice.

Most of us spend more time doing actions we think of as meaningless and less time doing those things we find meaningful. There are three solutions to the burden of being mired in meaningless activity.

The first is to find ways of spending more of our time doing what we find meaningful. Of course, most people would say: "No, I can't find more time for what feels meaningful to me. I'm too busy with the meaningless stuff." But sometimes we can be surprised by what can happen when we identify what we really want to do.

Vivian, a sixty-eight-year-old woman, had spent most of her life working in a government job she hated, while spending her spare time collecting dolls. Doll collecting was her passion and gave her tremendous meaning as she shared her delight with girls and other women. But she never pursued doll collecting as a career because she felt she couldn't support herself with her "little hobby," as she referred to it.

Only after retirement did she decide to open up a small doll shop, where she displayed her collection and began buying and selling dolls and related products. She said that "work" for her was now like playing, and she eagerly spent most of her time in the shop or going to antique stores and shows looking for additions to her collection. To Vivian's surprise, her business quickly grew. In two years she was earning more money from her doll shop than she'd ever made as a civil servant!

"I wasted all that time at a job I hated when I could have been doing this if I'd only given it a chance," she told us. "When I look back at all the time I wasted filling out forms and shuffling paperwork, I only wish I could get it all back."

Many of us can learn from Vivian's experience, as we aim our life toward greater meaning, identifying those things for which we have great passion and pursuing them.

Of course, it's also true that what's most meaningful to us may only result in money spent with no money being earned. Still, it's important for each of us to at least examine our life for meaning and consider doing more of what feels inherently worthwhile.

Perhaps we'll be surprised that there's a bigger chance of spending more time feeling fulfilled than we thought.

The Art of Conscious Waitressing

Vivian's story is inspiring, but what if you're stuck in actions you don't find meaningful? For many of us, what we find most meaningful may not be turned into a full-time passion. Instead, many of us may have to work at a job we've never considered meaningful at all. This was Tara's situation.

Tara found that she could best earn a living for her family as a waitress, even though her sense of meaning came in the other parts of her life. However, after going on an enriching Spiritual Diet, she found herself "waking up" in the midst of waitressing and she also discovered *the second way to find meaning—discovering meaning in what we're already doing.*

Tara learned to focus her mind and be aware of her movements, her sensations, the actions of those around her. And as she continued doing this, the world "gradually opened up." She said that as she became generally more conscious, calm, and aware of her surroundings, she quite naturally found herself doing her own version of "the art of conscious waitressing."

Tara became aware of the wonderful aromas around her and learned to savor them. She became more aware of her body, relaxing herself even in the midst of hurry. She practiced breathing to feel the tension and to let it go. She began to move more gracefully and with less fatigue. As she became more alert and less tired, she became more aware of the happiness and satisfaction she could bring other people. She enjoyed their words of appreciation and realized that for some, she offered the only kind words they might hear in a day and served their only hot meal. This alertness made her more connected with her customers, and realizing that she made a difference in people's lives made a difference in her life.

She became more aware of the art of being a conscious waitress and gave herself credit for doing it well. After a time, she told us, "The restaurant is a new place for me. It's always been just 'work.' But now I get a lot more out of it than just money to pay my rent and car. Now, at the end of my shift, I might be tired, but I feel like I did something worthwhile and I'm in a better mood to go home to my family."

Tara's change of attitude is exactly what spiritual seekers are encouraged to do in monasteries, nunneries, and spiritual retreats. Menial chores are to be done with consciousness and care, with love and grace, with peace of mind and a sense of dedicating the work to God (Buddha, Jesus, Allah, the Great Spirit . . .).

In this way meaning can even be found in menial or tedious jobs. We can learn to appreciate the hidden purposes they do serve (providing for our family, offering a service to others . . .).

It's also important to look for opportunities to change our circumstances wherever possible, so they become more meaningful. We shouldn't just accept our lot and be passive.

Those of us with fewer responsibilities can more easily take risks than those with many responsibilities or obligations. But often if we pay attention and concentrate on the changes we want to make, opportunities will present themselves. Many spiritual philosophies tell us that thoughts are so powerful that we can, to some degree, create our reality with them. Opportunities are often visible if we have a calm and clear mind that's open to seeing them. Being awake within our activities and following the Spiritual Diet provide us with a calmer and clearer mind that can more clearly see and seize these opportunities.

The third way to have meaning in our lives is to identify our life's missions and do the activities that support them.

Our Mission in Life

My life is my message.

GANDHI

While *meaning* **most often comes from acts that feel inherently valuable,** *mission* **is a goal (or set of goals) that is important to us and gives certain acts value that might not otherwise feel valuable.**

For example, changing a dirty diaper might not feel worthwhile in and of itself, but if your mission is to be a good parent, then the act of diapering a baby has value because it supports this mission.

Having a mission that we feel is important provides us with a central focus that makes our life feel worthwhile. What we set as our mission comes from what we feel we're *meant to do,* our *reason for being.* A mission is a goal or set of goals that seems important to us.

Carrying out an important goal while using our greatest talents is what we refer to as our *calling.* For some it may be a mission to fulfill a specific and rare talent, like having a great voice and working to be a great singer, or having unusual athletic ability and training to be a professional football or soccer player. For others, their calling may be raising children or healing the sick.

Usually, our lifelong mission is broken into a series of smaller missions. For example, if being a good parent feels inherently worthwhile, then our top-priority missions would include creating a stable primary relationship and a healthy home, the financial ability to afford kids, getting pregnant, having a safe delivery, and learning effective child rearing (including diaper changing).

If helping others live healthier, happier lives is the overriding mission, then smaller missions might include getting into and through medical or dental or psychology school, followed by getting internships and employment or setting up practice, teaching or supervising younger health practitioners, writing articles or books.

By giving meaning to those activities that support our mission, we make our life meaningful. When we're doing meaningful activities that support an overall mission, we feel great satisfaction that our life is deeply enriching and "nutritious." Typing may not be inherently meaningful, but it becomes meaningful when we're typing a paper that helps us fulfill our mission of graduating from school.

Think about your own mission in life. It doesn't have to be something for which you'd ever get a Nobel Prize. Nor does it mean that every moment must be devoted to it. What is important is that we wake up, now, in the midst of our activities, that we clarify how much meaning our present activities give us, and that we determine whether or not we're carrying out the mission that gives our life a sense of purpose.

12 Purposes in Living

Understanding our mission(s) begins by looking at our life and discovering what we find most important. The following is not intended to be an exhaustive or complete list, but it does contain many of the most commonly shared purposes or missions in living.

If you like to quantify, you can number each of the following from 1 to 10 for how high or low a priority each is to you personally.

TO SURVIVE — Life is hard, and for some of us, life's meaning lies in merely surviving. After all, thousands of people go to bed each night and don't wake up in the morning. Like they say, half the job is just showing up. Get the bills paid, put food on the table, avoid being run over and you've got it made, for you live another day.

TO PROCREATE — Evolutionary psychologists, geneticists, and billions of people around the world would agree that the main purpose of life is to help humanity continue and evolve. From this broad perspective having children is the most meaning-filled activity, as it helps our species and our particular genetic material go on to the next generation. As the Bible says in Genesis, "Be fruitful, and multiply." And as the philosopher Novalis put it, "Where children are, there is the golden age."

TO HELP AND PROTECT — There's a Sufi story about a seeker who was praying when a crippled beggar came by. The holy one cried out, "Great God, how can a loving Being see such things and do nothing to help?" Out of the silence God thundered, "I *did* do something. I made *you*."

In whatever ways we can, we help and protect. Albert Einstein said that "the ideal of success should be replaced with the ideal of service." We can be of help not only to people but also to pets and to nature.

TO HEAL — There's so much suffering in the world, and whether our gifts lie in the direction of healing the body, the mind, the emotions, or the soul, we can help others to heal and be healthier in both body and soul.

As the Jewish philosopher and physician Maimonides wrote, God "has endowed man[kind] with the wisdom to relieve the suffering of his brother [and sister]." Our life is more worthwhile when we soothe another's pain and heal another's wound.

TO LOVE — Millions of people feel that our basic nature, the heart of human life, is love and that our main purpose is to feel and show love.

Thomas Merton wrote, "Love *is* the spiritual life ... Love means an interior and spiritual identification with one's brother [and sister], so that he [and she] is not regarded as an 'object' to 'which' one 'does good' ... Love takes one's neighbor as one's self." We can express spiritual love each and every day and that's why we're here. Whether it's to our children, spouse, or pet, a grandparent, a stranger in need, or a vegetable garden, showing that we care helps our fountain of love flow forth.

TO BE PART OF A COMMUNITY — President John Kennedy expressed this purpose when he said, "Ask not what your country can do for you. Ask what you can do for your country."

Barbra Streisand expressed this purpose in life when she sang "People who need people are the luckiest people in the world." We can realize that all these purposes are shared with others on similar life paths, creating an existential community of shared meanings and missions. Good social relationships, friendships, family, a sense of belonging and commonality are what makes life meaningful.

TO BE HAPPY — The Bible says, "He that is of a merry heart hath a continual feast." The Dalai Lama says, "The purpose of life is to be happy." Not just in the sense of satisfying our personal whims and wishes, but to be at peace with our self and the world, satisfied in the midst of our real life.

Life is to be lived to the fullest. Our senses exist in part to provide satisfaction and pleasure, and they should be enjoyed. The same is true for sex. We should be open to what life offers and find delight in it whenever we can. We should let go and enjoy the drama and the circus all around us. There's time enough to be dead when we're dead. No sleepwalking through life for me. Life is to be lived to the fullest and enjoyed. That's what makes life meaningful.

When we're happy, we're nourished and fed by our good feelings. We can experience a natural spiritual joy when we open to living life fully, processing our sensations, thoughts, and emotions so as to flow freely within. We can enjoy the good with the bad and savor what's set before us. Our life is meaningful when we're happy in this mature way.

TO ENTERTAIN — We can express our talents in the service of giving others enjoyment. Whether it's with jokes and stories or singing and piano, a gourmet dinner or a barbecue, we can lighten the load people are carrying. Helping others to enjoy life makes life worthwhile.

TO TEACH — Henry Adams said, "A teacher affects eternity; he can never tell where his influence stops." A side benefit is that when we teach others, we also teach our self, for we continue to grow and learn when we teach. In this we help our self and future generations to be better than our own in some way.

TO GROW— We are put here to learn and to grow. Each of us may have different lessons to learn or a place to fill in the world. Some mystics say our ultimate task on earth is to learn what we're supposed to learn. Rabbi Schachter-Shalomi says, "In mystical Judaism, we believe in reincarnation. It's called *gilgul*. We believe each time we incarnate, we move a step forward. Coming down one time prepares me for the task I have to do the next time. Whatever I conclude in this lifetime, if I come back again, I can take up from where I left off—not with the same memory, mind you, but with the same traces and vibrations and merit and clarity and God-connection that I had. Then I can go farther in the next incarnation to provide more input. If I learned a lot this time around, I get to teach the next time around!"

We're here to continuously evolve. As Bob Dylan sang, "If you're not busy bein' born, you're busy dyin'." Learning and growing make life meaningful.

TO CREATE— Pir Vilayat Khan, head of the Sufi Order in the West, says, "The purpose of our life is being creative. The building blocks with which we create are us. To be creative, we need to create the world as us. In fact, that's the whole purpose of life. The Universe becomes created in each individual."

We are the world. Whether it's through spirituality, music, art, sculpting, needlepoint, cooking, gardening, writing, or our personal/universal development, being creative gets us to unwrap our gifts, releasing life's potential, making life fun and worthwhile.

TO LIVE A SPIRITUAL LIFE— The purpose of life is to make Spirit a living reality, bringing God (Jesus, Buddha, the Tao . . .) to life by making our own life sacred.

The philosopher Ernest Becker wrote, "The Deity is experiencing the world through you, your consciousness and your perception are part of His Self-knowledge and Self-delight. Possibly man's [and woman's] role is to serve as a progressively richer, more attuned, purer vehicle for Divine self-consciousness."

So a meaningful life is a heroic one in which we awaken to the sacredness within, using our authentic talents and abilities in the service of Spirit. If our gifts include baking, perhaps we bake some muffins (aware in the moment while pouring and mixing) and bring them to a senior center. Or if our gifts include being a good parent, we treat all children with care and respect; maybe we adopt a child in need or teach elementary school. If our gifts include writing, then we write in the service of life and Spirit.

Mahatma Gandhi said that our mission in life is to manifest God's will through actions: "My experience tells me that the Kingdom of God is within us, and that we can realize it not by saying "Lord, Lord," but by doing His will and His work."

As we go more fully into the Spiritual Diet, we find that many things seem contradictory. One of them is that when we know how to rest and feel a sense of completeness through basic being, then we no longer care about meaning and purpose. We transcend the intellectual question of meaning when we allow our self to be with what is, as it is, here and now.

To search for the meaning in life means that we're separate from life. When we're integrated into our life, the question doesn't arise. Toni Packer says, "What is the meaning of life? When there is no feeling of separation, then there is just living. There is just life. No one is standing outside of life and therefore worrying about whether this is pointed toward something else. Everything is what is."

We return to the Basic Spiritual Diet—awake in the present, alert and resting content and complete, here and now, breathing in and out.

When we think about our work, we usually think about how

it's accomplishing various goals (helping pay the bills, feeling personal satisfaction). But ultimately, as philosopher A. J. Bahm put it, "Right livelihood is life living itself, for itself, not for something else; the more you search for the purpose of life, the more you find it in the way life lives itself (including living itself as a search for its own purpose in living)."

We can go beyond purpose to meaning. Brother David Stendl-Rast puts it this way: "Life in my experience has meaning more than purpose. It's like a dance or play. A dance has no particular purpose. The main thing about a dance or play is that you give yourself to it and that it has meaning. You dance not in order to get somewhere; you sing not in order to get finished as soon as possible. But you sing in order to sing; you dance because it's meaningful to you."

Beyond meaning and purpose, the point of life is to be. We sing and dance in order to sing and dance. We live in order to live. There is no secret beyond basic being. Ultimately, that's what life's all about. Being here, being now.

Whether we do it through consciousness, our talents, or our actions, a meaningful life is one in which we see that everything—including our self and all we do—is a manifestation of Spirit.

When we're living meaningfully and with a sense of mission in life, we have greater peace of mind, our personality relaxes its grip, and spirituality can more fully come to the foreground.

Thinking about our purpose in living and being conscious of our meaningful activities, we can begin to consider ways we can more fully manifest them in our life. We can aim our activity toward that which is meaningful to a greater degree. Then we can relax more fully in the midst of daily life knowing we're always in the midst of accomplishing our purpose, even if we never do it perfectly or all the time. We don't need to be perfect; perfection is just personality's desire.

Problems in Purpose

Problems can arise when we look more closely at our daily life, and when we try to change our life to be more meaningful, in keeping with our life's mission.

Sometimes we've been so far away from having meaning in life that if we realize a disconnection or a lack of meaning, we're tempted to drop our life as it exists and start over.

Midlife crises are often provoked by someone "waking up" and realizing his or her life isn't the way he/she wants it to be. He or she realizes how much time has passed by and that there is a finite amount left in this lifetime.

People in this aggravated state often make poor decisions and can cause damage and pain to those around them as they try to change their lives too rapidly or too radically.

Many of us, when we wake up within our activity and find ourselves dissatisfied, must have patience with ourselves and the situations we've created. We can use the Basic Spiritual Diet to relax and stay with our present life while working to change what can be changed.

It's important to reasonably assess our situation. For example, sometimes we have great meaning in our life but we fail to recognize it or we simply take it for granted. In this case it's necessary to appreciate our life fully. The change in our perception of our life actually changes our life.

Whatever change is called for, we must exercise self-control and self-discipline to live a life that carries us beyond the confines of our own personal wishes, needs, impulses, and attachments. The Native American perspective expressed by Onondagan elder Leon Shenandoah illustrates the point: "Look behind you. See your sons and your daughters. They are your future. Look farther and see your sons' and daughters' children and their children's children even unto the seventh generation. That's the way we were taught. Think about it—you yourself are a seventh generation."

When we think long-term, we feel more deeply connected with the world beyond our self and feel a meaningfulness to our existence. When we act responsibly, life-affirmingly, we find our self better able to rest in the midst of activity.

What Can I Do?
The "Purpose in Life" Recipe

We want to be at home in the midst of our life, finding both meaningfulness and rest within our actions.

1. Aim your actions at what you find most meaningful and know your different missions in life. Review your purposes for living described above, being clear about what's most significant to you. Look to your passions for clues and keep your primary missions clearly in mind as you go through the day, week, and year. And use your missions as a gauge to help manage your effort, time, and attention. By using your primary purposes in this way, you'll maximize the meaningfulness of your daily life.

2. Look for ways to make activities you now consider boring more meaningful. If it's a routine chore, then be conscious of your senses, attune to your feelings, or realize the purposes it's serving. Use it as an opportunity to breathe and be with your current Spiritual Diet Recipe, and learn to relax and be conscious, even in the midst of boring activities.

Appreciate the small yet significant daily acts we perform which may be routine but are still manifestations of our daily meaningful missions (like providing food for ourselves and our families, keeping our house clean, getting to work). And act responsibly, with the long run in mind.

Once we've begun practicing breathing awareness and being present while instilling our life with purpose and rest in the midst of activity, then the Spiritual Diet shifts focus to the ways there are "too much me."

Chapter 10

 _____

Too Much Me

Everybody has his own territory of self, like
islands separate from everyone else's islands.
You're always trying to protect that island so
nobody else can take it over. You defend it and
you beautify it as much as possible in order to
make it the best island around.

A. H. ALMAAS

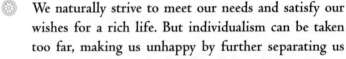 We naturally strive to meet our needs and satisfy our
wishes for a rich life. But individualism can be taken
too far, making us unhappy by further separating us
from our unity with all other living things. We can

learn to spiritually enrich ourselves by growing beyond our individual self to interconnectedness with the One.

Numero Uno

In this world it's everyone for themselves. Once in a while someone will do you a favor, but mostly if you don't look out for numero uno, you'll get taken.

I often feel isolated, even when I'm with other people. I can be in a meeting or at a party talking to people and still feel alone. I know I'd be happier if I could be closer to people.

Sometimes I feel depressed, but I don't know why. I can't understand what's making me so unhappy.

The first day Kathleen taught the class of southwestern American Indian children was the kind of disaster about which every teacher has nightmares. It wasn't that Kathleen was inexperienced. She'd taught in the public schools for fourteen years and spent her entire adulthood volunteering her services to various charities and church projects.

This was all the worse because it was so unexpected. She'd heard that Indian children were particularly respectful of adults, and eager to learn. Yet, as soon as the new desks had been moved into the new schoolhouse on the reservation, and the students had arrived, Kathleen suffered her first setback.

Not only did the children apparently not like the desks provided by Kathleen's church (at great difficulty and expense), they also refused to sit in them, or even sit in rows. Indeed, nothing would do but to move the desks outside the room, while the chil-

dren spontaneously sat on the floor in a circle. Even in this position they could hardly sit still, and kept relating to each other
through hand signals, eye contact, and touching each other's arms
or knees. Then at pauses in the lesson, they spontaneously broke
into a song that seemed to mock their teacher. Worst of all, when
Kathleen gave them a test to determine ability level, they shame-
lessly whispered the answers to each other and even unapologeti-
cally looked on each other's papers.

Losing patience, Kathleen called a halt to the test and said that
what they were doing was called cheating, which she explained was
like lying or stealing. When the children finally understood her
point, they were very upset, got up, and filed out, some crying, others indignant, and nothing Kathleen did or said had any effect on the
mass exodus.

That night, Kathleen considered what to do with such unco-
operative and undisciplined students, and the next day, when they
failed to come to school, she resolved to go and visit their parents.

When she arrived at the grouping of village homes, the children and adults went inside. Only one old woman remained in the
open.

The woman's gray hair was unbound to her waist, and her face
was as wrinkled as a dried apple. Yet in spite of her age, her eyes
shone bright and black and were calmly welcoming.

Kathleen was invited to sit with this tribal elder, Walks-with-
the-Sun, and wasted little time relating the impossible behavior of
the children, pointing out that something needed to be done if she
was expected to teach.

Walks-with-the-Sun looked at Kathleen for a long time before
at last speaking slowly and carefully. "For your people, all things are
separate," she began, "and our People are hard for you to understand. For you one person is one person, another is another. What
belongs here does not belong there. You have your children. Another
has their children. A mountain is only a mountain, the sky is only

the sky. Each one of you is alone. For our People it is different. For us all is One."

She studied Kathleen for a moment, as if to see if she understood. Then Walks-with-the-Sun waved a weathered arm in a sweeping gesture to include everything. "We cannot separate the earth from the wind and the rain or the trees from the sunlight. They are part of all that is. To separate them is like the wind saying, 'I will be just the wind by myself. I will decide when to blow and not to blow.' Yet the wind is a part of the One and cannot be fully without the others. The wind brings the clouds, and the clouds bring the rain, and the rain brings the lakes and the woods. The animals, the People, the village, the earth, and all that is, is of the Great Spirit. And it is One.

"For us, all children are our children, for we are all one family. Therefore when we sit, it is our way to sit as one. When we speak, we speak together as one. When we think, we think together as one. In our world we are never alone. We are always one with all things.

"For you the world is separate. It is the Other, and for your whole life you live alone in the midst of the Others. For you everyone is a stranger."

When Kathleen told us this story, it had already been almost fifty years since she'd first taught on the Indian reservation. Yet, she remembered it as if it had only been moments before, and said that it was the most profound moment of her life as she first understood the true meaning of spiritual unity.

"I had been dedicated to what I thought was a spiritual life, and yet from the Indians I realized that my sense of community with other people and with the world of nature was almost nonexistent. I was experiencing what I later realized was a sense of tremendous isolation and loneliness. I was trying to completely fill my emptiness with my relationship to God, while completely ignoring my spiritual connection to all of God's creation."

For most, connection with the world around us is as foreign a concept as it was to Kathleen. Yet many native people traditionally feel this connection on an intuitive level in each moment of their daily lives. They are grounded and secured by their sense of being part of the larger One. Such native people are never lost or lonely, even without other humans, for they still experience their connection with the Great Spirit who lives through the trees, hills, flowers, and sky.

We moderns often live spiritually alone. Some of us have a connection with God—far off in heaven—but with little else. Many of us have no spiritual connectedness at all, and we're almost totally cut off from life beyond ourselves.

This is why Kathleen's realization of her own isolation is one common to many of us. Particularly as we progress spiritually, we often become more aware of our feelings and often experience a profound sense of aloneness or of "something missing." This is because we are inescapably connected spiritually to all other living things and are pulled toward this idea quite naturally.

Many religions say that we come from the One before we differentiate into our individual body. We then feel separate from the One while still having an intuitive sense of connection back to our Source. Our culture and our beliefs generally determine the extent to which we develop an individual identity and how conscious our spiritual connection remains as we develop our personality.

For these Indians and many other primal people, their individualism was more limited, and their spiritual and tribal connection stronger and more conscious.

For mainstream Western industrialized society, our individuation is greatly encouraged and our spiritual connection often only minimally cultivated. And yet, it remains always in the background, endlessly calling us home. The call of our spiritual connection creates a longing, a deep sense of isolation, that can be hard to identify.

Excessive Individualism

In the modern world, the sense of separateness or isolation, which we call "excessive individualism," is so common a burden that most of us don't realize it's weighing us down, even though its symptoms (isolation, loneliness, insecurity, anxiety, depression) may cause us tremendous difficulty.

It can be difficult to realize that we're spiritually isolated. We're like a fish swimming in the ocean who's unaware that it's surrounded by water. Similarly, we can be swimming in excessive individualism and never realize it.

Why? In our culture, this natural and necessary individuality is emphasized and cultivated. We are taught to take care of ourselves by ourselves. We are taught to have our own thoughts, our own answers, our own opinions, and we learn that as adults we'll have to take care of ourselves and our needs on our own.

To prepare us for this lifestyle of individuality, we are taught to compete, to abhor losing and to fight to win, even at great sacrifice. While we're taught to share, the concept of individual rights and ownership is the cornerstone of our social system—including our philosophy and economy and our legal and political systems.

This is not to say that our way of life is "bad." Indeed, our Western philosophy of individualism has obviously brought about tremendous economic advantages by creating an extremely efficient and wealthy society capable of supporting millions of members. And advances in nearly every field of life have come about because individuals dared to think and risk and work to manifest their unique talents and gifts.

The downside of our very successful society and of our individual strivings is that we rarely discuss the price we pay in our social connectedness and spiritual underdevelopment. It is a form of the psychospiritual bankruptcy that our society experiences.

Teens in Transition

Few people ever tell us that if we pay too much attention to ourselves and our separation from other living things, in time we lose awareness of our true connection to everything around us, making us unhappy and weighted down.

We see this particularly with older children and teenagers. As young children, we still feel our intuitive connection with the One and often express this magical sense in childhood play and by having a strong connection with family and friends. But as we grow up and are encouraged to disconnect more and more from these primary spiritual relationships, we often end up without any sense of connection at all.

In most cultures and religions, the transition to adulthood has traditionally been marked by some kind of ceremony designed to connect the growing child with Spirit and the adult community. Examples include communions, bar and bat mitzvahs, walkabouts, and vision quests.

Yet in modern society, many children are never given this connection. Even those who go through such ceremonies may never experience a spiritual connection, since their social aspects (whom to invite, what to serve, what to wear, the gifts received) play such a powerful part in the event.

As a result, many children lose the magic and connectedness of childhood as they grow older, and have nothing with which to replace it. Teens then naturally turn to their peer group and fads, which often take on even greater significance than they otherwise would, in an attempt at replacing what's "missing."

Their near total identification with their peer group makes every nuance of these peer relationships seem of cosmic importance. Every situation risks being "terminal": who says what to whom, who likes you and who doesn't, who's good-looking and who isn't ...

This dependency on personality and lack of connection puts them at risk of feeling like lonely outcasts. They think their newly developing, individual adult personality is all they are. If it's wounded badly enough, they think they'll "die."

This also makes adolescents and young adults especially vulnerable to drugs, alcohol, depression, and other symptoms of disconnection. Many slip into despair, dreading the future and all its problems (career, financial, environmental). Some turn to rebellion or acting out as they break rules in their struggle to find and solidify their unique personality. Others take the opposite tack and fail to develop themselves and their abilities, hiding in the herd, not taking any risks.

Children need help in knowing and unpacking their individual gifts and abilities, and in developing the skills to survive and succeed in modern society. They need to learn how to balance their personal identity with their connectedness to Spirit.

Too Sweet

Excessive individualism is like sugar. It's great in certain amounts, but too much ultimately poisons us. It's so attractive (and addictive) that sometimes we don't even recognize it's the very thing making us feel so bad.

The sugar of individualism fuels a negative cycle. The more of it we take, the more individualized we become; and the more of a separate individual we become, the more we're disconnected from our spiritual nature. This leads to our feeling bad and wanting to feel better. But then, instead of eating a more spiritual and nutritious diet, maybe we eat more sugar. We become even more individualized and competitive in order to gain the ego food (recognition, success, wealth, power, prestige, possessions) that we crave in our attempt to get rid of the bad feelings caused by our sugar addiction in the first place.

We are, in fact, doing exactly what we're applauded for doing, which is why excessive individualism is the invisible burden we so often feel, but can't really identify or see that we're carrying. We become too full of ourselves, overweighted with "too much me."

Moralectomies

Since excessive individualism makes us feel that we're supposed to look out for ourselves to the exclusion of others, it's easy for us to look at the world as a competition. We think to ourselves, "It's me against the world" and "I want mine before they get it."

The result can be a *moralectomy* in which our moral backbone is removed or remains undeveloped, along with our compassion, caring, and consideration. The psychic hole that's left is morally, socially, and environmentally threatening, particularly when it's the philosophy of many influential entities (including corporations, professionals, the media, and others whose main concern is so often their own profits), regardless of the harmful effects on us all.

A few obvious examples: tobacco companies who, in spite of the proven harmful qualities of their product, spend millions of dollars to hook people on cigarettes regardless of the immense cost in illness and suffering; car companies who block lower-polluting cars in favor of the more profitable, higher-polluting models; the media who operate on the philosophy that "If it bleeds, it leads," and bombard us with violent, frightening, and gut-wrenching news items, giving us an inaccurate and unnecessarily negative view of the world; lawyers who fight to help their clients escape on any technicality, regardless of the truth, honor, or justice.

Excessive individualism can also be applied to groups of individuals separating themselves from other groups. For example, politicians seeking to enhance their own power will often stir up nationalistic or racial hatreds. Many religious leaders preach the idea that one religion or people is better or "holier" than another.

Individual separateness and self-interest fan our fears and insecurities. This disconnection from our basic spiritual connection leads to the pitting of one group against another, igniting hatreds that lead to destruction and suffering.

All of these examples are variations on the theme of wanting to seem special as individuals by feeling superior and separate from others. We like to think to ourselves, "I know more than you" or "I'm better (smarter, richer, more successful, more spiritual, more moral, better looking) than you."

Some people or groups have taken their individualism to such excess that they feel little or no connection or sense of responsibility to anyone but themselves and, as a result, damage us all.

Of course, most of us don't carry our individualism to such extremes. However, the more "successful" we become by being highly competitive individuals, the more we can become isolated and separate from our fellow earth creatures.

This isolation creates such difficulties spiritually and can also create physical ailments as well. This has long been understood by the more evolved individuals in society, who realized long before Western medicine got around to it that they needed to treat the "whole person." These individuals have often devoted their lives not only to healing the physically based illnesses but also to identifying and addressing those symptoms caused by personal and spiritual ailments. One who knew this was Jonathan's dad, Dr. Lou.

DR. LOU'S SKELETON

Dr. Lou was an old-fashioned physician who looked like a cross between the comedian Groucho Marx and the newscaster Walter

Cronkite. Solo practice, house calls, up three flights of stairs to see a patient with the flu, delivering twins in the middle of the night. If patients couldn't pay, well maybe they'd pay later, and if they didn't pay at all, it wasn't all that important.

Dr. Lou had a calling to help and heal and was a good example of a person with the right livelihood who earned a living in a life-affirming way, without excessive individualism. Even though Dr. Lou's shoes were worn to the point of having holes in his soles, there was never a hole in his soul.

Dr. Lou offered his patients a good sense of humor mixed with a healthy dose of wisdom. He had what he called his "bare-bones philosophy of life." When he'd hear that someone was having job difficulties or fighting with their spouse or smoking, he'd point to a skeleton in his office and say, "The hipbone's connected to the thighbone. And whether we realize it or not, all parts of our life are interconnected. Good physical health is related to all the rest of what we do." Dr. Lou understood that everything is One.

Cosmic Dust to Cosmic Dust

The history of human thought has evolved over time, in many ways mirroring the developmental stages that are normal and natural to each of us individually as we grow from infancy to adulthood.

As infants we're the center of our universe. Everything revolves around us because we know of nothing beyond ourselves. Similarly, early human thinkers concluded that we were the center of the universe and all things revolved around us. This sense of self-importance was so essential to earlier societies that anyone suggesting a different idea would literally face torture and execution for voicing what was considered blasphemy.

As time went on, humans realized that we are not the center of the universe, but just one of many planets circling the sun. But then our ancestors decided that our sun must be the center of the universe.

So, too, in childhood, we realize that we are not the center of the universe, but rather that there are many children and we are one of many (though our perception of the world may stretch no further than our brothers and sisters, friends, and schoolmates).

As adults, we can see that we are truly one of many, and while we are unique as individuals, we are perhaps not even that significant in the larger scheme of things. Likewise, astronomers now teach us that there are billions of suns in the universe, and while our planet is no doubt unique in many ways, it's easier to imagine that there are many other solar and planetary systems with life, perhaps even similar to life on earth.

The person who begins to mature spiritually comes to realize the Oneness of what is, and the connectedness between himself or herself and all of creation. Similarly, the growing realization among scientists is that our earth and indeed ourselves can't truly be separated from the universe at large, since we are all made of the same elements. Indeed, the biochemical seeds of life are very likely to have come from meteors and cosmic dust that showered the earth for billions of years.

Whatever hand we believe is our Creator's, and however we believe creation came about, we are all unquestionably the same carbon-based biochemical life-forms created from the same universal cosmic material. We are an incredibly complex, unique manifestation of this eternal, life-creating matter. But no matter how particular and individual we are, we can't escape the absolute Oneness of the universe.

Still, this is difficult to grasp, since we're so used to feeling far more separated from those around us. As modern people with personal lives, homes, and careers, few of us would elect to live in the noncompetitive Indian fashion, so much more simple and connected than the lifestyle we're used to, nor are we advocating such a change.

What's needed are ways to stay spiritually connected, even in the midst of our Western society's overemphasis on individualism.

Holy Is to Be Whole

The cure for excessive individualism lies in balancing our life with other "higher" values that lead us to spiritual wholeness, summarized by the Hawaiian proverb "We overrides Me."

Monotheism, the belief in one God, can be seen as a metaphor for the Oneness of Life.

Ram Dass says, "The Hebrew, Christian and Islamic traditions are all monotheistic because there is only one awareness... There is 'one' behind the many—one awareness and one completeness, which includes the many and also manifests through the many."

Jesus was asked, "Which commandment is the greatest of all?" He said, "Hear, O Israel: the Lord our God is One... and there is a second one that is like it: You shall love your neighbor as yourself. On these two commandments all the Law and the prophets depend."

In the Gospel of Thomas, discovered in 1945, Jesus says, "If one is whole, one will be filled with light, but if one is divided, one will be filled with darkness." Jesus teaches us that division, the basis of personality, is darkness; wholeness, the nature of Spirit, is light.

He also said, "I and the Father are One" and "we are all sons [and daughters] of God" and "When you make the two one, and the inside like the outside ... then you will enter the Kingdom." These examples show Jesus' direct understanding of the wholeness of the human family and its infusion with Spirit.

Jesus spoke from Oneness and knew that the bridge across which we reach Oneness is love. Thus the Christian emphasis on loving one's neighbor as oneself, on the ideas of compassion, altruism, and forgiveness. Each teaching brings our personality into alignment with natural spiritual wholeness.

Rabbi Schmelke of Nikolsburg wrote, "All souls are One. Each is a spark from the original soul."

In ancient Greece, the philosopher Heraclitus said, "For those who are awake, the cosmos is One."

Freud explained it psychologically: "The ego feeling we are aware of now is . . . only a shrunken vestige of a far more extensive feeling—a feeling which embraced the universe and expressed an inseparable connection of the ego with the external world."

Those who are attuned to consciousness, presence, and awareness see the Oneness and the nonmaterial realms of existence. They see beyond personality's individual desires and have the vision to see the broader, deeper reality in which we're always living.

> **Growing beyond our individuality means developing a larger, more encompassing perspective that lightens our load.**

Holy is to be whole. Whole is to know Oneness, not as a concept within our small animal brains, but the Whole beyond thought, the Spirit beyond thought and knowing, to the experience of Oneness where the knower and the known are merged. Each is part of a whole, and each whole is part of a still greater, more encompassing whole, endlessly unfolding, eternally evolving. The true One is beyond words and ideas, yet we can increasingly experience it as we grow in Spirit.

Finding Oneness

Most of us are not disconnected to the point of having moralectomies, nor are we as spiritually connected as were some of our primal ancestors. Most of us moderns are feeling some combination of connection and separation.

Moralectomy ....*Spiritually connected*

You can get a sense of your own connectedness by reading the following and asking yourself the degree to which you agree or disagree, circling the answer most appropriate for you:

1. **I'm often bored and irritated when others talk about themselves.**
   strongly disagree   mildly disagree   mildly agree
   strongly agree

2. **What I do with my children is my business and no one else's.**
   strongly disagree   mildly disagree   mildly agree
   strongly agree

3. **People should know what they want and not let anything stand in the way of achieving their goals.**
   strongly disagree   mildly disagree   mildly agree
   strongly agree

4. **People who buy land should be able to do whatever they want with it.**
   strongly disagree   mildly disagree   mildly agree
   strongly agree

5. **When I go into a room of people, I usually feel uncomfortable.**
   strongly disagree   mildly disagree   mildly agree
   strongly agree

6. I work to be a winner and hate to be a loser.

strongly disagree   mildly disagree   mildly agree
strongly agree

The more strongly you agree with each of these statements, the more individualism you're experiencing and expressing.

1. People who have difficulty listening to others talk about themselves usually have trouble relating to others' thoughts and feelings. The more connected we are spiritually, the more we can see others as part of ourselves. For example, many parents can more easily listen to their own children talk about themselves than they can anyone else, because they're identified and connected with their offspring.

2. Those who feel that their children are solely their business tend to see children as their "property," related to them and to no one else. In the past, children were seen as personal property and could be beaten or abused by their parents. Now society has seen that all children are connected to all of us, and we share a communal responsibility for their welfare. Hence the many recent laws designed to prevent abuse and to protect children from harm. The spiritual view is that *all* children are *our* children.

3. This point of view encourages the "me first" philosophy that we as individuals have a right to go after what we want with no concern for the repercussions to others or anything else. The spiritual viewpoint is that we need to take into account the needs of others in whatever we do, for we are all interconnected.

4. This point of view indicates that we as individuals actually own the land and should be free to plunder its resources in any way to suit ourselves even if it harms those who come after us. We may think and act as if we're immortal and the earth is a passing thing, when actually it's we humans who come and go, the earth remaining for billions of years.

Those who are spiritually connected with nature see the earth and the natural world as eternal creations of God, and we are only temporary custodians charged and obligated with a sacred trust to do what is in nature's best interest.

In the Native American way of seeing the world, the same Oneness is described by Chief Seattle: "All things are connected. Whatever befalls the Earth befalls the sons [and daughters] of the Earth. Man did not weave the web of life; he is merely a strand in it. Whatever he does to the web, he does to himself."

5. When we feel disconnected from others, we often feel nervous and fearful of rejection or criticism. This makes it difficult to be with them, particularly if they're strangers. And this is especially true in situations where we have to make a presentation and the focus is on us. A common suggestion to overcome the fear of public speaking is to imagine the audience naked or in some demeaning condition. This is a typical "me"-oriented way of making ourselves feel better by feeling superior. The spiritual view is to see that we are all a part of the One and to realize that our audience is our spiritual family.

6. People with this winner/loser mentality are eager to separate themselves from others, and want proof that they are "better," thus further separating themselves from others. Naturally, "winning" in our society goes hand in hand with success, wealth, and power. This allows us to buy, to own, to control, to meet our individual wishes and have our life be the way we want it to be. There's a humorous variation on the Golden Rule that says, "He who has the gold makes the rules." Wealth creates power, but taken too far, it becomes a spiritual hole and a curse separating us from life's most satisfying connections.

The spiritual viewpoint does not separate winners and losers as being better or worse, but rather aims at doing the activity for the joy of doing it. A playful story illustrates the point:

Jesus went to his first soccer game with some friends, and the Muslims were playing the Catholics. When the Catholics scored, Jesus jumped up and yelled "Hooray!" Then when the Muslims scored, he jumped up and yelled "Hooray!" The man behind him was confused and asked Jesus, "Hey, who are you rooting for?"

"Everyone," Jesus said. "I'm enjoying the game."

Reserved for Me

It's easy to separate our spiritual practice from what we do every day. Many spiritually experienced people compartmentalize their spiritual practice from their everyday lives, lives in which we're expected to be highly efficient, individualized competitors, working and striving for ourselves and our families.

An interesting example of this occurred when two friends, Hank and Matthew, spent the afternoon walking through a meditation garden. They talked about spirituality and their church community, specifically discussing the disconnection and isolation so many feel. It was clear that they had given a tremendous amount of serious attention to leading a spiritual life, even while being successful businessmen.

Driving to a nearby restaurant, they were delayed by traffic, and once they arrived at the restaurant unavoidably late, they discovered that their reserved table had been given away. Unfortunately, their only hope for service at that restaurant was if one of the people with an upcoming reservation decided to cancel. Immediately, Hank struck up a conversation with a couple waiting to pick up their reservation, and told them that the food was better at the restaurant next door, convincing them to leave. Having successfully gotten a table, Hank and Matthew continued the conversation about selfishness and separateness, without any apparent awareness of their highly competitive and self-focused behavior. Spiritual practice can be saved for an hour or two on the weekend and thus kept separate from daily life in the real world.

Our competitive society constantly encourages us to think of our own needs and wants first, working to have others lose out to our desires and priorities. It's so easy, many of us act out of self-interest without even thinking there might be an alternative.

Old Patterns, New Patterns

Sometimes old patterns cause us to avoid connecting with people, nature, or pets. We may have been bitten by a dog in the past and now find dogs scary. We may have been lost in the woods and now find nature uncomfortable. A parent or trusted friend may have hurt us or given us a philosophy of fearing other living creatures.

Sometimes such patterns can be easily observed and changed. Others are deeply ingrained and can take years of concentrated effort to modify.

Whatever it is, we must start where we are and understand what holds us back from our connection with others. Hank was the youngest of four boys and was constantly picked on while growing up. As a child, he had to learn to defend himself and fight for his turn and territory or he'd get nothing. Looking out for his own interests was an old, deeply ingrained pattern.

Darlene had a highly critical mother and grandmother, and she learned to look for the flaws in everything and everybody. Darlene was cynical and skeptical, with a cutting wit and an automatic snide or sarcastic comment for any and all. She even prided herself on being "an equal-opportunity bitch." When Darlene became conscious of her family history and pattern, she began using the Spiritual Diet Recipe of seeing the small examples of good in herself and others.

It took several months, but she was able to begin making real progress in letting go of her harsh, cynical, and distancing style.

We can become more aware of ourselves by identifying what's holding us back from connectedness. We can, for example, go through our day aware of our reaction to the people around us. Do I feel open and comfortable with them, or am I nervous and on guard?

Do it now. Clearly observe your attitude and look into the patterns that keep you from connecting with others. When someone new enters the room, what do you tell yourself? Inwardly, are you getting a red, yellow, or green light? And why? Be aware of the feelings that divide you from others and question them.

Obviously, some of us are on guard with good reason. We all know dangerous people are out there in the world. Competitive or critical family or coworkers can be difficult to connect with. But, as we can see, it's also true that we may have old patterns that may no longer apply, yet still keep us separate and lonely. Whatever the reasons and their sources, we can begin to correct our social and spiritual malnourishment.

Too Little Me

Our focus has been on the dangers and costs of "too much me," but some people have the opposite problem—too little me.

Some people have fears and shyness (because of a lack of confidence, from excessive criticism, or because of some real or imagined failure), and they pull inside like a turtle in its shell and fail to develop a strong enough sense of self to successfully survive in modern society. The artistic and the sensitive among us often find themselves responding to harshness through withdrawal and wariness, and many spend their lives feeling like strangers in a strange land.

As mentioned above, many teenagers and young adults find the adult world frightening and intimidating and remain underdeveloped as they hide in a herd mentality of fads and fashion. They fail to discover and develop their talents and uniqueness and are vulnerable to giving up and dropping out of school and society.

Those with "too little me" can identify healthy goals based on their values (see Chapter 4), their basic needs (Chapter 6), their good feelings (Chapter 8), and whatever gives them meaning in life (Chapter 9). They can learn to be better swimmers and jump into the River of Life.

Feeding Our Deficiency

Our separateness causes a feeling of missing something, a lack or deficiency in our daily diet. Once we begin to see our disconnection, we can begin to feed our deficiency and be healthy and whole.

Anna Lemkow writes that the "essential unity with others is expressible through sympathy, empathy, solidarity, compassion, love and identity . . . a sense of unity arises from the intuitive or spiritual or mystical level of consciousness." But how do we begin? We can learn from people like Audrey.

AUDREY'S PHONE CALL

Some people have a tremendous sense of connection that comes naturally to them. Such people may not even think in spiritual terms or may even scoff when others praise their kindness. Such a woman was Diane's mother, Audrey.

Audrey never saw anyone or any living thing as truly separate from herself. She couldn't stand in a line at a theater for more than five minutes without getting to know the people both in front and in back of her, and sometimes others along the line as well, since others so often responded to her friendliness.

Audrey's powerful sense of connection made her house the welcome repository for cast-off animals of any kind. She took every abused, neurotic, epileptic (or whatever else) dog, cat, horse, or hamster into her house and heart, rehabilitating and finding homes for all she could, and keeping the rest.

She was a leader of the Brownies, Cub Scouts, Boy Scouts, and Girl Scouts and the president of the PTA, and that was in her early years. Her volunteer apex was in running a program at a large community hospital to train service-minded teenage girls as hospital volunteers, rewarding them for their service at a large annual charity ball that she organized.

Her activities were so broad and varied that her friendships were global, and she could have a telephone call from any of hundreds of people with whom she kept in touch.

Another of Audrey's great talents and joys was cooking. One Thanksgiving, she was supervising our family and friends in an elaborate preparation of the dinner when the phone rang, and Audrey picked it up.

From her side of the conversation we could tell that whoever it was, was in a different time zone, had two children, had an Afghan hound that wouldn't stay in the yard, and was planning a vacation to Naples in May.

With the phone cradled between her shoulder and chin, Audrey continued stirring and tasting and directing all of us in mime fashion as the conversation went on.

Each of us began putting together hints and guessing who the caller might be—

"It's got to be that woman who had the Afghan and moved to Cleveland," one of us guessed.

"No. It's that Italian family she met last year. They were going to Naples," another offered.

"No, it's just Aunt Doris. They were thinking about getting a new dog," someone else ventured.

An hour later, when the conversation wound down and ended with Audrey giving her address, we were all even more puzzled.

"So *who was it?*" we chorused when she hung up, all of us wondering who'd made the right guess. "Someone we know?"

"Oh, that?" Audrey said, surprised by our question. "Oh, that was just a wrong number."

No doubt about it, Audrey was connected with others as few ever are. When asked about it, she would just say, "I never think of really not knowing someone—I just don't know their name yet, and they don't know mine. But that's just because we haven't met yet."

Audrey was naturally connected with others, a gift that came to her without effort. And while many of us may never be so easily involved with others, we can see the connectedness that's possible from people such as Audrey.

Connecting Through Intellectual Understanding

We can begin learning to reconnect spiritually just as we begin re-lieving all of our burdens, by breathing with attention in the present and then focusing on our natural connectedness that's always calling us home.

But what if we don't feel any sense of connection?

For many people, our sense of connection can more easily begin with an intellectual understanding before it can become a more heartfelt and intuitive one. So let's begin by looking at the connections that we can understand intellectually.

Each and every moment, we're connected to all life around us through the great sacred bellows of our lungs, silently, invisibly, and constantly inhaling and exhaling.

Breathing in, we inhale oxygen produced by plants and trees. Breathing out, we exhale carbon dioxide, which is used by plants and trees and turned back into oxygen and returned to us and the living world once again to be used as the fuel of life.

This circle of life energy goes on constantly, and we play our part, each of us turning the wheel of life with each breath in and each breath out.

Our breath connects us not only with plants but with all other living things past, present, and future. The molecules of the air we're breathing right now were breathed by the dinosaurs on land, the great whales swimming in our oceans, and will be breathed by future earthlings of all species.

Feel yourself within the cycle of the ebb and flow of a great bellows. Consciously breathe and be here now with this awareness of our intimate, life-giving connection to all other living creatures.

Do it now. Look around you at the plants outside or in your house or office. You are connected with them in this inescapable web of breath and life. Breathing can feel especially connecting when you breathe in the fragrance of a flower, or a forest glade, or the dry, crisp desert air. This not only connects us but is delicious breathing.

The sea is one sea. A change in temperature anywhere means a change all over the world. The warming ocean known as El Niño causes extreme weather thousands of miles away in North America.

Astronauts come back from space forever changed by the experience of seeing the world as one without borders. Many of the astronauts who've flown around the earth have been awestruck by the majesty and wholeness of our home planet. As we travel through space, we're all flying and spinning together.

Billions of us are sharing the same planet, looking up at the same moon, stars, and sun, living under the same vast sky, breathing in and out the same air. The world is whole and we can experience our universality and our connectedness.

> The more we're aware of our connection to our earthly home and to spiritual oneness with all living things, the more we discover our connection with the One.
>
> Conversely, the more connected we are with the One, the more fully we can be connected with all of life in and around us.

Since Oneness is our essential being, we're automatically drawn toward connectedness. It is our true nature calling us home.

Connecting by Being Nurtured by Nature

For some of us, it's easiest to begin reconnecting by learning to connect with nature. A comfortable place that's safe and natural helps us focus on our spiritual connection. Even if we can only go for a few minutes, we can let ourselves relax and be at home, but without the interruptions and responsibilities.

Even in a local park or a neighborhood garden, we can see the many forms of life, the grasses and trees, flowers, birds, and insects all living together. Hear the sounds. Take a beginning and a second breath for attention and presence, and close your eyes and listen to the wind. Hear the rise and fall of birds singing and insects buzzing and chirping, creatures chattering and scurrying. Sit within it and hear the gentle rhythm, not unlike a symphony with its own instruments, crescendos, and pauses.

> Sink into the being of it and feel your place within the web of life, as you rest, awake and alive. The One in the many, the many in the One. One planet in One universe inhabited by One spiritual force, manifesting in infinite, ever-evolving forms, one of which is the family of humankind.

Connecting Through Friends and Family

As we breathe and be, it's important to look carefully at our connection with other people. Many of us can begin best by reconnecting with our own families and closest friends. As you breathe consciously and rest within, recognize your feelings for the people closest to your heart. As you become more centered and present, observe the judgments and criticisms you may have that keep you from being emotionally closer.

Listen to them more. Understand the other's viewpoint. Set aside meaningless differences. Let bygones be bygones.

Show love to those we love. This seemingly obvious suggestion is commonly overlooked, as we vent our frustrations and irritations on those we love the most and with whom we feel the safest to unload our negativity. As Ella Wheeler Wilcox wrote,

We flatter those we scarcely know,
And please the fleeting guest,

And deal full many a thoughtless blow,
To those who love us best.

Connecting Through
What We Have in Common

We can already experience our Oneness on many levels and in many ways:

We can feel our Oneness with others through our shared emotions. We can feel what the other feels and have empathy and compassion.

We can know our Oneness when we share similar thoughts and ideas with friends and enjoy conversations with others with whom we "speak the same language."

We can sense our Oneness with others when we share sensations in common (as when we watch a sunset or split dessert with a friend). Our shared sensations highlight our Oneness.

We can be One in activity as when we share a ride in the country or go to a movie or work on a puzzle with our spouse. Doing the same thing at the same time brings out our Oneness in action.

Often we reject others because they don't have the same opinions and affiliations as we do, and yet we can also find our overlooked similarities—bridges over which we can relate.

Breathe mindfully and be present. Find compassion for yourself and the bruises of past problems with others and have compassion for the suffering of others.

Take a deep, relaxing breath and be less judgmental.
Open to heartfelt compassion and widen your circle of
connectedness.

Be aware of our shared spiritual connection. When we see the Oneness of Spirit, we grasp the essence of the world's major religions. Then we understand why Mahatma Gandhi said, "I consider myself a Hindu, Christian, Moslem, Jew, Buddhist and Confucian."

The more aware of our spiritual connection, the less insecure we are with other people. As we feel a deeper awareness of our own being and can better see others' true humanity, we are less intimidated, less insecure, and less fearful of interacting with others.

Albert Einstein said, "A human being is a part of the whole that we call the universe, a part limited in time and space. He experiences himself, his thoughts and feelings, as something separated from the rest—a kind of optical illusion of his consciousness. This illusion is a prison for us, restricting us to our personal desires and to affection for only the few people nearest us. Our task must be to free ourselves from this prison by widening our circle of compassion to embrace all living beings and all of nature."

Identify with others. Try to look at their lives through their eyes. When we do this, we see that others are just like ourselves, with many of the same desires to live comfortably, to provide for their families, and to have the joy of living meaningful lives even as they, like ourselves, are beset with many of the same fears and difficulties. In this way we find compassion for others, and through this compassion we can experience a deeper connection through understanding that we share our common human condition.

Connecting Through Pets

Wherever we feel a sense of spiritual connection and love is where we should cultivate it, and millions find it most readily with their pets.

Especially for the many people who are separated from loved ones through distance or death, and for those who have great difficulty trusting and connecting with other people, pets provide a ready and willing partner through the "pet connection"—friend, family, and nature in one.

While we obviously have profound differences, we also have tremendous commonalities with our fellow creatures, be they cats, dogs, or monkeys. In fact, we humans have over 95 percent of our genetic structure in common with chimpanzees.

People who are deeply connected with animals point out that most pets are trying to tell you what they need, if you pay careful attention to what they're "saying."

The problem is often that most of us don't, or don't know how to, pay careful attention. Amy, one of Diane's writing students, knowing that Diane loved and raised cats, complained about her own cat, Snowball, who had been a perfectly behaved cat for many years, but was now suddenly urinating in the living room, and nothing she tried made any difference. Snowball had always jumped out the window to use a cat box on Amy's enclosed patio, but now she refused to go out the window at all. Amy was so upset about the problem, she was almost ready to get rid of Snowball.

Amy was directed to an expert on cat behavior who quickly diagnosed the problem. Snowball always went out the window using a stool that she jumped on and then from the stool out the window. But the stool had recently found its way into the garage, and Snowball had apparently hurt her leg, perhaps miscalculating the jump. Now unable to make the higher leap, she chose the most prominent place to send her message.

Once Amy understood what was going on, she said she realized Snowball had been consistently trying to tell her what was wrong by leaning up against her and licking her sore leg, an apparent attempt at communication Amy had totally ignored.

It's sad to think of the huge number of instances when animals have been misunderstood and gotten rid of because of not being able to communicate with their owner. Thinking of someone having life-and-death power over us, whom we couldn't make understand our language, gives us some notion of what it might be like for pets.

Being and consciousness are universally present in living creatures. Through conscious breathing and being present, we can connect with our pets in a profound way that may surprise us.

Take a full, restful breath and let yourself be with your pet for a moment. Often when we do this, we discover how truly present many animals are—naturally able to be with us here and now, content just living.

Find whatever helps you the most and do it. As we grow more comfortable with our spiritual connection, it often manifests itself in caring and nurturing. Our focus moves from our self as our sense of self enlarges to be able to embrace all others as part of our self.

Finding Our Connection

Since Oneness is our true spiritual nature, we're automatically drawn toward connectedness. We call friends and family, we care about pets and special places. We join clubs and other organizations that make us feel a sense of belonging. We have children and loved ones—all forms of merging and belonging.

We might even be extremely separated when we begin looking for ways to experience our natural connection. But once we start to experience what's behind the effort to feel connected, we can even see ourselves in a flower. As the poet William Blake wrote:

> *To see a world in a grain of sand*
> *And a heaven in a wild flower,*
> *Hold infinity in the palm of your hand*
> *And eternity in an hour.*

We begin by using our breath to observe our self, until we see the observer or watcher within. As we keep watching, we realize we're both the watcher and that which is seen, or, as Krishnamurti repeatedly said, "The observer is the observed."

When we see this, we realize that who we are is fundamentally fine. And what others think or don't think doesn't change our basic Being in the slightest. We know we won't be able to please everyone, we may be rejected or criticized, but rejection makes no difference to the essence within us. Our personal reactions can be observed, felt, digested, and then let go.

COOKING IN OUR OWN JUICES

I'm in a room of people, seeing them, hearing them, understanding them, connected with them. I can be present and awake, regardless of what they do or think. We're here, mirroring what is, including our personal wishes and fears.

Seeing myself in them and them in me, we're all here together, all wanting to feel safe and accepted, all manifestations of spiritual consciousness in individual human form, thinking we're separate from each other.

I can breathe consciously and be present in the midst of the crowd, safe and free, alert and alive, not needing them or me to be different than we are (including our personal desires to have things be different than they are). We're here. We're what we are, for we're all in the soup together, cooking in our own collective juices.

What Can I Do?
The "Collective Soup" Recipe

1. **Breathe to be aware and present** in the midst of the ever-unfolding process of life, of which we're an integral part. The Collective Soup Recipe combines the Basic Spiritual Diet with any of the courses on the diet, so we're enriched and evolve beyond our self, growing more intimate with larger life.

2. **Connect with life through understanding, nature, family, friends, and pets.** Find the ways in which you are already connected and strengthen whatever means are available to connect with life.

3. **Create community with others.** We can overcome excessive individualism by becoming more conscious of our connectedness to others and the world beyond our self, and by valuing other aspects of life in addition to the material.

We can join spiritual organizations—churches, synagogues, and temples. *We can say "Hello" and speak to our neighbors* and read local news so we feel connected with others around us. *We can join a neighborhood watch group* to help protect and care for our local streets. When we see a neighbor's child having a problem, we can help or *take responsibility to call or visit the child's parents* to make sure they know something's wrong. When we pick up our child at school, we can *speak with other parents and ask about their children.* We can *appreciate and care for our home environment,* be it a local park, a nearby state beach, or our own street. We can *thank* the checker at the supermarket, the sanitation worker, and the letter carrier. We can *volunteer* at community organizations to help our fellow humans and animals, whether it's cooking at a soup kitchen, donating blood to the Red Cross, joining the local PTA, coaching a kids' soccer team, or helping at an animal shelter.

4. Focus on the nonmaterial. We can focus more of our time and energy on nonmaterial aspects of life, including family, friends, neighbors, spiritual awareness, nature, music, athletics, reading, being of service . . . so as to feel healthy and fulfilled in nonmaterialistic ways.

Spirit: Pay attention to the One, of which we're all a part.

Personality: But I don't feel connected. I feel on my own, insecure and fearful. I hate to admit it, but I need to feel special and better than others to feel good about myself.

Spirit: You're a manifestation of all that is most powerful and special in the universe. Connect with this and feel relieved of insecurity and fear.

Personality: It's not so easy to feel good.

Spirit: Because you're excessively connected with your personal identity, and overlook your connectedness with that which is beyond your personal self. Breathe mindfully in the moment, and like a living mirror, you'll reflect the larger universe, eternally unfolding in myriad forms.

When we see our interconnectedness with the world, we realize that we *are* the world and experience a merging of boundaries. Like an iceberg melting back into the ocean from which it was formed, with a sense of harmony and lovingness, personality can merge into Oneness. Then we can feel what it's like to experience true freedom and feel fully alive.

Chapter 11

 ─────────────────────────

Barefoot
in the Spring

I have set before thee life and death ... choose life.

DEUTERONOMY 30:19

The true saint goes in and out amongst the
people and eats and sleeps with them and buys
and sells in the market and marries and takes
part in social intercourse, and never forgets God
for a moment.

ABU SA 'ID IBN ABI L-TKAYR

✻ Our many burdens make millions live halfheartedly. We can enjoy a vibrant, juicy life and find spiritual nourishment when we lighten our load and live more fully.

The Winter of Our Lives

As a child I knew how to have fun, but I seem to have forgotten along the way. Now I'm stuck in adulthood with a load of responsibilities weighing me down.

I'm so preoccupied and busy I feel like I'm only half here much of the time. Maybe that's why I don't enjoy myself more than I do.

I had a chance to start a new job, but I couldn't make the move even though it would have been good for me. I'd like to take more risks, but something's holding me back.

A close friend of mine said I'm too nervous and uptight. Maybe she's right and that's why I get headaches.

PAPA'S BIGGEST MISTAKE

It was Papa's (Diane's grandfather's) eighty-eighth birthday. He'd blown out the forest of candles, and we were sitting around the family dinner table eating his favorite (chocolate) cake. There was a lull in the conversation and Diane said in a playful tone, "Well, Papa, so tell us what you've learned in the past eighty-eight years."

Papa looked up and seemed to consider the answer before saying seriously, "Well, I'll tell you. I've missed out on a lot that I could have had. And I've got nobody to blame but myself."

Everyone felt the gravity of his tone as he continued. "When I was a scrawny kid growing up in St. Louis, I had a lot of trouble. I was small for my age and at twelve was working after school. On payday the rough kids in the neighborhood would always try to chase me down so they could beat me up and take my money. As time went on and they got older and meaner, I thought that one day they would kill me, and I was always scared everywhere I went. But then everything changed.

"I'll never forget it. One dark day in November, a big black dog—mostly Labrador—wandered into our house through an open back door. The poor dog seemed to be starving. I fed him and got my mom to let him stay. The next day, Shadow (that's the name I gave him) followed me to school and waited outside until I got out. Then after school he followed me to my job at the biscuit factory and he waited there, too. When those guys showed up, boy, they had a *big* surprise. You should have seen their eyes when they started chasing me and then saw Shadow. That dog turned around and bit the biggest one's hand and they all ran away. After that they never bothered me if Shadow was along, and believe me, Shadow went everywhere I did.

"On Sundays, we'd swim together at a creek outside town. I'd spend hours throwing sticks into the creek and Shadow wouldn't rest until he'd found the exact one I'd thrown, and brought it back proud as he could be. Then we'd fall asleep on the bank of the creek under the willow trees, my head on his chest."

We're a family of animal lovers and all of us could relate to Papa's friendship with Shadow.

"That's a wonderful story," Audrey (Diane's mother) said, before adding with a note of bewilderment, "but in all these years you've never mentioned having a dog and you always told us you didn't want one."

Papa nodded, cocking a bushy gray eyebrow. "Well, I guess that's because of what happened next. Shadow was with me fifteen years until I was in my twenties and we were in the Depression. I was working long hours at three jobs. It was winter, but I still left a window in the hallway open to let Shadow in and out when he wanted. All I can figure is that he must have jumped out and he was just too old or too cold to jump back in. I know he must have been out there barking, but I was always so tired at night I just didn't wake up. Anyway the next day I found him out there already too far gone to help him. I tried to warm him up, but it wasn't any good. He died right there in my lap.

"I was so angry at myself. My best friend who'd saved me and given so much to my life was gone. It just tore me up."

Papa spoke slowly. "Never got over him. I felt so bad I made a promise to myself that I'd never get another dog as long as I lived. And I never did."

Everyone was silent, as Papa's words made each of us aware of the losses and the grief we'd experienced. "That's heartbreaking," Audrey said.

"But that's just it!" Papa slapped a hand on the table. "It *did* break my heart. I never told it or even wanted to think about it because my heart was broken. That's just what I'm trying to tell you. Life goes on, and that promise that I made—and kept—was just plain foolish. I've missed out on having and loving another dog all these years, because I was afraid to love and lose again. So *I* lost out in the long run. Dumbest mistake I ever made."

The Burden of Not Living Fully

Papa's experience, though unique in many ways, has a universal quality as well. All of us have had life experiences that have hurt or scared us. Pain in life is inevitable. We all lose pets and people we love. We all have disappointments, setbacks, even tragedies. What is optional is how we relate to life's inevitable negative experiences.

These experiences may be a single traumatic event, or they may happen slowly over many years such as in the case of children who are routinely emotionally and/or physically abused.

Sometimes we remember these formative events and can identify clearly both the cause and the effect, as in Papa's case. Other times, events are clouded in our memories. Many abused children, for example, don't remember clearly (or want to remember) being abused, and later thoughts, feelings, actions, and reactions may puzzle even them.

Whether we remember or not, it's difficult to positively and effectively deal with a situation like this. As a result, we either consciously (as in Papa's case) or unconsciously try to separate the experience from our awareness by erecting an internal barrier that blocks us from feeling the guilt, sadness, or anger associated with it.

Our mind is very powerful. If someone says to us, "Don't think of ice cream," we immediately think of ice cream. Even if we resist, the thought has been planted in our mind and we're more likely to notice ice cream in an ad or a restaurant.

Negative experiences are analogously planted in our minds, and it's extremely difficult not to focus on them in some form. The energy we use doing this takes energy that could have been spent on other things. As a result, it contributes to our "weight of the world."

The more of these burdens we carry, the more we're limited in our ability to be fully aware, to experience our basic goodness, to experience sensations, to avoid addictions and harmful habits, to think clearly, to handle our emotions, to live a meaningful life, and to be able to connect with others. As a result, those of us trying to wall off our difficulties may feel exhausted (or be experiencing many other possible chronic symptoms).

Recipes in the Real World

The Spiritual Diet is designed to help us lose the burden resulting from unprocessed feelings. It helps us see what burdens we're carrying and then gives us the tools to create our own recipes to diet them off. We hope that as you've read the previous chapters, you've considered which of these burdens you're carrying. (If not, go back now, and look at "Identify Your Burdens," page 71.)

Once they're identified, we hope you'll begin breathing for awareness and presence. The Basic Spiritual Diet can be followed by a recipe of your own choosing. It can be a prayer or mantra that addresses one of your burdens. If you have identified your burden, but haven't put together your recipe to help diet them off, the following are sample solutions used by two of the people we discussed earlier.

ANDREW'S RECIPE

In Chapter 6 Andrew made a commitment to go on the Spiritual Diet. He identified his burdens as being excessively focused on the material and out of touch with his emotions, particularly emotions of closeness and love.

Beginning with the Basic Spiritual Diet, he learned to focus his awareness more and more, just doing it here and there at first, until he was comfortable breathing to be aware and present. As he became more conscious in the midst of his life, he began to see what he later called his "craziness," which was centered in a constant state of anxiety and compulsiveness. He began to see the negative effects that his burdens were having on him and those around him, and made up his own Spiritual Diet Recipe: a beginning and a second breath to be aware and present and a mantra to counterbalance his burdens by saying to himself, "Ahh! Now it's enough," and later, more simply, "enough" with the in-breath and "ahh!" with the out-breath.

When he finally pictured all he had that made his life full enough, he felt grounded in the present. Andrew said he'd always imagine these as a series of snapshots of his family and house and all that made him secure.

After several weeks he reported that he never imagined that anything so simple could make such a profound difference. "It was as if every time I would be conscious and see my drive and need, I'd realize how much I was still controlled by my raising. They were like old tape recordings installed in my brain, telling me how to live, even though deeper down they were never right for me. Then every time I would say, 'Ahh! Enough right now, or Enough!' it would be like erasing some of the tape. The more I did it, the weaker the old feelings became until I could see they weren't really part of a deeper me at all."

After practicing this for a time Andrew began to think more clearly about what was more meaningful, and when he was aware and present, he would sometimes meditate on what was the "right" thing for him to be doing.

He realized that he wanted to be with his children while he still had the chance, but having such a demanding schedule made it extremely difficult. So he decided that, since he couldn't change himself overnight, the best way for his personality was to do it in a structured way by scheduling time in his appointment book. He began by writing a small "ahh!" on each page of his book and then made a schedule so he'd really follow through: Wednesday night at 7:00 was reading to Kathy, Thursday night at 7:30 was playing with Marty, Saturday at 6:30 he went out with his wife, and so on. He had his secretary work around this schedule, which he made "sacred." He discovered that by adding structure he could give his family the closeness that they all wanted.

Being with his family more and being conscious of his unhealthy patterns of materialism and driveness, Andrew began to change.

As time went on, Andrew worked on one burden after another, and his life slowly became more centered in things that were really important to him and less centered in working endless hours for more material objects, which he realized was fueling many of his difficulties, such as needing things to be exactly under his control. At one point, he changed his recipe to include "loosening my grip," noticing immediately that it had an amazing effect on his level of stress.

He'd been raised as a Christian but had lapsed, and decided at one point that he wanted to feel closer to his spiritual source. So he started going to church and saying to himself "Jesus" with his inhalation and "is with me" with his exhalation.

MIRIAM'S RECIPE

Miriam (see Chapter 8), the daughter of Holocaust survivors, had been raised with a deeply ingrained pattern of sadness. Miriam began the Spiritual Diet the same way as Andrew, just being more aware and present each day. She also began seeing that her burdens included not only a pattern of sadness but being almost completely out of touch with physical sensation and pleasure.

Having identified her main burdens, she went through her day remembering whenever possible to breathe to be present and aware. When told that the average six-year-old laughs three hundreds times a day and the average adult laughs about seventeen, Miriam said she laughed once or twice. She started to counterbalance her sadness by recalling those things that made her happy and by watching more comedies, her main source of laughter. Her Spiritual Diet Recipe became breathing to be present and aware, and then saying to herself on the inhalation, "happy right now," and on the exhalation, "La Chaim" ("To Life," in Hebrew).

From doing this she discovered that she had many things that she was thankful for and that made her laugh and feel happy—when she paid attention to them. Much of her inherent happiness was just covered over by sadness. She also realized that working in a hospice was exactly in keeping with her pattern of feeling down, and exactly the opposite work for what she now needed.

As she spent more of her time awake and present, she felt stronger and decided that she needed to switch jobs. She couldn't leave her job without finding another, so she began looking around and realized that she could use her training as a registered nurse in many different ways. She began looking into birthing instruction and went back to school to be a midwife, later working with a group of midwives who run a birthing center. She said this gave her a whole new outlook. "Now," she says, "instead of constantly waiting for people to die and lives to end, I'm constantly enjoying babies being born and lives beginning."

Losing the weight of this sadness helped Miriam have better feelings generally, which helped her want to address her burden of not being in touch with her body, which had led her to overeating.

She decided on another recipe, and when she sat down to eat, she would breathe to be present and aware, saying "La Chaim," and focus on her body and her senses—the aromas, the sight of the food, the feel of it in her mouth and going down. She said that a lot of times she'd find herself with a little smile from her "private prayer." Later, she changed her prayer to breathing in, saying to herself "tasting all," breathing out, "feeling satisfied," in "tasting," out "satisfied."

With these spiritual recipes, she found it much easier to pay attention to what she was eating. She started choosing better foods and found herself eating more slowly and eating less. As her conscious awareness grew, she also found herself feeling less of a victim of her hunger and started eating smaller meals more often. In time, her awareness expanded from the narrower confines of tasting to include her other sensations as well, and for a while she changed her recipe to "listen, taste, see, feel, smell." Little by little, her senses came more and more to prominence. After a while, she started taking regular walks and lost physical weight as well.

She later said, "Using this spiritual recipe is really helping me to wake up to life. It was all going on before, but I wasn't there to notice or enjoy it. It's really why I was eating so much, because I was numb to almost any other pleasure so that eating was all I could enjoy. Now it's as if I'm really able to be alive for the first time. Last week was the first time I've ever initiated sex with my husband. And it was much better than it usually is."

This, then, is the real point to it all. Losing the weight of the world is great by itself, but even better when we can replace the burdens with living fully.

THE EASTER PRESENT

As for Papa, he found that talking about Shadow for the first time in all those years was like lancing a boil, and after more discussion, he could see that, by blocking his feelings for animals (because of his guilt and sadness about Shadow, and his fear of loving and losing again), he'd cut off his feelings in general. By bringing his awareness of caring to consciousness, he could grow beyond his "stuckness" and his painful feelings and open his heart again.

By the time Easter came around, Papa was ready to receive the black Lab puppy the family bought him. He said it was as though Shadow had been "resurrected." It was love at first sight and, as he held his wiggly new puppy, Shadow II, Papa got his smiling face licked a hundred times that Easter day.

What Can I Do?
The "Living Fully" Recipe

1. Each time you awaken (be it morning, afternoon, or evening), **take a couple of slow, full breaths** to be aware and present, happy to have been given another day of life. Begin by being fully in touch with your senses—what you hear, see, smell, taste, and feel. Take a minute, stretch, and get up. Standing, slowly bend and allow your body to move as it will. You may want to use music or just allow your own life energy to flow through you. You can do this for as little or as long as you want and as is convenient.

The point is to be conscious of your body and physical energy. In this way we loosen up and start our day more fully alive.

2. Breathe consciously in the present with what is, as it is. Use the Basic Spiritual Diet. This basic process enables us to relax in the moment, opening us up to living fully. If we find it valuable, we can use prayer or mantra to help us stay centered and awake right now, on more intimate terms with our life moment by moment. Whenever possible, bring yourself fully into the present, even if only for a fleeting moment. Keep Huang Po's words in mind: "It's right in front of you." We can breathe more fully to bring more oxygen, blood, energy, and life into our body and mind.

3. Have compassion for yourself, your fellow humans, and other living creatures. We can see our shared reality of difficulty and confusion in the face of life's insecurity, complexity, and mystery. Some problems don't have good solutions and we just have to live with them. We're all flawed, imperfect, incomplete personalities, yet we can all find greater peace of mind in the midst of reality as it is, and learn to truly live more fully.

4. Use the "digestion" process with the flow of life energy. Be aware and present with feelings. Let them flow in and out of your awareness and experiencing. Sad, scared, mad, happy, loving. Let them come and go. Juicy and alive. Don't dwell excessively on worries—they'll weigh you down and keep you from living fully. Counterbalance your pain, anger, and fear, recalling the ways you are also feeling good, happy, and secure. Have a plan. Do what you can and move on.

One of the early Christian desert fathers, Abba Or, advised in the second century to "either flee from people, or laugh at the world and the people in it, and make a fool of yourself in many things."

If we're going to live a normal life, we can still have a perspective in which we're involved but also detached, able to laugh at ourselves, gaining the freedom to relax and live fully.

5. Take small risks during daily life to help you overcome your limitations. Tell someone that you like their smile or that you're angry with or hurt by them or ask for that raise you deserve. Risk going beyond your personality's boundaries to feel alive. Plan a weekend of horseback riding or dancing or celebrating with friends or river rafting or hot-air ballooning or a walk in the woods or a mountain bike ride. Whatever makes you feel alive. Rock climbers and sky jumpers say they're intensely alive when their life is on the line. You may not want or need to risk your life to get your adrenaline pumping and your heart going. Push yourself a bit beyond your limits and breathe in the midst of the activity. Breathe! Just do it! We're alive and kickin'.

6. Limit the damage done to you each day. For example, we can reduce tension and bad feeling by not watching negative TV news shows. Studies have shown that when we watch negative news stories we become sadder and more anxious, and our worrying about our personal problems is greatly increased. (Reading negative news in newspapers has much less negative impact than watching TV.)

7. Use your darkest friends, your mortality and impermanence to help you appreciate and make the most of each day.

Physician Bernie Siegel says, "In many cases, people who've become aware of their mortality find they've gained the freedom to live. They're seized with an appreciation for the present: every day is my best day; this is my life; I'm not going to have this moment again. They spend more time with the things and people they love and less time on people and pastimes that don't offer love or joy."

Being conscious of our impermanence can be our friend and ally, helping us to appreciate the moment we're in right now, loving what is, sensing the cosmos as the body of Spirit. We can awaken to our essence which existed before our birth and survives beyond our death.

The Native American Indian Crowfoot's last words were, "What is life? It is a flash of a firefly in the night. It is the breath of a buffalo in the wintertime. It is the little shadow which runs across the grass and loses itself in the sunset."

Think about our impermanence and use an end-of-life perspective, the advice we might give when we're at the end of our life. What do you think will stand out to you as having been most important? Emphasize those aspects of life that you believe will really count. Usually people respond that, when all is said and done, the people they were close to meant the most to them. If that's true for you, go out of your way to be with the people that mean the most to you.

Plutarch wrote, "The whole of life is but a point in time; let us enjoy it while it lasts." We don't get to live forever in the form we're in. The Spirit within us lives forever, but the unique life we're living now is short.

Make sure you're doing your best to live meaningfully (see Chapter 9) and know your mission in life.

8. Have faith and trust in Spirit so personality can keep the big picture in mind. Personality fears, Spirit trusts. Spiritual security means letting go and living fully, with faith and trust in our spiritual nature. The Spiritual Diet asks us to live each day as fully as we can, trusting that in the big scheme of things, everything is as it's supposed to be. Even though our personal needs and wishes may not be met the way we want, the Great Spirit is moving through life exactly as it's supposed to. We don't get rid of our problems and frustrations, we have to live fully in the midst of them. And all our effort leads us to relaxing into the suchness of what is, as it is, with awareness and experiencing for all. So take a leap of faith, and trust that all is going fine.

9. Be juicy and alive! One day a searcher went to see a Zen master to discover the meaning of life and asked about the master's beliefs. After being told by the master that he didn't have any beliefs, the seeker asked, "Well, if you don't have any beliefs, what's your theology?"

The Zen master answered, "We dance."

The heart of wisdom tells us to love and to dance with life, learning to caress the divine details along the way. That's why the philosopher Nietzsche said, "I would believe only in a god who could dance," and why Zen master Hakuin said, "In singing and dancing is the voice of the Law."

Watch children play and find the child within who knows how to have a good time. Recall what made you feel fully alive as a child. Did you love riding your bike or swimming or running or drawing? What made you feel free and able to enjoy yourself? So much of adulthood is taken up with accomplishing and succeeding, how about resting without being productive or successful?

We can find our own way of dancing with life. Whether our "dance" means quilting, reading, woodworking, gardening, or baking cookies with our kids, we can do what we inherently love doing and simply breathe and be awake and present and alive in the midst of it all for no reason at all.

The key nutrients on a vibrant spiritual diet are: consciousness, presence, and intimacy with life as it's being lived. Open to new experiences and keep awake in the moment while doing them. Learn a new game. Read a book you've always wanted to read. Lie in an open field.

10. **When you lie down** in bed to go to sleep, sink in and enjoy the safety and comfort of your familiar sleeping place. We can appreciate the day we've just completed and enjoy good thoughts about what we've experienced.

When you get up, live in keeping with the spirit of the traditional Jewish toast: *La Chaim! To Life!*

PICKING DAISIES

We can appreciate each day we awaken and make good use of it. Nadine Stair, an eighty-five-year-old woman, wrote, "If I had my life to live over, I would start barefoot earlier in the spring and stay that way later in the fall. I would go to more dances. I would ride more merry-go-rounds. I would pick more daisies."

Enlightenment is allowing personality to fade into the void, filling us with conscious awareness of, and presence with, what is, as it is. Then we are everything and nothing, beyond division and distinction.

ENJOYING THE GAME

George Santayana wrote that "there is no cure for birth and death save to enjoy the interval."

When we loosen our grip and accept ourselves as perfectly imperfect and uniquely ordinary, then we can enjoy whatever's happening without our personality being excessively attached to the outcome.

In the first century A.D., the Jewish philosopher Philo said:

The face of the wise man is not somber or austere, contracted by anxiety and sorrow, but precisely the opposite: radiant and serene, and filled with a vast delight, which often makes him the most playful of men . . .

According to Moses, the goal of wisdom is laughter and play—not the kind that one sees in little children who do not yet have the faculty of reason, but the kind that is developed in those who have grown mature through both time and understanding. If someone has experienced the wisdom that can only be heard from oneself, learned from oneself, and created from oneself, he does not merely participate in laughter: he becomes laughter itself.

Does Living Fully Mean Losing Ambition?

Does living fully and seeing the spiritual perfection of life mean we just accept our regular lives as they are and not work to change them? Does it mean we accept unfair treatment or avoid arguing when we think another's wrong? No. We do what we need to do, with life-affirming values such as the Golden Rule and basic goodness as our guides.

The Spiritual Diet gives us *more* tools to solve our problems, not fewer. By losing our burdens, we develop clearer thinking. When we think more clearly, we can see which of our problems can and should be solved and which are not really problems at all or are not problems that can be solved at this time.

But let's say that we have a problem. What do we do?

First, we create a plan, deciding what to do.

Then we make the necessary effort.

Now we can stop worrying. We're doing our part. The secret is to let yourself accept and work with the outcome. If you have feelings about it, you properly "digest" them, and you work with the situation you now face. But all the while, you know that you're doing what you can, and even though we try hard, the outcome isn't entirely under our control. We can drop unnecessary worrying, self-criticism, guilt, and blame.

This does not mean we stop meeting our needs or reaching our goals. Ambitions are still an important part of life. Personality naturally tries to take care of itself, doing the best it can with its personal life, but it also learns to trust Spirit. If life gives me roses, great; if life gives me thorns, well, personality doesn't have to like thorns, but it can pay attention and trim them off or handle them carefully. We do what we can to make what we want happen, accept the results, and work with what we get.

Living fully, we sink into the suchness of it. But this doesn't mean we make less effort.

We do what's appropriate in the world of our home and job. Let's say you're in charge of a large, complex event (like a wedding, birthday party, research project, conference, meeting). Does this mean that you stand back and just let whatever happens happen, and be at peace with it? Living fully with acceptance means only that you accept the outcome, not that you don't make the effort. Life is effort. We work with the outcome as well. Our body and personality survive and succeed through our skills. We can't get away from utilizing these skills. And so we do. We lay down plans. We go forward. Decisions are made and followed up on. Everything is planned, checked, and rechecked. If there's a snag, we work to fix it.

⊛ **We work to make it as we think it should be. But *then* we *accept* the result, even as we may still work to change it.**

A speaker cancels at the last moment. A microphone doesn't work.

With a relaxed breath and the proper digesting of our fear, we can laugh and enjoy the challenge and go on. It's all working out as best it can in the Big Picture. There's always your inner awareness of spiritual calm in the midst of the hassle.

If all efforts fail, then this inner awareness of Spirit is the reality and you're simply mindful when you can, and aware of yourself being aware. We identify those things we can change and those things we can't. We make the effort and accept the outcome. Then we make more effort, and again accept the outcome . . . on and on.

In this way, our Spirit and personality are more fully balanced. We are not wasting our energy on repressing feelings, or on our thoughts jumping around like jabbering monkeys on a sugar high. Once our ability to be aware and present makes us more conscious of the essence of our life, we have far more clarity and energy to help us do what is "right" for ourselves *and* others, and we can reconnect with more of the life that is constantly surging around us.

Rabbi Kushner writes, "When your life is filled with the desire to see the holiness in everyday life, something magical happens: ordinary life becomes extraordinary, and the very process of life begins to nourish your soul!"

This process works on itself. The clearer we become, the more we're able to do and the more we want to do. And our life can feel as if we're finally in a rhythm that works. We can see our future more clearly. We can make better decisions. Generally, our life feels richer as we experience more fully and let things go.

Think the World Alive

When we learn to be "in the flow," "walking with Christ," "on the Warrior's path," "living within God's Grace," "in the eyes of the Lord," "a Living Mirror," we are completely in the suchness of it. The American Indian Blackfoot elder George Goodstriker succinctly expresses the vision that leads to spiritual harmony: "We see God in Water, Sun, Air—everywhere."

When we see Spirit operating in our life, we have greater faith and trust, and our life moves more easily, freely, and smoothly. The flow of consciousness, presence, and basic goodness moves between us, and we are part of it and it is part of us. And this connection offers us tremendous support and strength.

The more we're able to flow with whatever is happening at the time, and deal with it all consciously, the more we see that events are often going in ways that are of value to us in the Big Picture. We meet someone we're "supposed" to meet, who has an answer (or a question) we need to hear. An opportunity appears to do something that makes our life more meaningful, and we're awake enough to re- alize it. An accident is avoided. We intuitively know something, but there's no "normal" way we could have known. We see and under- stand others more fully and accurately. We communicate more hon- estly and clearly.

When we are more conscious and present, we are better able to go with the flow of the energy and events pulsing through our life.

It's like a river in which we're all swimming. Yes, some of us bump along the edges where it's shallow, and the rocks and branches catch us, and scrape and bruise us. No one's life is without such events, and some of our lives seem easier than the lives of others. What is important is that we learn from our experiences as we live more consciously, and shape and mold our life accordingly.

Difficult experiences are part of life and can help us learn how to move better with the flow by increasing our ability and motivation to make more positive decisions and take wiser actions. By evaluating experience, we learn to more expertly swim in the waters of our own life.

Awake, alert, alive. Being juicy and alive is what it's all about, the end in itself. We do it in order to do it. In this way we reach a stage of life that's beyond personality's struggling, while enmeshed in normal, daily life. Being awake and aware of what is, being intimate with life, is our deepest natural state. In so doing we feel a peace and contentment in the midst of whatever we're doing, wherever and whenever we're doing it.

Then we realize what it means to live lusciously, dining on a nutritious daily Spiritual Diet so we truly lose the weight of the world.

Chapter 12

Luscious Living:
A Daily Spiritual Diet

Your daily life is your temple and your religion.

KAHLIL GIBRAN

The Lord lives among the pots and pans.

ST. TERESA

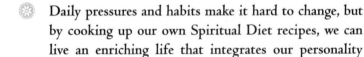 Daily pressures and habits make it hard to change, but by cooking up our own Spiritual Diet recipes, we can live an enriching life that integrates our personality

and spirituality and helps us lose the weight of the world.

The Ultimate Challenge

"I want to meditate or pray or at least have some quiet time, but I never seem to get around to it," said a successful New York literary executive. "I have so many responsibilities and move so quickly from calls to manuscripts to meetings that I can't find the time."

There is one final burden we must lighten. If we're to lead a harmonious, balanced life, we must merge the personal with the spiritual in the midst of our real, stressful, and preoccupying daily life.

Our old patterns have a life of their own and pull us back to the familiar. So it's easy to read about the Spiritual Diet, try it out a little, then set it aside and forget all about it. But to get the most benefit, we need to use what we now know until we've established new patterns of thought, feeling, action, intent, etc.

> Our ultimate challenge is to be both a doer and a witness, to "be" in the midst of "becoming," to merge personality with Spirit. Finding this harmonious balance is the ultimate living out of the Spiritual Diet and the final way to lose the weight of the world.

Perfectly Imperfect

A Zen master of great spiritual consciousness came to teach at a monastery. When he was welcomed by the other monks at the evening meal, he spoke to them in a moving and poetic manner, about the need to concentrate on the perfection of all things just as they exist here and now.

The following day, he set everyone to work repairing the roof, cleaning the grounds, weeding the garden, and scrubbing the kitchen. This intense undertaking went on for several days. Finally, the exhausted monks, usually more focused on sitting meditation than on doing daily deeds, reported that the major projects were finished. The new master nodded and immediately gave out new assignments—repairing tiles, painting walls, cleaning out the cellar, and rehanging the gate.

"But, Master," a clever young monk asked, "why are we working so hard to change things when you instructed us to contemplate the perfection of things as they are?"

The master said, "Everything is perfect just as it is, but there are still a lot of ways to improve it."

Our effort to be more conscious and present doesn't mean we have to put our regular, day-to-day life on hold. Daily life is ever evolving, and our careers and chores go on as before. As we grow in awareness and presence, we're increasingly able to spend more time, living more fully, here and now with what is, as it is, in the midst of fixing, cleaning, and filing.

As we practice our Spiritual Diet, we come to experience the perfection of reality while also seeing the endless ways life can be improved.

Personality sees what can be changed.

Spirit sees perfection of *what is.*

We must provide for our self and our family and lead normal, productive lives while resting in eternity. Perfection can be seen while returning messages, weeding the garden, sending a fax, or taking out the trash.

By practicing our Spiritual Diet, we can foster personality's cooperation with spirituality.

What happens when we use the Spiritual Diet? We feel more complete. We realize what is deeper in us than our thoughts, desires, and actions, and we find greater comfort with our self as we actually are, imperfect as we may seem. When we're at home with our real self, at peace in our real life, our load lightens.

The door to the Universal opens when we, the individual, relax our grip and rest with awareness here and now with what is, as it is.

Suddenly we may glimpse eternity.

Maybe it's a blade of grass or an ocean sunset; maybe it's a loved one's face or a moving story in the news. Anything can awaken us right now where we are.

A feast has been set before us. The secret is that when we learn to live intimately with awareness of the here and now, savoring the experiences flowing through us, we realize that everything is ambrosia.

If we open our heart and our mind, we find our self in a world beyond words and concepts. It's a matter of having eyes to see, ears to hear, and a mouth with which to taste. At any and every moment, we can allow the light of awareness to shine on whatever appears within and around us, even if only for this instant, right here, right now. When personality/Spirit is lived as one, everything is a feast to be savored.

One of the greatest and most uncompromising masters of the twentieth century was Jiddu Krishnamurti. Born in India, raised in England by the Theosophical Society as the Messiah, Krishnamurti rejected this role and disbanded the organization built for him, saying each must find his/her own way in life. Listen to a moment of his original deep awakening to living fully:

On that first day while I was in that state and more conscious of the things around me, I had the first most extraordinary experience ... I could feel the wind passing through the tree and the little ant on the blade of grass I could feel. The birds, the dust and the very noise were a part of me. All day long I remained in this happy condition.

I was so happy, calm and at peace. I could still see my body and I was hovering and within myself was the calmness of the bottom of a deep unfathomable lake. Like the lake, I felt my physical body an unfathomable lake. Like the lake I felt that my physical body with its mind and emotions could be ruffled on the surface, but nothing, nay nothing could disturb the calmness of my soul ...

Never more could I be in utter darkness. I have seen the glorious and healing Light. The fountain Truth has been revealed to me and the darkness has been dispersed. Love in all its glory has intoxicated my heart; my heart can never be closed. I have drunk at the fountain of joy and eternal Beauty. I am God-intoxicated!

A moment of such spiritual intensity is highly unusual, but we know it's possible for each of us. We can't control it. It's beyond our control. But we can feel at home and set a place for it at the table of our life. We can relax, breathing and awake in the present.

At Home on the Range

In a flash, we're aware that we're present. We take a beginning breath in and out, to be conscious. And a second breath in and out, to be here and now. Oxygen from earth's vegetation in, carbon dioxide out for plants to turn into life energy. We feel our self as part of the great cycle of life.

Every day, we sit down to eat, and when we do, we can rest in our body as our body rests in our chair. We can feel our tongue in our mouth and taste a sip of soda or a bite of salad. The napkin feels good against our skin. We swallow and feel the liquid going down.

Outside, a dog barks, a wren twitters in a tree, a car whooshes by. Life goes on, breathing here, breathing now. Wherever we are, whatever we're doing, conscious as we eat and breathe and digest our food, moving on to whatever comes next.

Doing the dishes, standing in front of the sink, I'm feeling my body resting inside my clothes. Recalling a joke I heard today, laughing silently to myself, a smile crosses my face. Conscious and present, hearing the sound of the water. Breathing in, feeling the water on my hands, breathing out, seeing the dishes, the result of my family having food to eat and fluids to drink. Recalling my Give Thanks Recipe— "thankful," breathing in, "resting," breathing out; gratefulness in my heart. The warm water cleans away the dirty food, resting at the sink, alive, doing what needs to be done.

A flash of annoyance passes through me at an overheard news item on the TV. Clenched teeth, breath held in. Ripples of sadness and fear wash through me as the story of a missing child unfolds. Facial sadness, constricted breath. The dishes are cleaned one by one. One deep, relaxing breath in, "sadness," one full, restful breath out, "fear." Heart and breath constriction in my chest. Mental jumping monkeys— thoughts of tomorrow's meeting, this evening's commute home, my children's safety. Oh yeah, the Calm Monkeys Recipe—"thinking, worrying, let it go."

A wave of love and affection. Warm chest. Time pressure comes. The kids need baths and their homework isn't done. The phone rings. Off and running, conscious in the moment, the feel of the phone. "Hello." Lost in conversation.

Back to the dishes with awareness, presence, experiencing, letting go and opening to whatever comes next. Tomorrow's tight schedule flashes through my thoughts as I rehearse and prepare, preoccupied yet excited at the same time. A full, relaxed breath in, feeling vibrant and juicy energy flowing through me. The report's nearly done. The garbage needs to go out. Seeing my child play with the cat, a secret smile goes through me. Doing what needs to be done. I'm here, conscious, awake, complete in the midst of it all. A deep, slow breath. Ahhh.

In this way I'm at home in the midst of it all, for whatever I'm doing at the time is the most important thing right now. Each act and moment can be infused with mindfulness, though in reality awareness comes and goes, one conscious breath at a time.

We are conscious, then preoccupied with thoughts and plans, then awake and aware once again. I'm at the office, picking up messages, viewing my schedule, writing notes, attending meetings; feelings come, feelings go. Conversations with colleagues, rushing to an appointment, answering the phone. Pressured and irritated, I recall the need to counterbalance and take a relaxed breath in with contentment and a thankfulness for having a livelihood, a house and people I love. Stressed and happy, conscious and present.

Don't expect to be present and aware all the time. Awareness comes and goes. Let it come, let it go, let it come again, and again.

We follow the Buddha's advice about the Middle Way, seeking moderation in whatever we do. We don't need to feel incomplete if we haven't achieved sainthood or enlightenment.

Life size is just the right size. This is it! We've already arrived, even when we're trying to get somewhere else. We can put out the welcome mat and rest at home in the midst of it all.

Ramana Maharshi tells us, "Reality is simply the loss of the ego . . . There is no greater mystery than seeking reality though in fact we *are* reality. We think there is something hiding reality and that this must be destroyed before reality is gained. How ridiculous! A day will dawn when you will laugh at all your past efforts. That which will be on the day you laugh is also here and now."

A Feeling Mirror

In the middle of combing our hair, flossing our teeth, eating break-fast, driving our car, sending a fax, kissing our family hello and good-bye, or watching TV, we keep aware of the five basic emotions, and see our rejection and acceptance of them, while being awake here and now.

Sitting on a bus or subway, we can take a break from the news-paper and be aware. We say to our self as we're breathing and rest-ing, "Now I'm mad." We feel it and let it go, opening to the next wave of feeling that washes through us. Aware, present, contented. We can turn off the car radio and notice how we're feeling as the trees and people pass by. Breathing and resting, we notice we're still irritated and we can counterbalance excessive anger: breathing in and out, "loving" (accompanying our mantra with meaning, as we look for those aspects of life that, in fact, do make us feel love and care).

Our emotions are apparent as we breathe to be conscious and present, sitting at our desk trying to make an important phone call, "frustrated." Sitting in a meeting, breathing in and out, conscious of what we're all wearing, of how we're sitting, intonations in our voice. Hearing what's apparent and what's intended.

We see our dislike for bad feelings, our rejection of fear, frus-tration, boredom, sadness, and hurt. But now we can relax with these uncomfortable feelings, not to mention the rejection of them. Knowing our emotions come and go, we can relax and breathe with our feelings, like them and not.

MEANINGFUL MOMENTS

In the midst of it all, I'm aware of what's inherently meaningful in my life and I'm aiming my actions toward a life of purpose. I'm focused on being conscious of what's important and go toward it. Valuing being of help, I remember to be aware as I hold the door for an elderly person, able to smile in consciousness, contentment, and an inner warmth from doing even so small a kindness.

Awake to the moment, I rest in the midst of grocery shopping. Pushing the cart down the aisle, I feel a sense of peacefulness inside as I toss a can of soup into my cart. Grateful to realize the abundance of foods available to us, I settle down, doing the Basic Spiritual Diet, noticing the colors and the music and the people passing by, content and complete.

Filling Our Hole with the Whole

As we become more aware, we realize how important having a sense of connectedness is, and we offer an affectionate hug to our spouse or a close friend, feeling our caring and union. We realize our connection with all living things and with the sacred running through all of life.

We watch a movie and realize that the character's hurt and happiness are *our* collective hurt and happiness, as we share our common human experiences, bridging the gaps between us.

We drift back to long-lost loves—people, places, pets—and sense how they live on through us in our heart, memories, and Spirit. We recall special moments of wonder, whether in the woods or at the water, in a church or temple, at a museum or a monument. We drift back to a time we walked hand in hand and realized we were together on this huge planet spinning through space, the breeze brushing our face and arms, the sun shining equally down on all of us as One.

We see our connectedness here and now, as we realize we're reading these words along with many others who share our efforts to become more awake in the moment. We see the sun and the trees and the rain in the paper we're reading and realize our union with all of life.

The Secret of Success

Success does not come from achieving all of our personality's wishes and dreams, but from living fully and living intimately. Swami Sivananda said, "Put your heart, mind, intellect and soul even into your smallest acts. This is the secret of success." When we feel in touch and inwardly successful, we feel less afraid, less constricted, less held back.

Rabbi Leib said, "I did not go to the maggid [Jewish preacher] to hear the Torah from him, but to see how he laces and unlaces his shoes." We can see a person's state of consciousness from any- and everything he or she does. The smallest acts can be infused with awareness and presence. The average person would notice nothing special, but those who can truly see and hear bring awareness and presence to the mere act of lacing and unlacing shoes. Awareness in, lacing up, awareness out, standing up.

Aware and here, "Now I'm thinking," "planning for tomorrow," the sun warms my back, worrying and rehearsing, glad and tense, conscious for a moment. Alive in the midst of it all, breathing and resting where I am, contented and complete.

Maybe we're in a situation where we don't want to be present. We're in a traffic jam and we're late. We're creeping along and we're frustrated and irritated. Our breathing is constricted and our neck and shoulders are tense.

The last thing we want is to be aware of where we are and what we're really feeling. We don't want to be present. We want to be at our destination, not in this stupid traffic tie-up. Yet, focusing on where we are not only keeps us in touch with our own spirituality and the truth that "this, too, shall pass" but also helps on the more practical, personality level. We can relax and be within our body, thus enabling us to better cope with the situation we're in. We can be at home on the road.

If we want, we can focus on another aspect of the experience—the flowers by the side of the road, the person in the car with us, solutions to some problem we've been worrying about, recalling a wonderful moment, the Spiritual Diet recipe we're following that day, week, or month.

Trust and Faith

The world's religions teach us to have faith and trust:

Judaism: The Lord is my strength and my shield. My heart trusteth in Him, and I am helped.

Christianity: By grace are ye saved through faith . . . Have faith in God.

Buddhism: Neither eating, nor fasting, nor penance, nor sacrifice, nor observance of the seasons, purify a mortal who has not conquered his doubt.

Shinto: Free yourself from doubt and you will find your life quickened in the goodness of God.

The common understanding of faith and trust is that I put my life in the hands of some higher power (God, Jesus, Allah, Buddah . . .). We may pray for money, for love, or for our soccer or football team to win. But these are all ego-based spirituality in which God is viewed as a provider who'll fulfill what I pray for.

But deeper spiritual faith and trust is different and more difficult. Instead of pleading for God to serve personality, we should pray for our personality to serve God. Instead of just wanting my personal wishes fulfilled, **I pray to be able to go with the flow of life, trusting that, in the big scheme of things, Spirit is moving in the direction Spirit needs to be moving in, even though this may not follow my private plan.**

True trust and faith are a leap into life as it really is, without the personal supports we're used to. We can work with it and try to modify its flow to some degree, but ultimately there's a limit to what we can control, and we must find peace in the midst of it all. Instead of praying to get God to come to me, let my prayer be for me to go to God. As the saying goes, "In God we trust." Not *my* will be done, but *Thy* will be done. I surrender my personal dreams to the reality God places before me.

When we relax this way, in tune with our spirituality, it's far easier for us to see the paths that are open for us, and we have a greater ability to bring these paths to fruition.

Matt had spent his adult life working as a building contractor while he studied to be an architect. Contracting was a difficult job because of his workers' constant personal problems, and he was eager to be an architect working with fewer employees. But when he failed his architecture exam a second time, he came to Jonathan for help.

Matt realized he was extremely tense and felt that whatever he did wasn't good enough. His tension and feelings of inadequacy as an architect made the exam an obstacle. In time, we developed several Spiritual Diet recipes for Matt based on his needing to calm down (the Basic Spiritual Diet and saying "relax" and "ahhh") and to realize that with experience, he'd develop better skills as a professional ("all in good time") and that he was a good person with good values and deserved to feel good about himself and his life.

Matt said that as he calmed down, he realized he was making poor personnel choices that kept him overly stressed. He started "seeing" people more clearly and handling them more effectively. In a few months, he assembled a far more reliable and capable work crew, with far fewer problems, and his tension and frustration subsided dramatically.

When his next exam came around, he was calmer and more philosophical about it, feeling that contracting work was a lot more enjoyable now and that he could relax more because it would all work out fine in the long run. "I used to be really uptight and worried about every little thing," Matt explained. "But when I learned to relax and have faith that things were okay in the big picture, I got a lot more comfortable and confident, and I came to feel that even though I'm still a beginner, I do deserve to be an architect. I think that's why I finally passed my exam and got my architect's license."

Ordinary Holiness

Each of us is special and unique, while at the same time completely ordinary. When we learn to "see God everywhere," we caress the divine details and we're nourished by ordinary holiness. Each of us has certain abilities and gifts (which we may or may not actualize), while at the same time, we must accept that in myriad ways we have great limitations and are just like everyone else.

Author William Elliot interviewed many spiritual people for his valuable book, *Tying Rocks to Clouds*, and went to see Mother Theresa, who was tired, not feeling well, and without any time to do the interview. He writes:

> Mother Theresa in all her wonderful loving presence now appeared to me in a different way. She was no longer a saint; she was more than that. She was a human being. She was what we, as human beings, were meant to be all along. She was so deeply human and ordinary that she had touched that part of humanity that touched God, a humanity that can suffer, cry, laugh, and even die while staying connected with that essence that infuses us.
>
> "Anyway," Mother Theresa continued, and I suddenly became aware again of her presence, "you have the Dalai Lama [interview]. He's enough!" As she said that, she waved her hand in the air as though to say, "Go on. It's going to be all right; you've got everything you need."

We can all "touch that part of humanity that touched God." You've got everything you need to live fully. If everything is a manifestation of God or Spirit, then everything is fine as it is and it's up to us to come to grips with this fact of our human life.

A great Chinese master from the eighth century, Layman P'ang, wrote:

> *My daily affairs are quite ordinary;*
> *but I'm in total harmony with them.*
> *I don't hold on to anything, don't reject anything;*
> *nowhere an obstacle or conflict.*
> *Who cares about wealth or honor?*
> *Even the poorest thing shines.*

My miraculous power and spiritual activity:
drawing water and carrying wood.

In our own ordinary life, drawing water means going to the sink and turning on the faucet. Carrying wood means turning on the heat and paying the electric bill. Regardless of our actions, Spirit is present at the sink, the thermostat, and our desk. We realize we already have everything we need. Spirit is evolving through us, fostering presence and awakeness in the midst of our ordinary life. That includes being in the midst of our enjoyment, as well as our insecurity and incompleteness, imperfection and impermanence.

At the same time that we are common and ordinary, we're also special and unique. Like fingerprints and snowflakes, no two of us are exactly the same. So in the midst of our ordinariness, we must be true to our individual style, needs, feelings, vision, and path. We must find our way, being true to our individual talents and abilities. Rabbi Zusya of Hanipol said, "If they ask me in the next world, 'Why were you not Moses?' I will know the answer. But if they ask me, 'Why were you not Zusya?' I will have nothing to say."

Both our specialness and our ordinariness can help us live fully and touch the spiritual dimension. We have to breathe consciously in the present and learn to communicate with Spirit.

Personality and Spirit Dialogue

Personality: I want what I want when I want.

Spirit: Be conscious of your desiring and be present with what is.

Personality: If I have a positive attitude and work hard to achieve my goals, I know I can get there.

Spirit: Work toward your goals. It's of great value to meet your needs. It lets you relax and have more peace in your life. But you can also see the limits of your personal wishes, know when to let them go, and keep awake along the way.

Personality: I thought you'd say to just *be* and go with the flow.

Spirit: We're here to live, to be conscious, and to grow. We can let ourselves be and go with the flow, but it's also of value to work hard, meet our needs, and achieve our aims. Personal desiring, however, is endless and so ultimately doomed to frustration. We can know this and see it.

Personality: I do see that no matter what I get or have, I always want something more or something else.

Spirit: Keep awake and present. Find the deeper part of your nature, even more essential than your personal goals. Besides, there's nowhere to go. Where do you think you're going? We've already, always arrived. This is it!

Personality: I never feel good enough, so how can I let myself rest until I've gotten where I want to be in life?

Spirit: Even though you say, "I'm not good enough yet," you can still relax, resting, consciously breathing and present with what is, as it is—including your self-assessment and your striving to survive and succeed, hurried, harried, and hassled. Even if you feel you haven't yet arrived while you're working toward your goals, you can still see your deeper nature, complete and content.

Personality: I might be able to try to be more aware.

Spirit: You can be where you are right now. Follow a breath in and out, here and now. Slow down. Be conscious in this moment. There's no need to force or manipulate yourself to be a certain way. No need to be perfect. No need to make this into another personal goal to pull you away from this moment. Do it now.

Personality: But it's got to be boring and uncomfortable to slow down.

Spirit: It becomes more comfortable over time. Don't worry about boredom and annoyance. We can just be here consciously, wherever we happen to be. Being aware, "bored and annoyed." Being here and now, repeating our prayer. Counterbalancing, "comfortable and relaxed," "loving," "This is it!"

After a while, it blends together and no matter what we're sensing, doing, thinking, or feeling, when we're consciously present we return to our home sweet home.

Personality: Maybe we can work together and I can lighten my load.

Spirit: Keep in mind that we already are together and have never really been apart. Awaken to this fact of life, and find love and contentment for no reason at all.

Mature Practice

Great artists and athletes make tremendous effort for many years, until they're one with their actions. Then, when we watch them perform their running, jumping, dancing, playing, we say they seem so relaxed and natural. It's as if they just do it—no big deal.

In reality, many years of work have gone into their naturalness and expertise. Years of effort lead to an inner knowing and a relaxation that lift us up and carry us along.

The great vaudeville star Eddie Cantor said, "It takes twenty years to make an overnight success." And in those "twenty years," we become one with our art or craft on whatever path we're following.

Along the way, we must expend great effort until we arrive at effortless effort. Then we're expertly swimming with the flow, doing our part, while being carried onward by life's powerful currents.

While the idea is a simple one, it's not easy. Throughout the Spiritual Diet we've tried to keep the message simple for the sake of clarity and ease of understanding. But the truth is that human life is anything but clear and simple. In reality, as Ken Wilber puts it, "We don't go from an acorn to a forest in a quantum leap. There are stages in all growth, including human." In the same way, a child with good balance takes many years of effort to become an accomplished gymnast or ballerina. We don't simply jump from babyhood with the light of Spirit in our eyes to being a wise woman or man.

Along the way, many stages must be mastered and grown beyond, each opening to a new set of challenges to be met and confusions to be resolved.

Along the way, we change. To grow and mature, we can make great effort, but eventually we must relax with faith and trust in that which is larger than ourselves.

Experienced spiritual seekers have different attitudes and perspectives than the less experienced.

The more our life is personality-dominated, the more we must use our personal will to create new patterns of awareness, presence, and experiencing which will lead us beyond the personal and beyond effort.

Along the way, we make effort and may want to be "further ahead" of where we are, but as Shunryu Suzuki tells us, "Even though you try very hard, the progress you make is always little by little." He adds, "If you continue this simple practice [breath awareness] every day, you will obtain a wonderful power."

On hearing these words, we want to "make progress" and desire "a wonderful power," even if it has to be "little by little." Mature people with highly developed awareness and presence are aware of their personal desires, expectations, and goals (especially when it comes to spiritual "progress"), and they settle down. Suzuki continues:

> "The result is not the point; it is the effort to improve ourselves that is valuable. There is no end to this practice."

So we must make great effort, but without attachment to some goal or outcome. Along the way, we can appreciate our effort and relax with contentment in the knowledge that we're fulfilling life's purpose, wherever we are along our path. We can mindfully take conscious, restful breaths here and now, again and again, regardless of our "progress."

We need patience and perseverance. It is not under our control when or how the merging of personality and spirituality will happen. Our expectation that it happen, that it be quick, or that it be any other way is a personal wish. We repeatedly point our awareness toward conscious presence as an end in itself and allow the natural process to occur.

The mature person understands the limitations of thought and words, as well as result-oriented effort. In the words of Sengts'an, the third Zen patriarch: "The more you talk about it, the more you think about it, the further from it you go; stop talking, stop thinking, and there is nothing you will not understand."

> Find space and quiet to foster psychospiritual growth on a regular basis. Discover what works best and do it regularly.

The mature person understands that any distinction is ultimately artificial, for all divisions are false. So, suggesting that progress can be made or there's a difference between the experienced and inexperienced, the mature and the beginner, or between personality and Spirit is inaccurate. But we can only see this once the effort has been made and we've understood the limits of result-oriented effort, thoughts, and words. When we experience wholeness, we realize the natural unity of all life.

When we've discovered the present, when we're centered in consciousness and presence, we understand Huang Po's words: "Enter deeply into it by awakening to it yourself. That which is before you is it, in all its fullness, utterly complete. There is nought beside."

The end is in the beginning and the beginning is in the end. Spirit is eternal consciousness, and it lives in each of us. It is always awake here now, even when we're lost in our personal preoccupations. We are both ever changing and never changing. The Seer and the Seen. The observer and the observed. Who am I? That which is within each of us—our timeless, spaceless knowingness. It's been called the Seer or Self or Eternal Witness.

So we watch and watch and watch until watchfulness happens. The Seer cannot be seen, the observer cannot be observed, for the Seer is emptiness and openness, the observer is consciousness itself. Awareness opens up and we're a living mirror.

> **Pure witnessing in the immediate moment makes us aware of the spiritual source beyond birth and death, time and space. The watcher is the watched, the observer is the observed. Who am I? The true answer comes in a flash. Just this. Just this!**

The nature of the living process that comes out of nothingness and creates everything existed before our birth and lives after our death. That's the stuff of which we're made. That's why spiritual teachers are forever telling us that each of us already, always has what we need. Our eyes are also God's eyes. Our life is also God's life. So from a spiritual perspective, where is there to get to and what is there to achieve?

Rajneesh said, "All effort will lead you to a point where you leave all effort and become effortless. And the whole search will lead you to a point where you simply shrug your shoulders and sit down under a tree and settle.

"Every journey ends into the innermost suchness of being—and that you have at every moment. So it is only a question of becoming a little more aware."

So we wake up in the morning and take a full, slow, *conscious* breath in and out, and a full, slow breath *here and now*, simply because we're alive. Just this! Just this!

What Can I Do?
Ways to Use the Spiritual Diet Each Day

1. Do one of your Spiritual Diet recipes each day. If you kept a Spiritual Diet Cookbook as suggested in Chapter 3, you no doubt have several from which to choose. If not, create your recipe(s) now from what you've learned along the way.

Each of us has psychobiological rhythms of activity and rest, most commonly ninety minutes of activity followed by five to twenty minutes of rest. The normal Western workday has this built into it: get up and dressed and have breakfast, work, coffee/tea break, work, lunch, work, afternoon break, work, home. Think of these downtimes as opportunities for a spiritual snack—anytime, day or night, we can attune to our natural rhythm and allow ourselves to use the normal periods of rest to practice the Basic Spiritual Diet and any spiritual recipe that lightens our load.

The more moments we use this Basic Spiritual Diet, the greater the impact. But regardless of the amount of time, this simple commitment and discipline has a ripple effect, sending spiritual waves through our daily life.

2. Use the revolving plan. One possibility is to use a revolving plan, alternating the Spiritual Diet recipes you've found to be most useful in lightening your load on a daily, weekly, or monthly rotation. Maybe one week you use the Basic Spiritual Diet; the next you say "relaxing" with each in-breath and "letting go" with each out-breath; the next, "happy" on the in-breath, "safe" on the out-breath; the following week, a prayer—"Jesus" on the in-breath, "loves me" on the out-breath; or "La Chaim" in, "ahhh" out.

3. Use the "digestion" process with your senses and emotions. The five steps of the fundamental process (discussed in detail in Chapters 5 and 8) will become second nature. **Aware and awake in the moment, open to experiencing what is, as it is, and letting go, allowing an openness and receptivity to whatever comes next—sight, smell, sound, touch, taste; happy, loving, mad, sad, scared.** No matter where we are along the way, simple awareness and knowing what's going on is the key. We **breathe and allow our self to be present with what is.** We are always aware now, no matter where we are.

Then **we attune to our felt experiencing.** We don't just know we're sad or glad, we feel the sadness or gladness in our face and breath and posture. We're conscious of the sad or glad thoughts jumping in our mind. We don't just know we have senses, we taste the bread and the mayonnaise in our sandwich, we see the greenness in a dollar bill and really hear the revving of our car engine and the humming of our computer. We feel, we sense, we experience, the juicy energy that life sends through us. We inhabit our body as we breathe in and out and notice the colors, sounds, tastes, and all the rest.

Then **we disengage and let it go.** Letting go helps us be less identified with everything, making us freer and lighter ("Anger comes, anger goes"). We're in the traffic jam, breathing and being, thoughts of things to do, feeling pressured, annoyance comes, annoyance goes, recalling our prayer or mantra, creeping along with the other cars, eternity leaps into view. Personality is stuck in traffic, but there's more to me than that, and Spirit is able to be conscious and present here now in traffic as well as anywhere.

Then we **open to whatever comes next**—sensation, feeling, thought, desire, and basic, life energy.

4. Counterbalance the overweighted with the overlooked. Most people are out of balance, too heavily weighted toward one or more emotions at the expense of others. If we're excessively angry, we can look for caring and love. We can act on our caring and we can use a recipe to remind us (saying "loving" to our self with each breath in and out). If we're overly scared and insecure, we can seek safety and assurance. If we're very unhappy and sad, we can find ways to lighten our heart and feel happier. If we're guilty and ashamed, we can emphasize basic goodness and nourishing our soul.

If we're caught in a world of routines and habits, we can make them meaningful by being aware in the midst of activity and emphasizing inherently valuable acts. If we're overemphasizing thinking, we may want to counterbalance our actions with being or thinking or feeling or sensing. If we're caught in a world of materialism and endless consuming, then along with an emphasis on the spiritual, we can also focus on expressing goodness, perhaps giving material things to those without even the basics.

We can be aware of what we overemphasize and counterbalance it with what we overlook.

5. The Fertilizer Method calls for us to use the smelly and disagreeable stuff of daily life (irritants, hatreds, boredom, annoyances, inadequacies, failings, pet peeves, and other forms of negativity) to serve as invaluable reminders to help us grow in awareness, finding that our "enemies" can be helpers and friends. Being put on hold, a late train or bus, a traffic slowdown, all block our forward movement toward our goals; we can use the frustrating moments to remind us to use in our Spiritual Diet recipe for the day.

6. Do it for God's sake. If we persevere, then we can integrate our spiritual nature into our personal world. When we do, we can see that:

It's all holy ground if we look with spiritual eyes.
They're all holy tastes if we have a spiritual mouth.
It's all holy sound if we hear with spiritual ears.
They're all holy smells if we breathe with a spiritual nose.
It's all holy territory if we have a spiritual touch.
Everything is holy if we feel with our spiritual heart.

The realization of spirituality in everything is why millions consider Mother Theresa to be a living saint. She said, "Do *everything* for God. God has given you many gifts—use them for the greater glory of God and the good of the people. Then you will make your life something beautiful; for this you have been created. Keep the joy of loving God ever burning in your heart and share this joy with others. That's all."

Bon Voyage

Dear fellow traveler, we wish you a good journey, and hope you follow Jonathan Swift's hope for us: "May you live all the days of your life." And may you live them with caring, connectedness, and compassion. And while you're living a good life and living fully and free, never forget Huang Po's comment that "it's right in front of you."

In the midst of eternity, we can

Simply be aware,
With sensitivity and care.

And even though we're at the end of this book, we can realize, as T. S. Eliot wrote, that

What we call the beginning is often the end
And to make an end is to make a beginning.
The end is where we start from.

A Heartfelt Prayer

Our shared human life is eternally evolving, and each of us dines on life's daily feast.

We remember Buddha's words:

Hard it is to be born,
Hard it is to live,
Harder still to hear of the Way,
And hard to rise and awake.
Yet the teaching is simple.
Do what is right.
Be pure.
At the end of the way is freedom.
Till then, patience.

With palms pressed together, breathing in and out, we offer a bow with awareness and presence to the eternal Spirit in us all, a bow of respect and appreciation to the universal life force which we all have in common with all living things.

We pray that our part contributes to our collective spiritual nourishment.

A deep bow of respect and appreciation:

May all beings be happy.

May we experience Spirit and personality as One.

May we shine brightly, embodying the light of awareness.

May we feel free, vibrantly alive, and on intimate terms with whatever life sets before us.

May we lighten our burdens and lose the weight of the world.

May our life be a delicious feast that nourishes our soul, bringing peace to our mind, love to our heart, and a smile to our face.

References and Recommended Reading

Diane Ackerman. *A Natural History of the Senses.* New York: Random House, 1990.

A. H. Almaas. *Diamond Heart: Books One, Two and Three.* Berkeley: Diamond Books, 1987–90.

A. J. Bahm. *The Philosophy of the Buddha.* New York: Capricorn Books, 1958.

Charlotte Joko Beck. *Nothing Special.* San Francisco: HarperCollins, 1993.

Hubert Benoit. *The Supreme Doctrine.* New York: Viking, 1955.

Herbert Benson, M.D. *Timeless Healing.* New York: Scribner, 1996.

The Bible. New Revised Standard Version. London and New York: Collins, 1989.

Norman O. Brown. *Love's Body.* New York: Random House, 1966.

Thomas Byrom, trans. *The Dhammapada: The Sayings of the Buddha.* New York: Vintage, 1976.

Jack Canfield and Mark V. Hansen. *Chicken Soup for the Soul.* Deerfield Beach, Florida: Health Communications, 1993.

Richard Carlson and Benjamin Shield. *Handbook for the Soul.* New York: Little, Brown, 1995.

Gorma C. C. Chang. *The Practice of Zen.* New York: Harper & Row, 1959.

Pema Chodron. *Start Where You Are.* Boston: Shambhala, 1994.

Deepok Chopra. *Unconditional Life.* New York: Bantam, 1991.

Thomas Cleary, trans. *Wisdom of the Prophet: Sayings of Muhammad.* Boston: Shambhala, 1994.

The Dalai Lama. *A Flash of Lightening in the Dark of Night.* Boston: Shambhala, 1994.

Ram Dass. *The Only Dance There Is.* New York: Anchor, 1974.

————. *Journey of Awakening: A Meditator's Guidebook.* New York: Bantam, 1990.

Barbara DeAngelis, *Real Moments.* New York: Dell, 1994.

William Elliott. *Tying Rocks to Clouds.* Wheaton: Quest, 1995.

Mark Epstein. *Thoughts Without a Thinker.* New York: Basic Books, 1995.

Richard Erdoes and Alfonso Ortiz, eds. *American Indian Myths and Legends.* New York: Pantheon, 1984.

Gia-Fu Feng and Jane English, trans. *Lao Tsu's Tao Te Ching.* New York: Vintage, 1972.

Rick Fields, et al. *Chop Wood, Carry Water.* Los Angeles: Tarcher, 1984.

Robert Fulghum. *All I Really Need to Know I Learned in Kindergarten.* New York: Ballantine, 1986.

————. *It Was on Fire When I Lay Down on It.* New York: Ballantine, 1988.

Daniel Goleman. *Emotional Intelligence.* New York: Bantam, 1995.

Al Gore. *Earth in the Balance.* Boston: Houghton Mifflin, 1992.

Thich Nhat Hanh. *The Blooming Lotus.* Boston: Beacon, 1993.

————. *Living Buddha, Living Christ.* New York: Riverhead, 1995.

Andrew Harvey. *The Essential Mystics.* San Francisco: HarperSan Francisco, 1996.

Andrew Harvey and Ann Baring. *The Mystic Vision.* San Francisco: Harper, 1995.

Pupal Jayakar. *Krishnamurti—A Biography.* New York: Harper & Row, 1986.

Jon Kabat-Zinn. *Wherever You Go, There You Are.* New York: Hyperion, 1994.

Aryeh Kaplan. *Jewish Meditation.* New York: Schocken, 1985.

Dainin Katagiri. *Returning to Silence.* Boston: Shambhala, 1988.

Pir Vilayat Inayat Khan. *Introducing Spirituality into Counseling and Therapy.* New York: Omega, 1982.

The Koran, A. J. Dawood, trans. London: Penguin, 1990.

Kreck and Crutchfield. *Elements of Psychology.* New York: Knopf, 1958.

Jiddu Krishnamurti. Edit., D. Rajogopal. *Think on These Things.* New York: HarperPerennial, 1964

————. *Freedom from the Known.* New York: Harper & Row, 1969.

————. *Meeting Life.* San Francisco: HarperCollins, 1991.

Ernest Kurtz and Katherine Ketchum. *The Spirituality of Imperfection.* New York: Bantam, 1994.

Frederick Leboyer. *Birth Without Violence.* New York: Knopf, 1975.

Michael Lerner. *Jewish Renewal.* New York: HarperPerennial, 1994.

Ramana Maharshi. *The Spiritual Teachings of Ramana Maharshi.* Berkeley: Shambhala, 1972.

Dennis Genpo Merzel. *The Eye Never Sleeps.* Boston: Shambhala, 1991.

Ronald Miller. *As Above, So Below.* New York: Tarcher, 1992.

Stephen Mitchell. *The Enlightened Heart.* New York: Harper & Row, 1989.

———. *The Enlightened Mind.* New York: HarperCollins, 1991.

———. *The Gospel According to Jesus.* New York: HarperCollins, 1991.

Thomas Moore. *Care of the Soul.* New York: HarperPerennial, 1994.

Wayne Muller. *The Legacy of the Heart.* New York: Fireside, 1992.

The New England Bible. New York: Oxford University Press, 1976.

Wes "Scoop" Nisker. *Crazy Wisdom.* Berkeley: Ten Speed, 1990.

Philip Novak. *The World's Wisdom.* San Francisco: HarperCollins, 1994.

Toni Packer. *The Work of This Moment.* Boston: Shambhala, 1990.

M. Scott Peck. *The Road Less Traveled.* New York: Touchstone, 1978.

Bhagwan Shree Rajneesh. *Nirvana: The Last Nightmare.* Poona, India: Tata Press, 1976.

———. *Only One Sky.* New York: Dutton, 1976.

Elizabeth Roberts and Elias Amidon, eds. *Earth Prayers, from Around the World.* New York: HarperCollins, 1991.

Sharon Salzberg. *Lovingkindness.* Boston: Shambhala, 1995.

Anne Wilson Schaef. *Native Wisdom for White Minds.* New York: Ballantine, 1995.

Bernard Siegel. *Love, Medicine and Miracles.* New York: HarperCollins, 1994

Huston Smith. *The World's Religions.* San Francisco: HarperCollins, 1991.

Shunryu Suzuki. *Zen Mind, Beginner's Mind.* New York: Weatherhill, 1970.

Chogyam Trungpa. *Cutting Through Spiritual Materialism.* Berkeley: Shambhala, 1973.

———. *Glimpses of Abhidharma.* Boulder: Prajna Press, 1978.

———. *Shambhala: The Sacred Path of the Warrior.* Boulder: Shambhala, 1984.

Frances Vaughn. *The Inward Arc.* Boston: New Science Library, 1985.

Michael Washburn. *The Ego and the Dynamic Ground.* New York: SUNY, 1988.

Andrew Weil. *Spontaneous Healing.* New York: Fawcett/Columbine, 1995.

John Welwood. *The Meeting of the Ways: Explorations in East/West Psychology.* New York: Schocken, 1979.

———, ed. *Ordinary Magic.* Boston: Shambhala, 1992.

Ken Wilber. *No Boundary.* Los Angeles: Center Publications, 1979.

———. *Transformations of Consciousness.* Boston: Shambhala, 1986.

———. *Sex, Ecology, Spirituality.* Boston: Shambhala, 1995.

———. *A Brief History of Everything.* Boston: Shambhala, 1996.

Michael Yapko. *Breaking the Patterns of Depression.* New York: Doubleday, 1997.

Yatri. *Unknown Man.* New York: Fireside, 1988.

Jonathan and Diane Kramer are available for workshops, seminars, and talks. Contact them at

8950 Villa La Jolla Drive, #2162,
La Jolla, CA 92037.
Phone: (619) 457-1314 or (888) 557-2637. (J. Kramer)
E-mail: jonmkramer@aol.com or ddunaway@aol.com

Index

JONATHAN M. KRAMER, PH.D., is a clinical psychologist practicing in La Jolla, California, with thirty years of professional therapy and counseling experience and over twenty years of personal experience meditating. Jonathan studied philosophy and religion at New York University and the New School for Social Research. His doctoral thesis was on Eastern spirituality and Western psychotherapy. He has taught transpersonal (spiritually based) psychology through the University of California and several other universities and colleges.

DIANE DUNAWAY KRAMER holds degrees in psychology and sociology and has been practicing spiritual techniques for many years. Diane is also a professional writer with over fifteen years of experience and is the founder and coordinator of the annual San Diego State University Writer's Conference, held since 1984. She has taught at seven colleges and universities over the last fifteen years and is a well-known public speaker.

Jonathan and Diane are married and have aimed at integrating their own spiritual search with their busy lives as psychologist, writers, university instructors, parents, and partners. They coauthored *Why Men Don't Get Enough Sex and Women Don't Get Enough Love.*